F# High Performance

Build powerful and fast applications with F#

Eriawan Kusumawardhono

BIRMINGHAM - MUMBAI

F# High Performance

First published: January 2017

Production reference: 1130117

Published by Packt Publishing Ltd.

Livery Place

35 Livery Street

Birmingham B3 2PB, UK.

ISBN 978-1-78646-807-9

www.packtpub.com

Credits

Author

Eriawan Kusumawardhono

Reviewer

Arthur Pham

Commissioning Editor

Kunal Parikh

Acquisition Editor

Sonali Vernekar

Content Development Editor

Nikhil Borkar

Technical Editor

Hussain Kanchwala

Copy Editor

Safis Editing

Project Coordinator

Ulhas Kambli

Proofreader

Safis Editing

Indexer

Tejal Daruwale Soni

Graphics

Abhinash Sahu

Production Coordinator

Shraddha Falebhai

About the Author

Eriawan Kusumawardhono is a veteran senior software development engineer (SDE) who has software development experience of more than 13 years, with 11 years of having developed in .NET, since the introduction of Visual Studio 2003. On usual working day he works at Allegro Development, a software development company, and in his spare time, he does speaking and training for software development and programming language communities in Indonesia. He is also a member of F# Foundation speaker program. He enjoys being a full-time technical polyglot software developer, mingling both OOP and functional programming at the same time.

He currently holds a Microsoft MVP award in Visual Studio development platform competency, from 2011 to 2017, for more than 5 consecutive years.

He lives in Jakarta with his wife, enjoying reading and cooking heterogeneous exotic food in Indonesia.

> *Many thanks to Microsoft, especially Microsoft Research, and Don Syme for developing F#, a functional programming that meets OOP nicely and truly pragmatic! I would like to give special thanks to Packt for giving me the chance to write this wonderful book and Nikhil for his continuous support and always giving me constructive feedback. I also would like to give a big huge thanks for my lovely wife, Dini Kusumawardhono, for always giving me unconditional love and support during the writing of this book and also her continuous understanding every day. I would like to dedicate this book to software development communities in Indonesia, and to all of the F# developer communities around the world. F# rocks!*

About the Reviewer

Arthur Pham has been working for Thomson Reuters as a Lead Quantitative Engineer since 2006.

He has spent many years designing and implementing derivatives pricing models and still loves learning new programming languages, such as F#, C++, Python, Flex/ActionScript, C#, Ruby, and JavaScript.

He currently lives in New York, NY, USA and can be contacted on Twitter at @arthurpham.

www.PacktPub.com

For support files and downloads related to your book, please visit www.PacktPub.com.

Did you know that Packt offers eBook versions of every book published, with PDF and ePub files available? You can upgrade to the eBook version at www.PacktPub.com and as a print book customer, you are entitled to a discount on the eBook copy. Get in touch with us at service@packtpub.com for more details.

At www.PacktPub.com, you can also read a collection of free technical articles, sign up for a range of free newsletters and receive exclusive discounts and offers on Packt books and eBooks.

https://www.packtpub.com/mapt

Get the most in-demand software skills with Mapt. Mapt gives you full access to all Packt books and video courses, as well as industry-leading tools to help you plan your personal development and advance your career.

Why subscribe?

- Fully searchable across every book published by Packt
- Copy and paste, print, and bookmark content
- On demand and accessible via a web browser

Customer Feedback

Thank you for purchasing this Packt book. We take our commitment to improving our content and products to meet your needs seriously—that's why your feedback is so valuable. Whatever your feelings about your purchase, please consider leaving a review on this book's Amazon page. Not only will this help us, more importantly it will also help others in the community to make an informed decision about the resources that they invest in to learn. You can also review for us on a regular basis by joining our reviewers' club. **If you're interested in joining, or would like to learn more about the benefits we offer, please contact us**: customerreviews@packtpub.com.

Table of Contents

Preface — 1

Chapter 1: Performing Common Optimizations in F# — 7

Understanding the nature of F# code — 8

F# runtime characteristics — 10

Relation between F# code and its generated assembly — 12

Immutability versus mutability — 13

Overview of common bottlenecks — 14

Common samples of misunderstood concurrent problems — 15

Introduction to concurrency in F# — 16

Defining asynchronous — 17

Misunderstood concurrency problems — 18

Introduction to concurrency support in .NET and F# — 20

Overview of F# tooling in Visual Studio — 21

Interactive support for F# interactive — 22

Introduction to debugging in F# — 29

Summary — 37

Chapter 2: Performance Measurement — 39

Introduction to the nature of F# code compilation — 40

General overview of F# compiler processes and results — 40

A quick overview of IL in F# — 43

IL tooling in .NET — 45

Using ILDASM and ILASM to understand low-level IL assembly — 46

Using CLR Profiler 4.5 — 56

A quick overview of CLR Profiler — 57

A quick walkthrough of CLR Profiler in action — 58

Ways to measure performance quantitatively — 66

Using .NET timers — 66

Running functions inside unit tests — 70

A quick introduction to unit tests — 71

Unit test support in Visual Studio — 71

Using FsUnit to implement a unit test in F# — 72

Summary — 80

Chapter 3: Optimizing Data Structures — 81

Overview and best practices of types in F# — 82

Static typing versus dynamic typing   82
Quick introduction to types in F#   85
Quick overview of generic type support in F#   86
Overall runtime strategy of handling data types   88
Introduction to memory storage allocation   88
Register   88
Stack   89
Heap   91
Best practices of types for storing and accessing data   91
Best practices in using F# collections   98
Comparing F# List to .NET List   102
Comparing F# Map to Dictionary   104
Choosing a value evaluation strategy   105
Scenarios involving evaluation strategy and memory allocations   109
Summary   111

Chapter 4: Introduction to Concurrency in F#   113
Introducing concurrency support in F# 4   114
Identifying blocking threads   116
Overview of the background technical reasons for the blocking nature of
I/O   117
Obvious trait of a blocking thread   119
Introducing asynchronous workflow   122
Getting to know asynchronous workflow   123
Using asynchronous with Dispose pattern   126
Operations in asynchronous workflow   132
Creating child asynchronous workflow   136
F# asynchronous workflow support for legacy .NET APM and EAP   138
Ignoring asynchronous operation asynchronously   143
Delaying asynchronous workflow   144
Handling cancellation in asynchronous workflow   147
Common conventions when implementing asynchronous operations   149
Introduction to interop with .NET TPL   150
A quick overview of asynchronous programming in .NET TPL   150
Summary   154

Chapter 5: Advanced Concurrency Support in F#   155
Using F# MailboxProcessor   156
Background case of having message agent   156
Introducing fire and forget pattern   156

Overview of a message agent 163
Overview of serialization 167
Introduction to F# MailboxProcessor 172
Overview of MailboxProcesor features 178
Further implementations of MailboxProcessor 180
**Managing side effects inside MailboxProcessor and asynchronous
workflows** 182
Parallel programming with .NET TPL 184
Overview of task-based parallelism 186
Quick start-using the parallel debugging tool in Visual Studio 191
Overview of data parallelism 194
Common potential pitfalls in parallel programming 197
Overview of handling mutable state 197
Summary 201

Chapter 6: Optimizing Type Provider 203
Overview of F# type provider 203
Comparing the type provider with other type generators 207
Interoperability with other managed programming languages 209
Understanding the type provider building blocks 210
Minimum requirements of type providers 210
Strategies of type provider implementation 211
Choosing strategies of type provider implementation 211
Sample usage of built-in type provider in F# 215
Quick sample of using SqlDataConnection type provider 215
Implementing your own type provider 223
Building the type's building blocks 227
Building type metadata infrastructure 228
Implementing assembly to provide base assembly 232
Implementing parameters for methods and constructors 233
Implementing generated constructor 234
Implementing generated methods 235
Implementing generated properties 236
Basic minimal implementation of type provider 240
Common pitfalls in implementing type provider 242
Summary 243

Chapter 7: Language Features and Constructs Optimization 245
Overview of language features and constructs optimization 246
Optimizing common F# language constructs 248
Best practices of interoperability of F# delegate with .NET delegate 248
Passing a .NET delegate as an F# function 250
Calling .NET delegate within F# 252

Best practices in pattern matching and active pattern 252
Comparing constant pattern matching with if constructs 254
Best practices in using active patterns 263
Considerations in catching exceptions in active patterns 267
Optimizing inline functions 268
Background overview of inline functions and related type inferences 269
Overview of F# type inference mechanism of generic type inference 269
Overview of automatic generalization in F# 270
Best practices in implementing inline functions 271
Identifying tail call in recursive constructs 276
Overview of recursion in functional programming 277
Tail call recursion in F# and .NET CLR 279
Identifying tail call optimized implementation 279
Advantages of having tail call recursive implementation 283
Limitations of tail call recursion in F# 284
Summary 285
Chapter 8: Optimizing Computation Expressions 287
Quick introduction to F# computation expression 288
Introduction to builders of computation expression 289
Using F# function/delegate over .NET Func 292
Relation of F# function computation expressions with arguments restriction 294
Walkthrough of planning and writing a computation expression 295
Understanding the use of type returned in computation expression 302
General computation expression design considerations 304
Implications of the design considerations of computation expression 308
Considerations of computation expression optimization 312
Summary 316
Index 317

Preface

It's well-known today that F# has been quite a first class citizen, a built-in part of programming language support in Visual Studio from Visual Studio 2010. F# is a programming language that has its own unique trait: it is a functional programming language, and at the same time, it has OOP support. F# has run on .NET until now, although we can also run F# as a cross-platform language, such as on Android (using Mono).

Although F# mostly runs faster than C# or VB when doing computations, F# has its own unique performance characteristics. Some of the performance characteristics might not be so obviously identified and code implementations might have implicit bad practices and subtleties that may lead to performance bottlenecks. The bottlenecks may or may not be faster than C#/VB counterparts, although some of the bottlenecks may share the same performance characteristics, such as the use of .NET APIs.

The main goal of this book is to identify the performance problems in F#, measuring and optimizing F# code to run more efficiently, while also maintaining the functional programming style as appropriately as possible.

This book focuses on optimizing F#. A basic skill of F# knowledge (including functional programming concept and basic OOP) is a prerequisite to start understanding its performance problems and optimizing F#.

What this book covers

Chapter 1, *Performing Common Optimizations in F#*, introduces F# and gives an overview of the common problems in F# code.

Chapter 2, *Performance Measurement*, helps you get to know what and how to measure and the tooling ecosystem to measure performance.

Chapter 3, *Optimizing Data Structures*, helps you decide the best and the most optimal use of F#-specific data structures and optimize them.

Chapter 4, *Introduction to Concurrency in F#*, provides a general introduction to the concept of concurrency and concurrency implementation support in F#.

Chapter 5, *Advanced Concurrency Support in F#*, provides best practices in implementing advanced concurrency support in F#, including interop with .NET TPL and avoiding performance pitfalls.

Chapter 6, *Optimizing Type Provider*, gives a quick walk-through of type provider implementation, while at the same time providing optimization and avoiding performance pitfalls in implementing your own custom type providers.

Chapter 7, *Language Features and Constructs Optimization*, explains best practices when implementing and using various F# language features and constructs without sacrificing the performance and correctness in functional programming.

Chapter 8, *Optimizing Computation Expressions*, explains best practices in using F# computation workflows and optimizing your own implementation of a computation workflow.

Who this book is for

This book is for F# developers who want to build high-performance applications. Knowledge of functional programming would be helpful.

What you need for this book

We need to ensure that we have met all of the software and hardware requirements and that we have their correct versions as well.

Basic requirements and setup environments

The following are the requirement specifications for an F# environment:

- Visual Studio 2015 Update 3. The minimum edition is Community Edition because it is the free minimum version of Visual Studio, which has extensibility support and Visual F# (also F# project templates) as part of the installation. Express Edition is not recommended because it has no F# project templates built in.
- .NET 4.6 as the minimum target runtime.
- Windows 7 SP1 (Windows 8.1 Update 1 64-bit or Windows 10 64-bit is recommended)

The following are the Visual Studio 2015 Update 3 hardware requirements:

- 4 GB RAM on Windows 7 SP1 or 6 GB RAM on Windows 8.1 and Windows 10.
- At least a Core 2 Duo or Athlon processor. It is recommended to have Core i5 as it is also a recommendation for a Windows 8.1 or Windows 10 machine. Also, using Core i5 will provide easier illustrations to see multi core in action when we discuss concurrency in Chapter 4 and 5.
- Approximately 12 GB to 15 GB of disk space with Windows 10 UWP installed (without Android development feature).
- DirectX 9.0c capable display adapter.

For more information, please check the requirement specification on MSDN:

```
https://www.visualstudio.com/en-us/downloads/visual-studio-2015-system-requi
rements-vs.aspx
```

 We recommend having at least 8 GB of RAM. This minimal memory size is recommended in order to have an optimal experience for not just running F# code. For large F# projects, Visual Studio IDE will load type information, metadata and debug symbols in the background, and Visual Studio's memory consumption will quickly climb to more than 3 GB. This is why 64-bit Windows is recommended as it allows us to use RAM higher than 4 GB.

Conventions

In this book, you will find a number of text styles that distinguish between different kinds of information. Here are some examples of these styles and an explanation of their meaning.

Code words in text, database table names, folder names, filenames, file extensions, pathnames, dummy URLs, user input, and Twitter handles are shown as follows: "We can include other contexts through the use of the `include` directive."

A block of code is set as follows:

```
[<EntryPoint>]
let main argv =
    printfn "Hello F# world"
    0 // return an integer exit code
```

If there is a line (or lines) of code that needs to be highlighted, it is set as follows:

```
[<EntryPoint>]
let main argv =
    printfn "Hello F# world"
    0 // return an integer exit code
```

New terms and **important words** are shown in bold. Words that you see on the screen, for example, in menus or dialog boxes, appear in the text like this: "Clicking the **Next** button moves you to the next screen."

Warnings or important notes appear in a box like this.

Tips and tricks appear like this.

Reader feedback

Feedback from our readers is always welcome. Let us know what you think about this book—what you liked or disliked. Reader feedback is important for us as it helps us develop titles that you will really get the most out of.

To send us general feedback, simply e-mail feedback@packtpub.com, and mention the book's title in the subject of your message.

If there is a topic that you have expertise in and you are interested in either writing or contributing to a book, see our author guide at www.packtpub.com/authors.

Customer support

Now that you are the proud owner of a Packt book, we have a number of things to help you to get the most from your purchase.

Downloading the example code

You can download the example code files for this book from your account at `http://www.packtpub.com`. If you purchased this book elsewhere, you can visit `http://www.packtpub.com/support` and register to have the files e-mailed directly to you.

You can download the code files by following these steps:

1. Log in or register to our website using your e-mail address and password.
2. Hover the mouse pointer on the **SUPPORT** tab at the top.
3. Click on **Code Downloads & Errata**.
4. Enter the name of the book in the **Search** box.
5. Select the book for which you're looking to download the code files.
6. Choose from the drop-down menu where you purchased this book from.
7. Click on **Code Download**.

Once the file is downloaded, please make sure that you unzip or extract the folder using the latest version of:

- WinRAR / 7-Zip for Windows
- Zipeg / iZip / UnRarX for Mac
- 7-Zip / PeaZip for Linux

The code bundle for the book is also hosted on GitHub at `https://github.com/PacktPublishing/F-Sharp-High-Performance/` We also have other code bundles from our rich catalog of books and videos available at `https://github.com/PacktPublishing/`. Check them out!

Errata

Although we have taken every care to ensure the accuracy of our content, mistakes do happen. If you find a mistake in one of our books—maybe a mistake in the text or the code—we would be grateful if you could report this to us. By doing so, you can save other readers from frustration and help us improve subsequent versions of this book. If you find any errata, please report them by visiting http://www.packtpub.com/submit-errata, selecting your book, clicking on the **Errata Submission Form link**, and entering the details of your errata. Once your errata are verified, your submission will be accepted and the errata will be uploaded to our website or added to any list of existing errata under the Errata section of that title.

To view the previously submitted errata, go to https://www.packtpub.com/books/content/support and enter the name of the book in the search field. The required information will appear under the Errata section.

Piracy

Piracy of copyrighted material on the Internet is an ongoing problem across all media. At Packt, we take the protection of our copyright and licenses very seriously. If you come across any illegal copies of our works in any form on the Internet, please provide us with the location address or website name immediately so that we can pursue a remedy.

Please contact us at copyright@packtpub.com with a link to the suspected pirated material.

We appreciate your help in protecting our authors and our ability to bring you valuable content.

Questions

If you have a problem with any aspect of this book, you can contact us at questions@packtpub.com, and we will do our best to address the problem.

1
Performing Common Optimizations in F#

It's quite well-known today that F# has been a first class citizen, a built-in part of programming language support in Visual Studio, starting from Visual Studio 2010. F# is a programming language that has its own unique trait: it is a functional programming language and at the same time it has object-oriented programming (OOP) support. F# from the start has run on .NET, although we can also run F# on cross-platform, such as Android (using Mono).

Although F# mostly runs faster than C# or VB when doing computations, its own performance characteristics and some not so obvious bad practices and subtleties may have led to performance bottlenecks. The bottlenecks may or may not be faster than the C#/VB counterparts, although some of the bottlenecks may share the same performance characteristics, such as the use of .NET APIs. The main goal of this book is to identify performance problems in F#, measuring and also optimizing F# code to run more efficiently, while also maintaining the functional programming style as appropriately as possible.

 A basic knowledge of F# (including the functional programming concept and basic OOP) is required as a prerequisite to start understanding the performance problems and the optimization of F#.

There are many ways to define F# performance characteristics and at the same time to measure them, but understanding the mechanics of running F# code, especially on top of .NET, is crucial and is also a part of the performance characteristics itself. This includes other aspects of approaches to identify concurrency problems and language constructs. This chapter describes the optimization of F# code and will cover the following topics:

- Understanding the nature of F# code
- Overview of common bottlenecks
- Commonly misunderstood concurrency problems
- Overview of tooling in .NET including Visual Studio to help understanding the running code
- Immediate testing of F# code in F# interactive
- Introduction to debugging in F#

Understanding the nature of F# code

Understanding the nature of F# code is very crucial and is a definitive prerequisite before we begin to measure how long it runs and its effectiveness. We can measure a running F# code by running time, but to fully understand why it may run slow or fast, there are some basic concepts we have to consider first.

Before we dive more into this, we must meet the basic requirements and setup.

After the requirements have been set, we need to put in place the environment setting of Visual Studio 2015. We have to set this because we need to maintain the consistency of the default setting of Visual Studio. The setting should be set to **General**.

These are the steps:

1. Select the **Tools** menu from Visual Studio's main menu.
2. Select **Import and Export Settings...** and the **Import and Export Settings Wizard** screen is displayed:

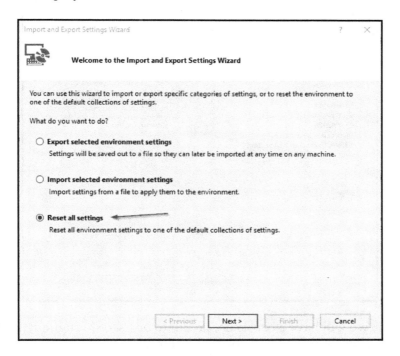

3. Select **Reset all Settings** and then **Next** to proceed.

4. Select **No, just reset my settings overwriting my current setting** and then **Next** to proceed

5. Select **General** and then click on **Finish**:

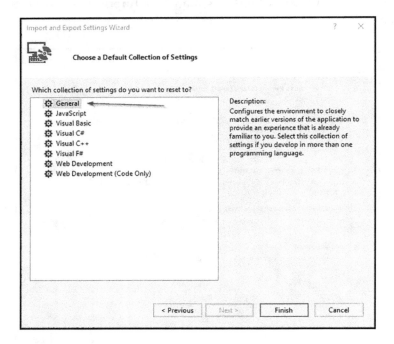

After setting it up, we will have a consistent layout to be used throughout this book, including the menu locations and the look and feel of Visual Studio.

Now, we are going to scratch the surface of F# runtime with an introductory overview of common F# runtime, which will give us some insights into F# performance.

F# runtime characteristics

The release of Visual Studio 2015 occurred at the same time as the release of .NET 4.6 and the rest of the tools, including the F# compiler. The compiler version of F# in Visual Studio 2015 is F# 4.0.

F# 4.0 has no large differences or notable new features compared to the previous version, F# 3.0 in Visual Studio 2013.

Its runtime characteristic is essentially the same as F# 4.0, although there are some subtle performance improvements and bug fixes.

For more information on what's new in F# 4.0 (described as release notes) visit:

`https://github.com/Microsoft/visualfsharp/blob/fsharp4/CHANGELOG.md`

 At the time of writing this book, the online and offline MSDN Library of F# in Visual Studio does not have F# 4.0 release notes documentation, but you can always go to the GitHub repository of F# to check the latest update.

These are the common characteristics of F# as part of managed programming language:

- F# must conform to .NET CLR. This includes the compatibilities, the IL emitted after compilation, and support for .NET BCL (the basic class library). Therefore, F# functions and libraries can be used by other CLR-compliant languages such as C#, VB, and managed C++.
- The debug symbols (PDB) have the same format and semantics as the other CLR-compliant languages. This is important because F# code must be able to be debugged from other CLR-compliant languages as well.

From the managed languages perspective, measuring the performance of F# is similar when measured by tools such as the CLR profiler. But from an F# unique perspective, the following are the unique characteristics of F#:

- By default, all types in F# are immutable. Therefore, it's safe to assume it is intrinsically thread safe.
- F# has a distinctive collection library, and it is immutable by default. It is also safe to assume it is intrinsically thread safe.
- F# has a strong type inference model, and when a generic type is inferred without any concrete type, it automatically performs generalizations.
- Default functions in F# are implemented internally by creating an internal class derived from F#'s `FSharpFunc`. This `FSharpFunc` is essentially a delegate that is used by F# to apply functional language constructs such as currying and partial application.
- With **tail call recursive optimization** in the IL, the F# compiler may emit `.tail` IL, and then the CLR will recognize this and perform optimization at runtime. More on this in `Chapter 7`, *Language Features and Constructs Optimization*.
- F# has inline functions as options. More on this in `Chapter 7`, *Language Features and Constructs Optimization*.

- F# has a computation workflow that is used to compose functions. This will be described in more detail in `Chapter 8`, *Optimizing Computation Expressions*.
- F# async computation doesn't need `Task<T>` to implement it.

 Although F# async doesn't need the `Task<T>` object, it can operate well with the async-await model in C# and VB. The async-await model in C# and VB is inspired by F# async, but behaves semantically differently based on more things than just the usage of `Task<T>`. More on this in `Chapter 4`, *Introduction to Concurrency in F#*.

All of those characteristics are not only unique, but they can also have performance implications when used to interoperate with C# and VB.

Relation between F# code and its generated assembly

The F# assembly (commonly known as DLL or executable EXE in .NET running on Windows) is the same as the C#/VB assembly upon compilation. The end product of the compiler is a .NET assembly.

An assembly may contain multiple namespaces, and each namespace may contain multiple files of modules, classes, or a mix of both.

The following table describes the F# relation of code and compiled code (assembly):

F# code	Description	Compiled code
Project	An organization of an F# project. It may contain F# script (FSX) and F# source files (FS). In the conceptual layout, a project may contain multiple namespaces that spawn across multiple files of FSX and F# script.	An assembly of either executable EXE or DLL class library
Namespace	A logical organization of modules and classes to help organizing within an organization, company, or functionality. For example: the `System.Web` namespace that contains many classes related to enable browser/server communication, including HTTP and HTTPS.	A namespace may spawn across different assemblies instead of a namespace for only one assembly

Module	A module in F# is equal to a C# static class or module in VB. An F# FS file may contain multiple modules, although it is not recommended to have this practice.	Part of a generated assembly
Classes and interfaces	A file can contain multiple classes and interfaces under different namespaces. It is recommended to have not more than one namespace for each file as this also minimizes compilation time when it tries to resolve references.	Part of a generated assembly

Immutability versus mutability

F# implementation of types and collection types are immutable. Immutable in this sense means it is read-only, and we can only initialize the object with an initial value and we can't change it afterwards.

Mutability means once we initialize an object, it can be changed afterwards. This is why it is sometimes called a *mutating object value* instead of a changing object value.

For example consider the following:

```
let anynumber = 0
```

By default, `anynumber` is immutable and the value of it will always be 0.

To mark a variable as mutable, F# has the `mutable` keyword and we can use `mutable` in the `let` declaration, as in this example:

```
let mutable anymutablenumber = 0
```

However, changing the value requires the use of the `<-` symbol in F#, for example:

```
anymutablenumber <- anymutablenumber + 1
```

Since the nature of F# is functional, a symbol can be both a data and a function. The content of the symbol is read-only, so does a function in it.

Immutability also has another advantage: it scales well across multiple threads or even in parallel, no matter whether it's a value or a function. The immutability guarantee means that it is free of side effects. It is then safe to spawn multiple symbols in parallel because the result of an execution will be guaranteed to have the same result. This is also simply called **thread safe**.

The fact that F# has a mixed support for functional and OOP at the same time (including having support for the inherent mutable state of OOP) may lead to bottlenecks as described next.

Overview of common bottlenecks

F# has common bottlenecks although they might be subtle as well.

In order to be able to quickly understand the bottleneck factors in F#, we will categorize the shared general bottlenecks of .NET as managed bottlenecks (also in C#/VB), and F#-only bottlenecks (this includes when using F# with other languages).

The following are managed .NET bottlenecks (from obvious to less obvious):

- String concatenations, such as using string `String.Concat` instead of `StringBuilder`. This is often overlooked because of a lack of awareness of the string's immutability.
- Usage of non-generic collections such as `ArrayList`.
- Incorrectly handling side effects, such as exceptions and I/O.
- Mutable objects usage, including casting.
- Complex objects that will be serialized and deserialized, for example: sending `DataSet` that has `DataTables` over HTTP.
- Ignoring performance profiling.

Side effects mean all of the elements outside the formal computation (it is often called the *outside world*) that we interact with, and this includes the changing global state. The outside world can be all of the things that we cannot fully determine as the end result. Examples of the outside world include:

- I/O: This is included as being part of the outside world because you cannot determine or guarantee any kind of work you pass to I/O to be successfully completed. For example, when sending a command to a printer to print a document, we cannot guarantee 100% success of the printing operation. We cannot even guarantee that the process of sending the data to the printer will be successful or not before the printer receives the data and begins to print the document.
- Global static mutable variables: A quick example of this is when we define a `public static` variable in the scope of ASP.NET. Every value change will always change the condition of any user of the ASP.NET application.

- Functions or properties that always have different results when they are invoked, such as DateTime.Now.

 DateTime.Now will always return different results and this is as expected because the result *must* change every time it is called or instantiated. It is not free of side effects, but it is still expected to always return a different result.

Side effects are not just for functional programming developers, as many of us are now becoming quite aware. There are no absolute side effect-free computations because we should learn and be able to correctly handle them. For example, even printing a screen to a console is also a side effect because it involves I/O, and it changes the state of the outside world.

The following are F#'s unique bottlenecks:

- Incorrect use of data structures and collections
- Incorrect use of auto generalization and other language constructs
- Incorrectly implemented concurrency problems, such as mixing synchronous and asynchronous although the original intention is asynchronous
- Slow performance when having to interoperate with other languages' class libraries such as C#/VB
- Scaling MailboxProcessor in F#
- Identifying when **tail call optimization** should occur
- Slow response when resolving type in type provider implementation
- Slow performance when implementing computation workflow

Common samples of misunderstood concurrent problems

Many of us, when dealing with concurrent problems, sometimes try to use a hammer for every nail. There is no silver bullet for all of the problems of implementing concurrency.

It is also recommended to understand concurrency, as concurrency is now becoming more relevant because of the many core models in the releases of modern microprocessors (or simply processors) in the last 7 years. This fact is also becoming a trend as the clock speed of the latest processors has been usually limited to 3.2 GHz for the last 3 years.

Microsoft's Visual C++ architect, Herb Sutter, has written a very thorough article in the form of a whitepaper famously known as *The Free Lunch Is Over*:

http://www.gotw.ca/publications/concurrency-ddj.htm

Let's understand first what concurrency is and the F# supports.

Introduction to concurrency in F#

Before we dive deeper into concurrency in F#, we should understand the definition of concurrency.

Concurrency is one of the main disciplines of computer science and it is still one of the main problems of computations.

Simply defined, concurrency is the composition of the order of independent process units or partially-ordered process units that can be executed in parallel or not in parallel, but not in sequential order. The term *order* in this context means ordered as sequentially.

The following diagram illustrates the concept of sequential (not concurrent) in action:

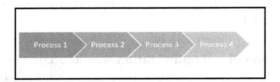

Process 1 to **Process 4** as shown in the preceding diagram is executed sequentially step by step. **Process 2** must wait for **Process 1** to be completed first, as do **Process 3** and **Process 4**.

This sequence is also called a synchronous process or is simply referred to as being synchronous.

The following figure is a sample illustration of a parallel concurrency combination of parallel and synchronous processes:

Processes 1A, 2A, and **3A** run in parallel, although each parallel lane has its own sequence of processes that are run sequentially.

The term parallel means that it is not just executing simultaneously in parallel, but parallel also means that it may run on many processors or on many cores, as is common in modern processors that have multiple cores.

Defining asynchronous

A simple definition of asynchronous means *not synchronous*. This means that if we have an asynchronous flow, the process is not run synchronously.

These are the implications of an asynchronous flow:

- Processes run not sequentially. For example, if the first process is running asynchronously, the next process doesn't have to wait for the first process to be completed.
- There has to be a way of scheduling and telling the scheduler to inform that the asynchronous process is completed. Typically, the asynchronous process is usually related to blocking I/O or some long computations.
- At first, the processes may look sequential, but the next process run may not be sequential at all.

This is a sample case of asynchronous: a customer is going to have dinner in a restaurant. The flows are:

1. *Customer A* orders some food or drinks, and the order is noted by *waiter X*. Usually, most restaurants have more than one waiter, but for this illustration, the waiter available currently to serve *customer A* is *waiter X*.
2. *Waiter X* then gives the list of the customer's order to *chef Y*.
3. *Chef Y* accepts the order, and checks if he is currently occupied or not. If he is occupied, the order is registered as part of his cooking queue. Otherwise, he will start to cook the order.
4. The waiter does not have to wait for the chef to complete his cooking. He can then serve other customers who have just arrived or there might be customers that want to add more food or drinks as well.
5. *Chef Y* finishes his cooking for *customer A*, and then gives a notification to *waiter X* to inform that his cooking for *customer A* is finished. Or he can inform all waiters to tell that the cooking for *customer A* is finished. This concept of informing to tell a process is finished is commonly called a callback.

6. *Waiter X* (or any other waiter) delivers the finished food to *customer A*.

The asynchronous model that uses a notification to inform that a process is completed is called **asynchronous callback**.

The result returned at the end of the execution later (or in the future) is called a **Future**. It is also the future, in a sense, when many processes are executed in parallel, having results later.

This is the official documentation of Future in MSDN Library:

```
https://msdn.microsoft.com/en-us/library/ff963556.aspx
```

For I/O operations, such as printing a document, we cannot determine whether the printing is successful or not, so the notification of the end process is not available. We can implement an asynchronous operation on I/O, and the fact that there is no observable notification of this is why this asynchronous model is called the asynchronous *fire and forget* model.

Misunderstood concurrency problems

Many developers, even seasoned or experienced developers, still think that concurrency and parallel programming are different. Actually, parallel programming is just one member within the concurrency discipline, together with the differentiation of asynchronous and synchronous processing models.

This is also one of the most misunderstood concurrency concepts or problems, and there are many more regarding how we approach concurrency.

These are some common organized sample cases of misunderstood concurrency problems:

1. Assuming all concurrent problems can be solved using parallel programming.

    Fact: Not all concurrent problems are easily solved with parallelism.

2. Assuming all implementation of asynchronous is asynchronous.

    Fact: This depends on how we implement async; sometimes the execution of an async construct is executed synchronously.

3. Ignoring blocking threads such as I/O.

    Fact: Blocking I/O threads should be handled asynchronously; otherwise, the current thread is always waiting indefinitely until the I/O thread is finished.

4. The synchronized lock is blocking.

   Fact: The lock is not a blocking thread.

5. Relying on the CPU speed.

   Fact: The CPU speed increase is becoming less of an issue. The research and development of modern CPUs is focusing on multiple core CPUs.

A few sample cases of concurrent problems are mentioned as follows:

The case samples of the first case are:

- **Ordering or sorting a collection**: Ordering is by default a sequential process, and it requires iterating all the elements of the collection. Therefore, it's useless to use parallelism.
- **Grouping data**: Grouping data is implicitly one of the sequential processes; it is also quite useless to use parallelism.
- **Printing reports**: Printing is part of I/O and I/O is intrinsically without support for parallelism. Unless the I/O is part of I/O parallelism, it is useless to use parallelism in this context.

Sample cases of the second case are listed as follows:

- Mixing `Parallel.For` that has F# async in it. The implications of having `Parallel.For` is by default taking a multiple core or a CPU to run it is not the same as running asynchronously, as it is not guaranteed to run as a combined async in parallel.
- Using `Thread.Sleep` instead of `Async.Sleep` to signify a *wait* operation. The call to `Thread.Sleep` will instead make the flow synchronous, as the `Sleep` method simply puts on hold the current thread as a *delay* synchronously.

 RAID array in the storage I/O is one of the best samples of parallelism in I/O. It stores data in parallel across multiple disks. It is faster than common I/O because data is stored in parts (not whole data to a disk) to several disks in parallel.

The third case is related to all of the I/O operations including sending data to a printer and saving large data into a disk. These operations are always blocking threads.

For the case of `lock`, Microsoft has issued official statements that `lock` in .NET used by C# and VB is executed without any interruption, and it only locks an object until it has finished executing the block in the synchronized lock. It's still allowing other threads to run without waiting for the thread that has the lock to finish.

This is the official thread synchronization of C# and VB in MSDN:

`https://msdn.microsoft.com/en-us/library/ms173179.aspx`

It is recommended to always check online the MSDN Library of the .NET class library, as this is always updated.

Introduction to concurrency support in .NET and F#

Concurrency support in F# is based on the existing work of concurrency support features in .NET BCL (the Base Class Library). It's also by design, since F# runs on top of .NET CLR and can use .NET BCL. F# also has its unique ways that bring more features other than just language features (for example, asynchronous computations).

The .NET BCL part of concurrency has basic support for the following:

- Thread
- Lock
- Mutex

Beginning with .NET 4.0, we have the **Task Parallel Library** (**TPL**). This library makes concurrent support easier. TPL consists of the following:

- Data parallelism (for example: `Parallel.For` and `ForEach`)
- Task parallelism
- Asynchronous task (this is also the base foundation of C#/VB's async-await)
- Parallel LINQ (often abbreviated as PLINQ)

For a more complete reference of concurrency support in .NET, please visit `https://msdn.microsoft.com/en-us/library/hh156548(v=vs.110).aspx`.

.NET has no support yet for fiber API in Win32 API. Microsoft currently has no definite plan for fiber support.

F# has its own unique features of concurrency supports. They are:

- Asynchronous workflow or computation
- MailboxProcessor
- Parallel async
- Parallel async combined with I/O

More on concurrency support in F# is available in `Chapter 4`, *Introduction to Concurrency in F#* and `Chapter 5`, *Advanced Concurrency Support in F#*.

Now it's time to dive more into some codes. To start writing F# code, we can use F# and Visual Studio combined. This includes IDE supports for F#.

Overview of F# tooling in Visual Studio

F# has been supported in Visual Studio since Visual Studio 2010, and in Visual Studio 2015 the support has improved with better syntax colorizations than Visual Studio 2010, not just IDE. This F# IDE support is officially called *Visual F#*.

This tooling is available as open source from Microsoft and it is available to be downloaded from GitHub at `https://github.com/Microsoft/visualfsharp/`.

And the F# compiler itself is open source and it is also available from GitHub (including the design proposal discussions) at `https://github.com/fsharp`.

The tooling is under the governance of Microsoft, but it is welcoming community contributions as it is available on GitHub. All of the community participations of tooling, compilers and the language specifications are under the governance of the F# Software Foundation (FSSF).

We can also support FSSF directly. For more information about FSSF, please visit `http://fsharp.org/`.

 The F# community projects are also managed by FSSF, and it is welcoming contributions as well. FSSF is an independent entity and it is not tied to Microsoft.

Visual F# in Visual Studio 2015 has mainly the following capabilities:

- Project template support, including the NuGet package addition and references to other projects in the same solution file. The other projects can be VB or C# projects, not just F#.
- `AssemblyInfo` support in a separate file. This feature has been available since Visual Studio 2015. Previously it was only available in C# and VB projects.
- The F# compiler, FSC, is used to compile F# into .NET executable and libraries in the form of DLL.
- Integration of the F# compiler, MSBuild infrastructure, and also Intellisense.
- F# libraries, a foundation to the functional programming constructs of F# and F# unique concurrency features such as asynchronous workflow and `MailboxProcessor`. It also contains many useful functions to further interoperate with C#/VB, including interoperating with .NET delegates.
- Interactive support for the F# interactive (FSI) prompt in the IDE.

For more information about F# tooling, this is the official MSDN Library link:

```
https://msdn.microsoft.com/visualfsharpdocs/conceptual/visual-fsharp
```

It is recommended to always consult the Visual F# documentation on GitHub first, then combine it with the online MSDN Library section of F#.

Microsoft has planned to rebuild all of the online MSDN Library to use the GitHub participation model, so developers can submit a pull request to modify or to amend any documentation page. Visual F# is now being reworked on as well, but there are some pages still left behind inside Visual F# GitHub repo.

To always check the latest development of F# documentation on GitHub, visit `https://github.com/Microsoft/visualfsharpdocs`.

Interactive support for F# interactive

F# interactive is a tool to interpret your F# code and run it immediately. It will also process and show the results, the types, and the syntax errors. The code can be run in the interactive prompt or taken from the source code and then run into F# interactive.

The concept of having interpreted code, executing it, and seeing the results is called REPL. **REPL** is abbreviated from **Read-Eval-Print-Loop**, and it was first available as the system's command-line prompt. There is nothing new about this REPL concept, as other programming languages such as Python already have had REPL before F#.

Compared to C# and VB, F# interactive is the first to have interactive REPL support since Visual Studio 2010. Unfortunately, there is no Visual Studio's Intellisense support for F# interactive yet.

There are two ways to use F# interactive:

- In Visual Studio IDE
- In Command Prompt

The most common usage of F# interactive is within Visual Studio IDE.

We have to set up the F# **Interactive** window to be displayed in order to use F# interactive.

These are the steps to display the F# **Interactive** window:

1. Open the **View** menu from the Visual Studio main menu.
2. Choose **Other Windows..** and then choose F# **Interactive**.

A window that hosts the F# **Interactive** within Visual Studio will appear and it will be ready to interpret our F# code:

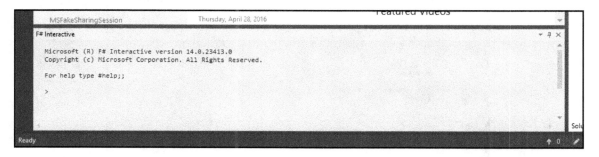

As a starter, type `#help` followed by `;;` to mark as closing statements to be evaluated. We now see some further options:

```
F# Interactive

Microsoft (R) F# Interactive version 14.0.23413.0
Copyright (c) Microsoft Corporation. All Rights Reserved.

For help type #help;;

> #help;;

  F# Interactive directives:

    #r "file.dll";;         Reference (dynamically load) the given DLL
    #I "path";;             Add the given search path for referenced DLLs
    #load "file.fs" ...;;   Load the given file(s) as if compiled and referenced
    #time ["on"|"off"];;    Toggle timing on/off
    #help;;                 Display help
    #quit;;                 Exit

  F# Interactive command line options:

      See 'fsi --help' for options
```

F# interactive can be used to not only interpret and run F# code but also as a way to see immediate results of a calculation.

Type 5 * 25;; and press *Enter*.

We now see the result of that calculation:

```
> #help;;

  F# Interactive directives:

    #r "file.dll";;         Reference (dynamically load) the given DLL
    #I "path";;             Add the given search path for referenced DLLs
    #load "file.fs" ...;;   Load the given file(s) as if compiled and referenced
    #time ["on"|"off"];;    Toggle timing on/off
    #help;;                 Display help
    #quit;;                 Exit

  F# Interactive command line options:

      See 'fsi --help' for options


> 5 * 25;;
val it : int = 125
>
```

We can also execute codes in the Visual Studio editor when we are opening F# source code file.

For example, create a new project using the F# tutorial project template:

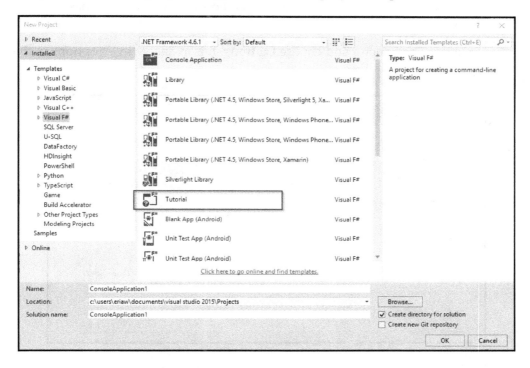

You may find that your display of Visual Studio is different from the previous screenshot. Actually, the aforementioned display depends on what Visual Studio edition we have. For Visual Studio Enterprise, more templates are available for us to use, such as the **Modeling Projects** to create UML.

For the purpose of F#, the project templates of the F# projects are the same for the Community Edition and above.

After creating the project, an F# project contains `Tutorial.fsx`.

Before we use F# interactive, we should turn on the option for displaying line numbers. It is also recommended to have this option always turned on, as it will provide easier navigation to the code we write:

1. Go to the **Tools** menu and choose **Options**. It is available in F# options in the **Options** dialog:

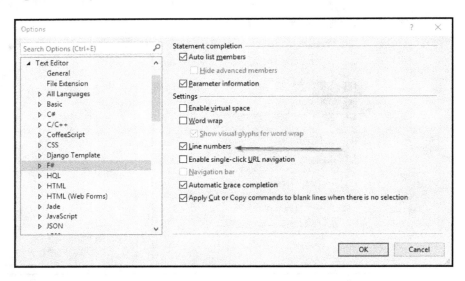

2. Now double-click `Tutorial.fsx`, and highlight lines **44** to **61**:

```
40  //       - OData access using type providers
41
42
43
44  // ---------------------------------------------------------------
45  //        Integers and basic functions
46  // ---------------------------------------------------------------
47
48  module Integers =
49      let sampleInteger = 176
50
51      /// Do some arithmetic starting with the first integer
52      let sampleInteger2 = (sampleInteger/4 + 5 - 7) * 4
53
54      /// A list of the numbers from 0 to 99
55      let sampleNumbers = [ 0 .. 99 ]
56
57      /// A list of all tuples containing all the numbers from 0 to 99 and their squares
58      let sampleTableOfSquares = [ for i in 0 .. 99 -> (i, i*i) ]
59
60      // The next line prints a list that includes tuples, using %A for generic printing
61      printfn "The table of squares from 0 to 99 is:\n%A" sampleTableOfSquares
62
63
```

3. Then press *Alt + Enter*. F# interprets the code. We can see the result of the interpretation in **F# Interactive**:

```
F# Interactive

 > 5 * 25;;
val it : int = 125
>
The table of squares from 0 to 99 is:
[(0, 0); (1, 1); (2, 4); (3, 9); (4, 16); (5, 25); (6, 36); (7, 49); (8, 64);
 (9, 81); (10, 100); (11, 121); (12, 144); (13, 169); (14, 196); (15, 225);
 (16, 256); (17, 289); (18, 324); (19, 361); (20, 400); (21, 441); (22, 484);
 (23, 529); (24, 576); (25, 625); (26, 676); (27, 729); (28, 784); (29, 841);
 (30, 900); (31, 961); (32, 1024); (33, 1089); (34, 1156); (35, 1225);
 (36, 1296); (37, 1369); (38, 1444); (39, 1521); (40, 1600); (41, 1681);
 (42, 1764); (43, 1849); (44, 1936); (45, 2025); (46, 2116); (47, 2209);
 (48, 2304); (49, 2401); (50, 2500); (51, 2601); (52, 2704); (53, 2809);
 (54, 2916); (55, 3025); (56, 3136); (57, 3249); (58, 3364); (59, 3481);
 (60, 3600); (61, 3721); (62, 3844); (63, 3969); (64, 4096); (65, 4225);
 (66, 4356); (67, 4489); (68, 4624); (69, 4761); (70, 4900); (71, 5041);
 (72, 5184); (73, 5329); (74, 5476); (75, 5625); (76, 5776); (77, 5929);
 (78, 6084); (79, 6241); (80, 6400); (81, 6561); (82, 6724); (83, 6889);
 (84, 7056); (85, 7225); (86, 7396); (87, 7569); (88, 7744); (89, 7921);
 (90, 8100); (91, 8281); (92, 8464); (93, 8649); (94, 8836); (95, 9025);
 (96, 9216); (97, 9409); (98, 9604); (99, 9801)]

module Integers = begin
  val sampleInteger : int = 176
  val sampleInteger2 : int = 168
  val sampleNumbers : int list =
    [0; 1; 2; 3; 4; 5; 6; 7; 8; 9; 10; 11; 12; 13; 14; 15; 16; 17; 18; 19; 20;
     21; 22; 23; 24; 25; 26; 27; 28; 29; 30; 31; 32; 33; 34; 35; 36; 37; 38;
     39; 40; 41; 42; 43; 44; 45; 46; 47; 48; 49; 50; 51; 52; 53; 54; 55; 56;
     57; 58; 59; 60; 61; 62; 63; 64; 65; 66; 67; 68; 69; 70; 71; 72; 73; 74;
     75; 76; 77; 78; 79; 80; 81; 82; 83; 84; 85; 86; 87; 88; 89; 90; 91; 92;
     93; 94; 95; 96; 97; 98; 99]
  val sampleTableOfSquares : (int * int) list =
```

We have tried F# interactive from within the Visual Studio IDE. Let's use F# interactive from Command Prompt.

We can also use *Ctrl + Alt + F* to activate or open **F# Interactive**.

To use F# interactive from Command Prompt, we call the executable FSI directly from Command Prompt.

The best way to run FSI is from Visual Studio's developer Command Prompt. This developer Command Prompt is available under the `Visual Studio 2015` folder on the start menu of the Windows desktop menu bar.

Select it, and now we have the **Developer Command Prompt for VS2015**:

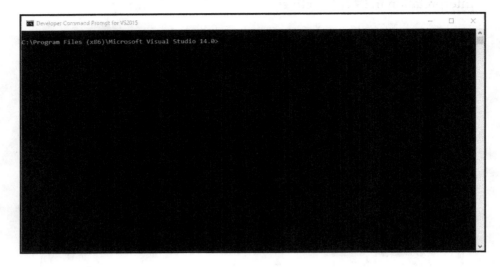

Type `FSI` and press *Enter*.

We can try to write some code to evaluate, such as:

```
let anynumber = 5 * 25;;
```

Press *Enter*. The immediate result will be displayed:

```
C:\Program Files (x86)\Microsoft Visual Studio 14.0>FSI

Microsoft (R) F# Interactive version 14.0.23413.0
Copyright (c) Microsoft Corporation. All Rights Reserved.

For help type #help;;

> let anynumber = 5 * 25;;

val anynumber : int = 125

>
```

To quit the FSI, type `#quit;;` and press *Enter*.

Using F# interactive from Command Prompt is faster but it is also not quite so user-friendly because we cannot evaluate multiple lines of code easily. It is easier to evaluate this in Visual Studio IDE.

For simplicity and ease of use, the rest of this book will always use FSI within the Visual Studio IDE.

For more information about F# FSI, consult the FSI reference from the MSDN Library at `htt ps://msdn.microsoft.com/visualfsharpdocs/conceptual/fsharp-interactive-%5bfs i.exe%5d-reference`.

FSI is also configurable. We can configure FSI further by leveraging the FSI class library in the `Microsoft.FSharp.Compiler.Interactive` namespace. More information on this library is also available at the F# FSI URL mentioned previously.

Introduction to debugging in F#

There is one aspect of understanding running F# code that is crucial: debugging F# code. We have to be able to debug F# code, especially when we have very large projects that have hundreds of F# code files, not to mention when each of the code files may have too many lines of code. For example, having to check a running F# code that has more than 2,000 lines.

The following are the advantages of the debug features:

- Isolating the error and focusing on it by inserting a breakpoint can ease the fixing of an error or bug. Developers are gaining more productivity because they can fix errors/bugs faster.
- Debugging can also provide insightful information about the correctness of any value returning from a function.
- Debugging can also be used to trace bugs further by examining the results from other referenced libraries as well. It is possible that we may use the referenced library incorrectly or the referenced library may also have bugs.

Visual F# in Visual Studio 2015 also has debugging capabilities. It was not as powerful when it was introduced in Visual Studio 2008 as additional add-on, but now the debugging experience is much better. It has been integrated with the Visual Studio extensibility model nicely, providing, for example, faster execution while running in the debug mode and having conditional breakpoints.

It is different from the C#/VB debugger because F#, although being a strongly and strictly typed language, currently has no support for evaluating expressions in the debugger's immediate windows in Visual Studio 2015.

Some experienced F# developers may argue that this additional debug feature is not a big concern at all as F# has a tendency to enforce type restriction and correctness at the fabric of F# as a programming language. But for most other developers, especially those who jump from C#/VB to F#, the overall debugging experience is still lacking some features.

Currently these are the differences between the F# and C#/VB debugger in Visual Studio 2015:

Feature	F#	C#/VB
Breakpoint insertion	Yes.	Yes
Condition in breakpoint	Yes.	Yes
Intellisense in editing condition in breakpoint	Not supported because Intellisense is not yet linked to the whole infrastructure of the Visual Studio 2015 IDE extensibility and the F# compiler. There is a plan to have this feature for the next Visual Studio release after Visual Studio 2015.	Yes
Lightbulb assistant	Not available. There is a plan to have this feature for the next Visual Studio release after Visual Studio 2015, but the exact planned release is not quite clear.	Yes
Expression evaluation in immediate window	Not available.	Yes
Locals value	Yes.	Yes
Auto watch value	Yes.	Yes

Other than the features in the previous table, basic debugging with breakpoints in Visual F# is essentially the same as debugging in C#/VB.

Let's take some code to debug. To quickly have some code, we can use the F# 3.0 sample from CodePlex at:

```
http://fsharp3sample.codeplex.com/
```

After downloading the ZIP file of the code samples, unzip it to a folder and open the `SampleProject.sln` solution file in Visual Studio.

You may read `Readme.txt` first before using the whole sample code. This readme guide is available in the `Solution Item` folder when opened in **Solution Explorer**.

Now, your screen should look like this:

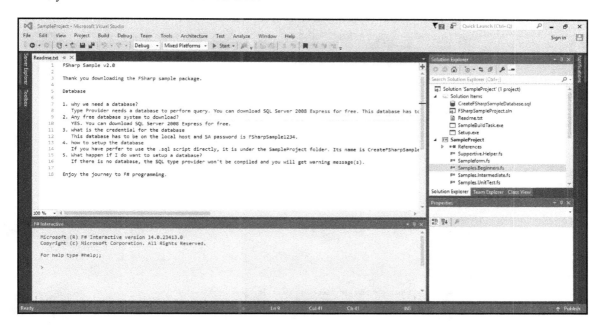

Some of the samples in F# 3.0 are not valid anymore. You have to register for Azure DataMarket to access the F# Type Provider of Azure DataMarket.

There are some compiler errors if we try to rebuild the solution without changing the code at all, and one of the sample type providers, ESRI DataMarket, is not working.

Based on those invalid type provider conditions, to build this sample solution successfully, you have to follow these steps:

1. Register with Azure DataMarket. You need to have your own Azure account key to access Azure DataMarket.
2. The ESRI sample has not been working since 2014. Please comment the lines from line 135 to line 157 in the `Samples.TypeProviders.AzureMarketPlace.fs` file.

3. Rebuild the solution. This will compile the whole solution and also resolve the type provider in the background for us to use.

4. Now open the `Samples.Beginners.fs` file. Put the debugger breakpoints at lines 19 and 20 by clicking the line.

5. To add breakpoints, you can simply toggle the highlighted column on the left before the line number like this:

```
Samples.Beginners.fs  -□ X  Readme.txt
     3   // We disclaim all warranties, either express or implied, including the
     4   // warranties of merchantability and fitness for a particular purpose.
     5
     6   [<Support.Helper.SampleAttributes.Sample("Basic")>]
     7   module Samples.Beginners
     8
     9   open System
    10   open System.Collections.Generic
    11   open Support.Helper
    12
    13   //-------------------------------------------------------
    14
    15   [<Category("Basic Data Types");
    16     Title("Integer Arithmetic");
    17     Description("This sample shows some basic integer arithmetic")>]
    18   let SampleArithmetic1() =
    19       let x = 10 + 12 - 3
    20       let y = x * 2 + 1
    21       let r1,r2 = x/3, x%3
    22       printfn "x = %d, y = %d, r1 = %d, r2 = %d" x y r1 r2
    23
    24
    25   [<Category("Basic Data Types");
    26     Title("Floating Point Arithmetic");
    27     Description("This sample shows some basic floating point arithmetic")>]
    28   let SampleArithmetic2() =
    29       let x = 10.0 + 12.0 - 3.0
    30       let y = x * 2.0 + 1.0
    31       let r1 = x/3.0
    32       printfn "x = %g, y = %g, r1 = %g" x y r1
    33
100 %  ▾
```

6. And we can also add breakpoints by right clicking and choosing **Breakpoints..** and then **Insert Breakpoint**.

7. Compile the code by initiating the **Build Solution**. Then press *F5* to run. The window of **F# Micro Sample Explore** is displayed:

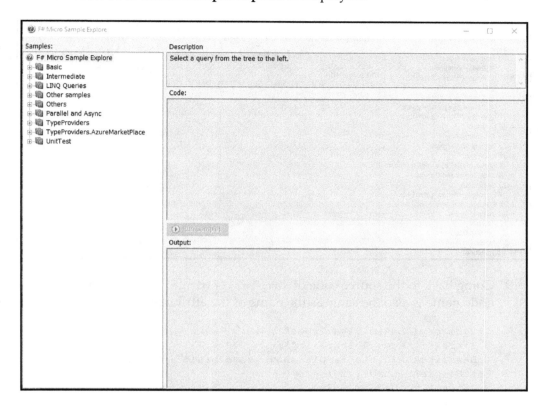

This sample is actually a showcase of many F# features, from basic language constructs, units of measure, type providers, and LINQ, to concurrency such as async and parallelism.

8. Now expand the **Basic** node on the left and choose **Basic Data Types**, and then choose the last node of **Integer Arithmetic**, as illustrated here:

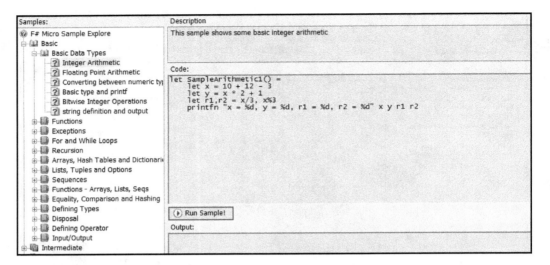

9. Going back to the source code of `Samples.Beginner.fs`, we can see that the node name is also the same as the name of the attributes in the code to categorize:

```
[<Category("Basic Data Types");
  Title("Integer Arithmetic");
  Description("This sample shows some basic integer arithmetic")>]
let SampleArithmetic1() =
    let x = 10 + 12 - 3
    let y = x * 2 + 1
    let r1,r2 = x/3, x%3
    printfn "x = %d, y = %d, r1 = %d, r2 = %d" x y r1 r2
```

10. Click the **Run Sample!** button and Visual Studio will stop the execution at the breakpoint:

```
 6    [<Support.Helper.SampleAttributes.Sample("Basic")>]
 7    module Samples.Beginners
 8
 9    open System
10    open System.Collections.Generic
11    open Support.Helper
12
13    //----------------------------------------------------------------
14
15    [<Category("Basic Data Types");
16      Title("Integer Arithmetic");
17      Description("This sample shows some basic integer arithmetic")>]
18    let SampleArithmetic1() =
19        let x = 10 + 12 - 3
20        let y = x * 2 + 1
21        let r1,r2 = x/3, x%3
22        printfn "x = %d, y = %d, r1 = %d, r2 = %d" x y r1 r2
23
24
25    [<Category("Basic Data Types");
26      Title("Floating Point Arithmetic");
27      Description("This sample shows some basic floating point arithmetic")>]
28    let SampleArithmetic2() =
29        let x = 10.0 + 12.0 - 3.0
30        let y = x * 2.0 + 1.0
31        let r1 = x/3.0
```

Now we can debug our code easily. We can also look at the value of the variables or symbols that are currently in scope by checking the value at the **Locals** window.

11. Press *F10* to step over, and now we see the evaluated value of x and y:

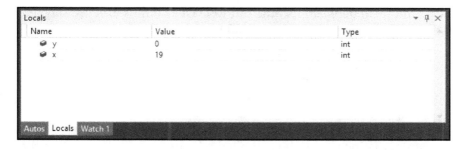

Any local variables in **Locals** and watch expressions displayed in the **Watch1** window always have the name, value, and type of the variables. The type displayed is using the F# keyword, not the full type name.

For example, int is displayed instead of System.Int32 as shown in **Locals**.

We can always check other values as well if we have another global or static global variable in the **Watch1** window. The values can contain immediate values from an expression, for example DateTime.Now.

Unfortunately, we have to write using the full namespace of `System.DateTime`, so we have to write the expression as `System.DateTime.Now`:

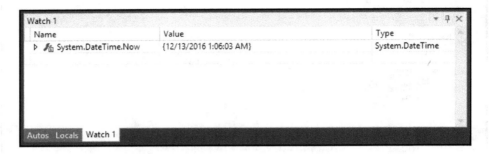

This requirement to have the full namespace proves that debugger support in Visual F# still requires improvements compared to its C#/VB counterparts. Typing the full object name may be error prone, as F# watch does not support Intellisense yet.

After we have finished debugging and bug fixing, it is recommended to change the compilation to the **Release** mode. The **Release** mode will have a smaller compiled F# code and it executes faster because it does not contain debug symbols and any other debug information attached to the compiled code.

To change back and forth between **Debug** and **Release** is quite easy. We can simply change the mode at the drop-down menu in the Visual Studio toolbar:

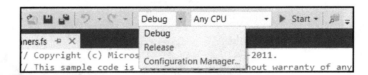

There is no apparent distinction on the compiled DLL or EXE filename, other than the smaller size of the release mode.

To summarize, the following are the differences of the **Debug** mode and the **Release** mode:

Elements	Debug	Release
Debug symbol (PDB)	Included	Not included.
Size of compiled code	Bigger than the release mode, excluding the PDB file	Smaller than the debug mode.
Code optimization	Not optimized, as it is focused for debugging and it is also synchronized	Yes, but the code will not be able to be debugged easily, as the code is optimized for executions. In .NET 4.6 and Windows 10, it is optimized further by compiling into native code using the Ahead Of Time (AOT) model instead of Just In Time (JIT).
Compilation symbol availability	DEBUG	Not applicable.
Execution	Slower than Release, as there is no optimization	Fast, since it is optimized for runtime, and there is no debug symbol overhead.

For more information about AOT and JIT, consult the MSDN Library at
`https://msdn.microsoft.com/en-us/library/dn807190(v=vs.110).aspx`.

Summary

We discussed the introduction to performing common performance optimizations, from the performance characteristics of F# and .NET to the most commonly used optimization concepts such as concurrency. We also have a basic knowledge to start troubleshooting performance problems by debugging using Visual Studio. But debugging running F# code is still a small part of performance optimization because debugging only provides an insight of the values and the states of objects in our code.

The debug support of F# tooling itself is not enough to fully understand the details of performance problems because most of the detailed performance optimization requires us to measure the benchmark of our code. The measurement of performance in order to objectively measure optimization will be described in `Chapter 2`, *Performance Measurement*.

2
Performance Measurement

Performance measurement is often subject to many debates, but we should approach the ways of solving performance problems as straightforwardly as possible while maintaining objective processes. The results must be as objective as they can. To correctly define that a performance optimization is needed or not, we must be able to measure the running code objectively. To ensure the objectiveness of the performance measurement, the result must be visible as quantitative (in numbers) and qualitative by analyzing how the code behaves when it runs, how fast it runs, and how big the code is in memory.

As a rule of thumb, it is easier to analyze quantitatively as data can be seen and compared more directly than when analyzed qualitatively. Understanding how to measure and how to interpret the measurement result can be used as a foundation for deducing the cause of any performance bottlenecks and can be further used in combination with qualitative analytics, such as deciding the best language construct and choosing the best strategy when dealing with concurrencies.

There are many ways to measure performance quantitatively, and we can use the existing tools in Visual Studio and in the .NET SDK/runtime. Understanding data qualitatively means that we have to understand the nature of the running code of F#, from the way it compiles to the way the result of the compilation works, which we can use to then reason the way the code runs.

 A basic understanding of the .NET SDK tool is recommended (including how to install it with Visual Studio) although this chapter will also describe the tools inside Visual Studio since Visual Studio 2015. Please ensure that the installation of .NET and Visual Studio is correct to ensure that the journey to measuring performance described in this chapter is a smooth one.

This chapter will cover the introduction to performance measurement, tooling, and the approaches to quantitative measurement with the following topics:

- Introduction to the nature of F# code compilation, including IL assembly generated
- Using CLR Profiler 4.5
- Ways to measure F# code performance using tools, libraries including timers, API in .NET, and Visual Studio's unit test to measure performance
- Collective time data gathering in unit tests

Introduction to the nature of F# code compilation

Before we measure .NET, we need to understand the nature of F# code and the nature of compiling the F# code. Of course, we can just analyze and look at the source code. We can also try to search for any patterns of non-performing code of known bottlenecks, which will be explained in Chapter 3, *Optimizing Data Structures* and Chapter 7, *Language Features and Constructs Optimization*.

General overview of F# compiler processes and results

All of the code in F# is compiled into byte codes of the IL assembly (as it's also an assembly language) either by the F# compiler or by using F# in interactive mode (by using FSI). This IL is then run in either **Debug** mode as Just In Time (JIT) code is further optimized by compiling it in **Release** mode. Running it in Release mode will yield compiled code to be optimized for .NET native by the Ahead Of Time (AOT) method.

For more information about .NET native, here is the official explanation in the MSDN Library:

```
https://msdn.microsoft.com/en-us/library/dn584397(v=vs.110).aspx
```

The IL is guaranteed to work well with other ILs as it has to conform to IL compliance before being enabled to run on top of .NET runtime. Therefore, running codes written in F# on .NET is essentially the same as running C#/VB codes on .NET. Both of them are coded in .NET IL. Therefore, any programming language compiler that runs on top of .NET has to support compiling into (sometimes called generating) .NET IL.

The IL is executed on top of .NET runtime. The .NET runtime itself is one of the implementations of **Common Language Runtime** (**CLR**). This CLR defines the environment to run any IL assembly, and it also provides isolation and virtualization as well. This concept is known as a *managed environment*. Although it's not tightly tied with an underlying operating system (OS), it can provide an interop service with the underlying OS. In .NET runtime, the call to the Windows API is provided as a Platform Invoke or simply called P/Invoke.

This is the latest official description of .NET CLR on the MSDN Library:

`https://msdn.microsoft.com/en-us/library/8bs2ecf4(v=vs.110).aspx.`

The .NET IL (Intermediate Language) is basically a .NET specific assembly that is part of the **Common Language Infrastructure** (**CLI**) implementation standard. The CLI defines rules, foundations, processes, and IL instruction sets (including the byte codes). This CLI serves as an infrastructure for all languages on top of .NET runtime (or other CLR compliants such as Mono). Microsoft had submitted an initial version of the CLI standard in the beginning of 2001, and the first edition of the CLI standard was released on December 2001. The CLI standard is always revised and synchronized with the release of .NET runtime rather than with the framework version. For example, the latest edition of CLI is now sixth edition and it conforms with .NET 4.0 CLR.

This is the official source of information about the IL and CLI standards in ECMA:

`http://www.ecma-international.org/publications/standards/Ecma-335.htm`

The CLI standard is also implemented in Mono, not just in .NET CLR. The .NET CLR itself defines the corresponding related version of the .NET Framework, and as there are different versions of .NET CLR and the .NET Framework, this is often overlooked.

The releases of .NET Framework versions are not the same as the releases of .NET runtime. For example, .NET Framework 3.5 (often called .NET 3.5) uses the runtime of .NET 2.0 runtime, whereas .NET 4.5 and .NET 4.6 use .NET 4.0 runtime. We should pay attention to this if we really want to understand the underlying foundation of .NET runtime/CLR.

Although most developers don't often care about IL, it may be useful to show you how the code is executed. This takes place at a very low level of the compiled code. It is easier to start from the source code before it's compiled, therefore it is recommended to start with the simple one rather than the code itself at a higher level.

It is also a best practice to always start from high level thinking first and to then go deeper to the lower level, as in IL.

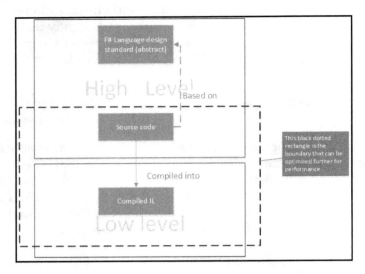

From the perspective of F# code, the highest level is the source code. The source code can be quickly checked for correctness by compiling it or by sending it to FSI. This is considered an important step as we can rely on the compiler when performing syntax and grammar checks. The language design of F# is more abstract than the source code, and it is used as our foundation for checking for correctness. This correctness checking is performed by the parser in the compiler. It is more abstract than the source code that has already been compiled successfully.

This is a common practice, and it is also understandable from a language design perspective; we cannot directly analyze it as it is not easy to apply optimization.

From the compiler side, the compiler interprets and compiles the code by steps in phases, from lexing to parsing the resultant compiled code as IL.

In general, F# compiles the code in the following steps:

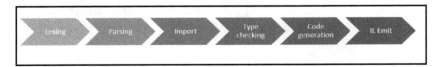

We will only focus on the behavior of the code as related in the phases from **Lexing** to **Type checking** and the result of the IL (related to the **IL Emit** phase). The **Code generation** phase heavily depends on the previous phases, and it will only produce abstract IL code before going to the next phase: the **IL Emit** phase.

At the time of the current release of F# 4.0, the steps are focused on the phases of the F# 4.0 compiler. The compiler is open source, and although we could dive deep into the work of the compiler itself, a deeper understanding of all the elements of the F# language specifications are beyond the scope of this book. From the perspective of performance optimization, we shall focus only on the code constructs, IL emitted, and instrumentations. We are not going to touch any further on the internal detail of how the F# compiler works.

If you want to know more, the previous steps are part of an open contribution process that is part of F# Foundation's missions because the F# Foundation always encourages open contributions to the F# compiler, language design standards, and other elements related to the F# Foundation architecture. This group is called the F# Core Engineering group.

The homepage of F# Core Engineering is at `https://fsharp.github.io/`.

These compilation steps are described in detail in the F# Foundation's F# Core Engineering group's F# compiler guide section on their GitHub page:

`https://fsharp.github.io/2015/09/29/fsharp-compiler-guide.html`

A quick overview of IL in F#

Let's start with the IL emitted by the F# compiler. Although the declared compatibility is as simple as it sounds, F# has a richer and more unique IL emitted than its C#/VB counterpart, but there are features in C#/VB that, currently, F# has no support for in the language yet. From .NET Core's perspective, the IL of F# and C#/VB are being developed at the same time.

This table summarizes the overall differences:

Feature	F#	C#/VB
Tailcall recursion (the `.tail` IL)	Yes. By default, F# will optimize simple recursion by translating it into a loop.	No. By default, tailcall recursion is not enabled in the Debug mode. But when enabled, IL emitted is not guaranteed to have tailcall IL.
Covariance/contravariance	Not available. Support is under review.	Yes.
Platform Invoke (P/Invoke)	Yes.	Yes.
COM objects	Partial. Because some COM objects can't be used as dynamic, they must be declared as `Type.Missing`, especially when writing code that interops with Office COM. This is as expected because F# has no direct support for late bounds.	Yes. Supports COM object as late bound by marking it as dynamic typed.
No PIA project and compile support	Not available. No definite plan in near future.	Yes. Not compatible with .NET Core by design because No PIA is only available on Windows.
.NET Core IL (for .NET Core, CoreCLR, and CoreFX) for cross platform support	The .NET Core is not yet released, but the development is keeping up with both languages.	Same state as F#. The overall source code of .NET CoreCLR is mostly written in C#.

For more information about the progress of .NET CoreCLR, have a look at the official open source repository of .NET CoreCLR at `https://github.com/dotnet/coreclr`.

Now, let's dive into the IL and the generated byte codes.

IL tooling in .NET

Visual Studio comes with .NET SDK by default, and we can use the whole tooling available in .NET SDK in conjunction with the IDE experience inside Visual Studio. This includes everything from compiling to checking the IL generated.

To quickly see the IL, we can use the existing tools in .NET that relate to the IL emitter and disassembler, ILASM, and ILDASM.

.NET itself, in particular .NET SDK, has many tools available for developers to perform development tasks, including ILDASM and ILASM. For more information about .NET tools in Visual Studio 2015, consult this MSDN Library:

`https://msdn.microsoft.com/en-us/library/d9kh6s92(v=vs.110).aspx`

These concepts of using ILASM to assemble IL assembly into machine code and ILDASM to disassemble are almost similar in terms of other assembler ecosystems. For example, the ILASM is conceptually equal to the Microsoft Macro Assembler compiler, known as MASM. It compiles Intel's processors (and its compatible) assembly language into byte codes that truly translate into code that the runtime can execute. ILASM takes the IL assembly and compiles it into a Windows PE (Portable Executable) file that can be in the form of EXE or DLL. ILDASM disassembles the byte code into the IL assembly code.

Unfortunately, there is no direct way to generate F# code into IL assembly code. In fact, the F# compiler compiles F# source codes into Window PE executable machine code as its final result. This is also true when compiling C#/VB source codes. We can see and check the generated assembly code by looking at the result of the disassembly first. We shall start with the easiest one: disassembly using ILDASM.

Using ILDASM and ILASM to understand low-level IL assembly

To illustrate the simplest sample to disassemble simple code, let's create an F# console project in Visual Studio 2015 and name the project as `FSConsole01`:

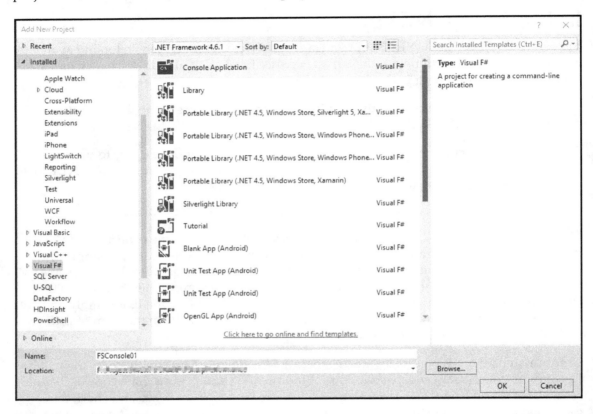

A file will be opened in the Visual Studio editor, named `Program.fs`, which contains basic entry point of the F# console project. Replace the line 6 with this code:

```
printfn "Hello F# world"
```

Then, build the project. We can directly build and run it by pressing *F5*, but the console will pop out and close instantly.

The recommended way to build is to use the key combination of *Ctrl* + *F5* to instruct Visual Studio to run the code without debugging. This action will also pause after the code has finished running in the console:

Press any key or close the window.

Let's examine the IL by disassembling the executable using ILDASM. Search for Visual Studio's **Developer Command Prompt for Visual Studio 2015** and select it:

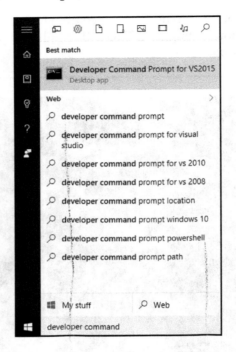

A window that shows the Command Prompt will appear. The window has a title bar of **Developer Command Prompt for VS 2015**. It is basically a Command Prompt (it is an instance of a Windows CMD Command Prompt) that has its environment variables set (including system's PATH environment variable).

NOTE: **Developer Command Prompt for VS 2015** is not available in the Visual Studio 2015 Express Edition installation. It is available in the Visual Studio 2015 Community Edition and above.

For more information about this developer Command Prompt, consult the MSDN Library:

```
https://msdn.microsoft.com/en-us/library/ms229859(v=vs.110).aspx
```

In the command prompt, type ILDASM and then press *Enter*. An **ILDASM** window will show the following:

To start disassembling FSConsole01, perform the following steps:

1. From the main menu, open the **File** menu.
2. Select **Open** and then go to the folder that stores FSConsole01.
3. Select the subfolder bin, the Debug subfolder.
4. Open FSConsole01.exe.

Let's resize a little bit so that now ILDASM will display the content of the EXE file as organized into metadata that contains IL:

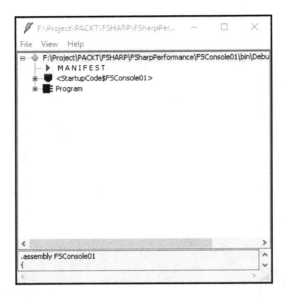

The ILDASM of `FSConsole01.exe` has three nodes:

- The **MANIFEST** node is a manifest of runtime information that contains the .NET runtime assembly it targets.
- **<StartupCode$FSConsole01>** contains the necessary metadata of the `AssemblyInfo`, the main class of Program, and other assembly attributes.
- **Program** contains the actual IL of the F# source code compiled into IL assembly, related to the `<EntryPoint>` attribute.

Now let's expand the Program node and select the **main : int32(string[])** node:

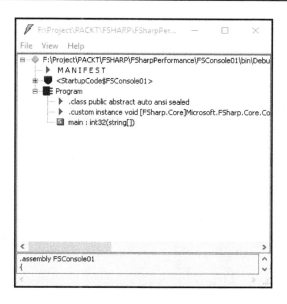

To further explore the source code, double-click the **main** node. ILDASM will display a new window that contains the IL assembly of `main`:

```
.method public static int32  main(string[] argv) cil managed
{
    .entrypoint
    .custom instance void [FSharp.Core]Microsoft.FSharp.Core.EntryPointAttribute::.ctor() = ( 01 00
    // Code size       19 (0x13)
    .maxstack  8
    IL_0000:  nop
    IL_0001:  ldstr      "Hello F# world"
    IL_0006:  newobj     instance void class [FSharp.Core]Microsoft.FSharp.Core.PrintfFormat`5<class
    IL_000b:  call       !!0 [FSharp.Core]Microsoft.FSharp.Core.ExtraTopLevelOperators::PrintFormatL
    IL_0010:  pop
    IL_0011:  ldc.i4.0
    IL_0012:  ret
} // end of method Program::main
```

Let's look again at the source code:

```
[<EntryPoint>]
let main argv =
    printfn "Hello F# world"
    0 // return an integer exit code
```

[51]

Now we will dive into the translation of IL.

The `let main argv` function declaration is translated into the following IL:

```
.method public static int32  main(string[] argv) cil managed
```

This is crucial and it's quite similar to the main console of C#/VB as it's also generated as a method that uses the `public static` modifier. In F#, the `main` method has `int32` as its return value instead of `void` in C# (Sub in VB).

The `EntryPoint` attribute is translated as `.entrypoint` combined with the instantiation of the `EntryPoint` attribute inside the method.

The `"Hello F# world"` string is loaded into memory as indicated by the `ldstr` IL assembly command. Then, the next line prepares the call to F# `PrintfFormatLine` (as compiled from the translation of the abbreviated name of `printf`) by calling the `static` constructor of `Microsoft.FSharp.Core.PrintfFormat` and then calling the `PrintFormatLine`.

This is the behavior of any call to the static method, and it is related to .NET CLR, not the convention or the IL result from F#. When calling any static method for the first time, the static constructor of the class that has the static method (if this constructor is available) is always called first. It behaves the same as in C# and VB.

Now let's examine the IL emitted by the recursive function in F# even further. Let's add the recursive factorial function. To make it more interesting, we are using pattern matching to match the conditions of the recursive calls. Add the following code before the main entry point:

```
let rec fact x =
    match x with
    | 1 -> 1
    | a when a < 1 -> 1
    | _ -> x * fact (x-1)
```

Run ILDASM and open the compiled `FSConsole01` executable. Navigate to the `fact` node and then double-click the node. We will see that the IL is translated into a loop in the IL assembly:

```
 Program::fact : int32(int32)                                       —    □    ×
Find  Find Next
.method public static int32  fact(int32 x) cil managed
{
    // Code size        44 (0x2c)
    .maxstack  5
    .locals init ([0] int32 V_0,
               [1] int32 a,
               [2] int32 V_2)
    IL_0000:  nop
    IL_0001:  ldarg.0
    IL_0002:  stloc.0
    IL_0003:  ldloc.0
    IL_0004:  ldc.i4.1
    IL_0005:  sub
    IL_0006:  switch        (
                             IL_001b)
    IL_000f:  ldloc.0
    IL_0010:  stloc.1
    IL_0011:  ldloc.1
    IL_0012:  ldc.i4.1
    IL_0013:  clt
    IL_0015:  brfalse.s   IL_0019
    IL_0017:  br.s        IL_001d
    IL_0019:  br.s        IL_0021
    IL_001b:  ldc.i4.1
    IL_001c:  ret
    IL_001d:  ldloc.0
    IL_001e:  stloc.2
    IL_001f:  ldc.i4.1
    IL_0020:  ret
    IL_0021:  ldarg.0
    IL_0022:  ldarg.0
    IL_0023:  call        int32 Program::fact(int32)
    IL_0028:  ldc.i4.1
    IL_0029:  sub
    IL_002a:  mul
    IL_002b:  ret
} // end of method Program::fact
```

There are three branch instructions: br.false and two br.s instructions. These three correspond to the match branches in the code.

In this sample recursive function of factorial, the recursive construct is optimized as a loop in the IL emitted. The usage of a loop also implies that the stack overflow will not happen as the code is not performing recursion; therefore, there is no need to store the function entry in the stack as with most recursive functions in other languages such as C# and VB. It is intrinsically faster and more efficient than using a stack frame to store the recursion returning point.

> The choice of optimization from a recursive into a loop is what separates F# from C#/VB. It is faster to have a loop than to use recursion that requires stack frames because stack frame usage adds more overhead of pushing and popping values in stack manipulations.

A deeper discussion on recursive function and tail calls is available in Chapter 7, *Language Features and Constructs Optimization*.

For more information on IL assembly instructions, consult the ECMA 335 standard.

We now have IL assemblies available to use. The output produced by ILDASM can be used to be the foundation of understanding IL deeper, but we need to be able to produce the whole IL assembly of the executable.

Using the existing `FSConsole01`, we are going to transform the compiled EXE to a text file that contains the IL assembly.

Open the **Developer Command Prompt for Visual Studio 2015** and change the folder to the `bindebug` subfolder of your `FSConsole01` project. Then, type the following:

```
ildasm FSConsole01.exe /OUT=FSConsole.IL
```

The `/OUT` parameter means that we are not going to display ILDASM UI because we are going to dump the IL into a file to contain the IL assembly code as a result of the disassembler of ILDASM. It is a recommended best practice to name the extension of the file as *IL* because it is a source code of .NET IL assembly code, although .NET will not register IL as a filename extension on Windows.

We now have `FSConsole.IL`. Open the `FSConsole.IL` using Notepad:

```
FSConsole.IL - Notepad                                                                          —  □  ×
File  Edit  Format  View  Help
//  Microsoft (R) .NET Framework IL Disassembler.  Version 4.6.1055.0
//  Copyright (c) Microsoft Corporation.  All rights reserved.


// Metadata version: v4.0.30319
.assembly extern mscorlib
{
  .publickeytoken = (B7 7A 5C 56 19 34 E0 89 )                    // .z\V.4..
  .ver 4:0:0:0
}
.assembly extern FSharp.Core
{
  .publickeytoken = (B0 3F 5F 7F 11 D5 0A 3A )                    // .?_....:
  .ver 4:4:0:0
}
.assembly FSConsole01
{
  .custom instance void [FSharp.Core]Microsoft.FSharp.Core.FSharpInterfaceDataVersionAttribute::.ctor(int32,
                                                                                                      int32,
                                                                                                      int32) = ( 01 00 02 00 00 00 00 00 00 0
  .custom instance void [mscorlib]System.Runtime.Versioning.TargetFrameworkAttribute::.ctor(string) = ( 01 00 1C 2E 4E 45 54 46 72 61 6D 6
                                                                                                        2C 56 65 72 73 69 6F 6E 3D 76 34 2
                                                                                                        00 54 0E 14 46 72 61 6D 65 77 6F 7
                                                                                                        70 6C 61 79 4E 61 6D 65 14 2E 4E 4
                                                                                                        61 6D 65 77 6F 72 6B 20 34 2E 36 2
  .custom instance void [mscorlib]System.Reflection.AssemblyTitleAttribute::.ctor(string) = ( 01 00 0B 46 53 43 6F 6E 73 6F 6C 65 30 31 00
  .custom instance void [mscorlib]System.Reflection.AssemblyDescriptionAttribute::.ctor(string) = ( 01 00 00 00 00 )
  .custom instance void [mscorlib]System.Reflection.AssemblyConfigurationAttribute::.ctor(string) = ( 01 00 00 00 00 )
  .custom instance void [mscorlib]System.Reflection.AssemblyCompanyAttribute::.ctor(string) = ( 01 00 00 00 00 )
  .custom instance void [mscorlib]System.Reflection.AssemblyProductAttribute::.ctor(string) = ( 01 00 0B 46 53 43 6F 6E 73 6F 6C 65 30 31
  .custom instance void [mscorlib]System.Reflection.AssemblyCopyrightAttribute::.ctor(string) = ( 01 00 12 43 6F 70 79 72 69 67 68 74 20 C
                                                                                                  20 32 30 31 36 00 00 )
  .custom instance void [mscorlib]System.Reflection.AssemblyTrademarkAttribute::.ctor(string) = ( 01 00 00 00 00 )
  .custom instance void [mscorlib]System.Reflection.AssemblyCultureAttribute::.ctor(string) = ( 01 00 00 00 00 )
```

Press *Ctrl + F* and search for `Program` and then we see that the F# compiler emitted the class declaration of Program as `public abstract`:

```
// =============== CLASS MEMBERS DECLARATION ===================

.class public abstract auto ansi sealed Program
       extends [mscorlib]System.Object
```

This is also a form of optimization by the F# compiler because the `Program` class as the entrypoint *doesn't have to be a concrete class*. This is different from C# as the default compile result is a concrete class. For example:

```
// =============== CLASS MEMBERS DECLARATION ===================

.class private auto ansi beforefieldinit Imperative.Program
       extends [mscorlib]System.Object
```

However, we can modify the corresponding C#'s `Program` class to have a similar abstract class explicitly in the code before building and compiling it again.

Let's directly modify the IL assembly code and compile it back to an executable using ILASM.

Search for this line of code:

```
IL_0001:  ldstr      "Hello F# world"
```

Change the `Hello F# world` to `Hello world!` and then save the IL using a different name, for example, `FSConsole01a.IL`.

Then, go back to the developer's Command Prompt and type this:

```
ilasm FSConsole01a.IL /exe
```

Then, execute `FSConsole01a.exe` on the Command Prompt; it should now display `Hello world!`, as shown here:

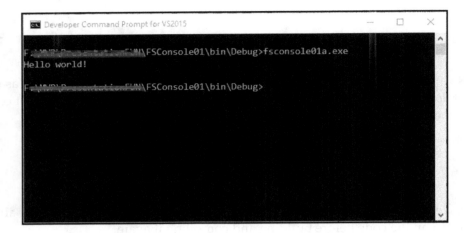

Now, we can have qualitative optimization based on IL! We also have learned this example of recursion as loop—one good example use case of IL analyzing. This IL use of a loop instead of recursion using a stack is also proof of optimization: F# is already one step ahead of other languages (especially non-functional languages) in terms of handling basic recursive functions.

We have grabbed the basic understanding of the F# compiler and IL. Now that we understood the underlying IL assembly generated by F#, we can profile it using the CLR Profiler, a profiler tool from Microsoft.

Using CLR Profiler 4.5

CLR Profiler is a profiler tool used to profile any compiled PE of .NET. It is free and open source, although it is not available by default in the current installation of .NET and Visual Studio 2015.

A profiler is basically a helper tool to analyze the elements of a running program that relates to performances, such as:

- Memory consumptions
- Execution time allocations in terms of classes and modules into smaller elements such as functions and subroutines
- Examining garbage collections (if the platform has support for garbage collection)

Based on the previous definitions, the CLR Profiler is simply a profiler to examine (or *to profile*) any application that runs on top of .NET CLR.

There are profilers toolings for .NET, not just CLR Profiler, out there, unfortunately not all the toolings are free. Fortunately, CLR Profiler has complete features to profile .NET application, and it is also free and open source. We can also build our own profiler based on the existing CLR Profiler.

A quick overview of CLR Profiler

CLR Profiler has been developed since .NET 1.1, although it is not supported anymore. The latest CLR Profiler is available for .NET 4.5, and it can only be used effectively for profiling any .NET 4.0 CLR-based application, including .NET 4.0 to .NET 4.6 applications. The next version of .NET may or may not be compatible.

CLR Profiler has been developed since .NET 1.1, and it is always released to match with the .NET runtime releases. For example, CLR Profiler version 2.0 supports .NET 2.0 runtime. This version 2.0 release supports .NET generics that were introduced in .NET 2.0 runtime. The version 3.5 supports .NET 2.0 SP1 runtime that was released with .NET Framework 3.5 and so do the next versions, as illustrated:

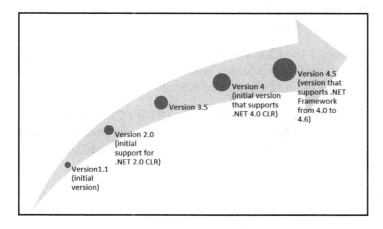

There were some maintenance releases of CLR Profiler between the themed releases from version 2.0 to version 4 that were in sync with .NET runtime, but these maintenance releases were mostly bug fixes that addressed minor test cases involving profiling Platform interop with Win32 API and COM. After the release of CLR Profiler 4, the maintenance releases are not available, particularly, because the source code of CLR Profiler is also open sourced.

An initial version of CLR Profiler, until version 2.0, was developed within a closed-source model, and it was then opened as open source. The repository of the CLR Profiler was located at CodePlex until now.

It was maintained originally by the CLR team, and was then lead by David Broman until now. The most interesting fact is that the CLR Profiler is written entirely in C++, using a mix of native Win32 C++ with managed C++. It can hook into the running code of the application to be profiled by first loading and examining the IL and then injecting some hooks as IL to monitor the execution.

To catch up with the development of CLR Profiler on CodePlex, have a look at this landing page:

`http://clrprofiler.codeplex.com/`

David Broman, Microsoft's original developer of CLR Profiler, has a blog on MSDN as well. His blog is available at `https://blogs.msdn.microsoft.com/davbr/`.

A quick walkthrough of CLR Profiler in action

On the download page of CLR Profiler, choose binaries. Since we are going to use CLR Profiler to profile our running code, we are going to use the compiled CLR Profiler instead of building and compiling it from the CLR Profiler source code.

After we have downloaded the CLR Profiler 4.5 binaries as a ZIP file, unzip it to any folder. It's recommended not to use a deep folder with nested folders because it may not be searchable, unless we put the folder into PATH environment variable.

This CLR Profiler can be used to profile 32-bit and 64-bit CLR executables and CLR DLL. There are two binaries for the 32-bit and 64-bit versions, respectively. For the most common case and best practices, we should use the 32-bit CLR Profiler to profile 32-bit CLR executables and DLL.

Before we use CLR Profiler to profile our executable, these are some limitations and warnings about the known consequences of running CLR Profiler to mention:

- CLR Profiler is an intrusive tool; seeing a 10 to 100x slowdown in the application being profiled is not unusual. Therefore, it is not the right tool to find out where time is spent–use other profilers for that.
- Log files can be huge. By default, every allocation and every call is logged, which can consume gigabytes of disk space. However, allocation and call logging can be turned on and off selectively, either by the application or in the CLR Profiler UI.

- CLR Profiler cannot *attach* to an application that is already running.
- CLR Profiler might get caught and be considered harmful by some antivirus programs such as Trend Micro, ESET, and even the older versions of Symantec and Kaspersky. These antiviruses might have treated CLR Profiler as harmful malware or security exploit software. This is truly a false alarm. CLR Profiler must be listed as *white list* for these antivirus programs. Also, update your antivirus detection data.

Now, let's examine our current `FSConsole01` project. Open the solution that contains your `FSConsole01` project and build it. To ensure that Visual Studio will not interfere with CLR Profiler, close the solution and close Visual Studio.

Go to the folder that you downloaded and extract the CLR Profiler. You shall see two subfolders and one file: subfolders named `32`, `64`, and a Word document file named `CLRProfiler.doc`. The DOC file is actually a complete documentation of how to use CLR Profiler. Open the subfolder of `32` and then execute the `CLRProfiler.exe` file by opening or by double-clicking it.

A Command Prompt and CLR Profiler UI is shown:

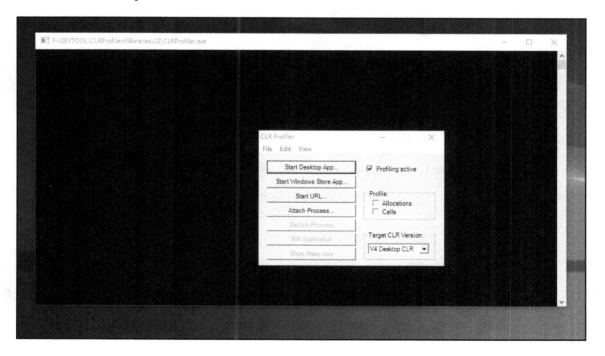

Ignore the Command Prompt, but do not close it, as it will also close CLR Profiler. Before you start profiling, check the **Allocations** and **Calls** under the **Profile** frame:

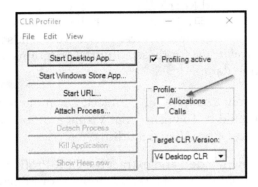

Also ensure that the checkbox of **Profiling active** is always checked.

This is the reason given in the CLR Profiler documentation as to why **Profiling active** is checked:

> *The Profiling active check box lets you turn profiling on and off selectively. You can do that either to save time (for example during application startup), or to profile selectively. For example, if you wanted to see what happens in your Windows Forms application when a certain button gets clicked, you would clear this box, start your application, then check the box, click your button, and then clear the box again. Another usage would be to turn this off when starting to profile your ASP.NET application, load a specific page, and then turn it on to see what gets allocated in the steady state for that specific page.*

Our FSConsole01 is a console application, and it is also a desktop application by nature although it is running as a console application. Therefore, we need to ensure that this checkbox of **Profiling active** is checked.

Click the **Start Desktop App...** button and open FSConsole01.exe in the bindebug folder.

Then, CLR Profiler will show a UI that acts as container of profiling summary:

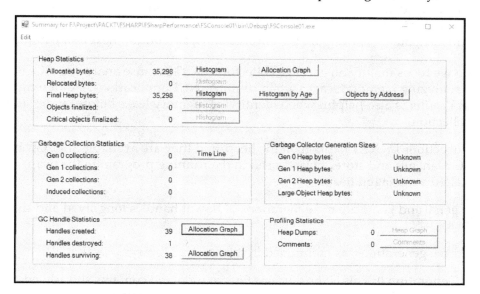

This summary is very important, as it is the starting point before starting to analyze the graphical data generated by CLR Profiler. The data summaries are grouped into sections.

The important sections of the summary are explained here:

- The section labeled **Garbage Collection Statistics** gives statistics about the garbage collections that happen during the program run. The garbage collector in the .NET CLR is generational, which means that many garbage collections only consider the newest objects on the heap. These are referred to as generation 0 collections and are quite fast. **Gen 1 collections** consider a bigger portion of the heap and are thus a bit slower, while **Gen 2 collections** (also referred to as *full collections*) consider the complete heap and can take a significant amount of time if the heap is large. Thus, you want to see a relatively small number of **Gen 2 collections** compared to **Gen 1 collections** and **Gen 0 collections**. Finally, **Induced collections** are the collections triggered outside of the garbage collector, for example, by calling GC.Collect from the application. The view reachable via the **Time Line** button will be explained in detail in a short while.

- The section **Garbage Collector Generation Sizes** gives the sizes of the various garbage collector generations. One additional twist is that there is a special area for large objects called **Large Object Heap bytes**. Note that these numbers are averages over the program run, which may not reflect the situation at the end of the run.

- The section **GC Handle Statistics** lists how many GC handles have been created, destroyed, and how many are surviving at the end of the program run. If the last number is particularly large, you may have a GC handle leak, which you can investigate by clicking on the **Allocation Graph** button next to the number.

So, why do we focus mainly on garbage collectors (GC)? Because analyzing GCs is very useful for analyzing memory usages when running .NET applications. Examining GCs using CLR Profiler is also helpful when identifying memory leaks before, at, or after garbage collection.

Garbage collections in .NET happen on the heap, and they are available after GC has started. GC manages and stores objects used in the running program in the heap, and this is why it is called a **managed heap**.

The terms gen 0 and gen 1 are the generations of how it handles long-lived and short-lived objects.

There are three generations, as mentioned in the MSDN Library:

- **Generation 0**: This is the youngest generation and contains short-lived objects. An example of a short-lived object is a temporary variable. Garbage collection occurs most frequently in this generation. Newly allocated objects form a new generation of objects and are implicitly generation 0 collections, unless they are large objects, in which case they go on the large object heap in a generation 2 collection. Most objects are reclaimed for garbage collection in generation 0 and do not survive to the next generation. This generation is also called gen 0 or simply Gen0.
- **Generation 1**: This generation contains short-lived objects and serves as a buffer between short-lived objects and long-lived objects. This generation is also called gen 1 or simply Gen1.
- **Generation 2**: This generation contains long-lived objects. An example of a long-lived object is an object in a server application that contains static data that is live for the duration of the process.

If there are many objects that are characterized as long-lived objects during the runtime of an application, GC overheads will always occur at the finalization of the garbage collecting. This stage of finalization means that many long-lived objects are often called as having a condition of high cost object finalizations. Analyzing the GC using CLR Profiler will provide us with data on when and where GC overheads occur, especially when GC has many objects to handle (this will be shown as handles in CLR Profiler).

We can reduce the cost of finalization by using objects that implement the `IDisposable` interface correctly.

This tip is explained in detail in the following MSDN article by Rico Mariani, one of the architects of .NET BCL: `https://msdn.microsoft.com/en-us/library/ms973837.aspx`.

In this article, it is recommended to use `IDisposable` interface for the following reason:

> *In many cases it is possible for objects that would otherwise always need to be finalized to avoid that cost by implementing the IDisposable interface. This interface provides an alternative method for reclaiming resources whose lifetime is well known to the programmer, and that actually happens quite a bit. Of course it's better still if your objects simply use only memory and therefore require no finalization or disposing at all; but if finalization is necessary and there are many cases where explicit management of your objects is easy and practical, then implementing the IDisposable interface is a great way to avoid, or at least reduce, finalization costs.*

The `IDisposable` interface has only one method: the `Dispose` method. It is crucial if we want to implement `IDisposable`, particularly, if the class that implements `IDisposable` is available to inherit (not marked with `SealedAttribute` in F#). Its detail implementation must obey the rules in the MSDN documentation:

- It should provide one `public`, non-virtual `Dispose()` method and a `protected` virtual `Dispose(Boolean disposing)` method
- The `Dispose()` method must call `Dispose(true)` and should suppress finalization for performance
- The base type should not include any finalizers

Unfortunately, there is no `protected` and `virtual` modifier support in F#; therefore, we could only use the F# default modifier on the `Dispose` method.

It is quite easy in F# to ensure that the `Dispose` method is always called after we are done using the object by using F# syntactic sugar of `use` or `using` keywords, which translate to always call for disposal after the object is no longer in use. It is quite similar to the syntactic `using` in C# and VB. More details on this can be found in `Chapter 7`, *Language Features and Constructs Optimization*.

For a starting point to understand more on .NET Garbage Collector, visit the MSDN Library article titled *Fundamentals of Garbage Collection*:

`https://msdn.microsoft.com/en-us/library/ee787088(v=vs.110).aspx`

Let's see a sample data of GC handles. In order to have this data presented to us, let's go back and focus our attention on the CLR Profiler's summary window.

Click the **Allocation Graph** button under **GC Handle Statistics** to see and check **GC handle allocations**:

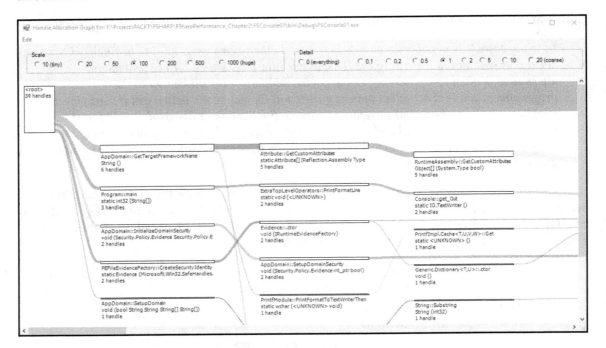

In the graph, there are some lines and rectangular bars that flow from the leftmost rectangle. These represent the flow of how many handles the GC has. The thicker lines represent the biggest number of handles. These handles are further described in detail as thinner handles that comes from thicker rectangles. In the following text, the rectangular bar represents the program elements.

We can also drill down further by double-clicking the element that we want to examine.

Let's examine the `Program::main` element:

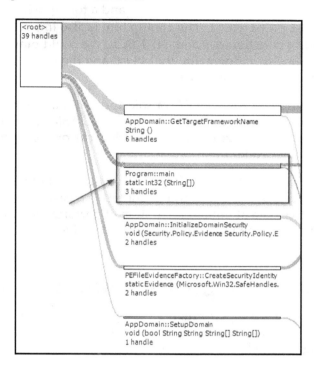

Double-click the rectangular bar above the `Program::main`. A new graph window will appear, and it will only display the handles from `Program::main`:

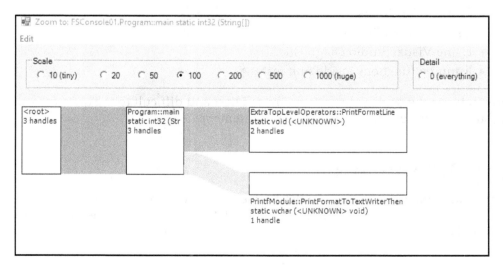

Hover the mouse over the rectangle that is labeled `ExtraTopLevelOperators::PrintFormatLine`, and a tooltip will show you that this object comes from `FSharp.Core.dll`. This tooltip hint is also important if we use references and not just F# core libraries and .NET BCL. We could pinpoint which part of an object holds many handles, drill down into the object, and then hover on it to see which object refers to which DLL library or executable.

We have used CLR Profiler to profile an F# console application. Combined with the knowledge of IL assembly language, CLR Profiler and ILDASM/ILASM provides us with a qualitative point of view for analyzing potential bottlenecks or even opportunities for further optimizations of our code.

Again, it's harder to analyze qualitative data than quantitative, but we can set the qualitative knowledge to further understand quantitative measurement because understanding qualitative data at initial preparation of performance measurement gives us reasoning capability when we analyze our running code using simpler quantitative ways.

Ways to measure performance quantitatively

There are many ways to measure performances of any running .NET code on top of CLR, including F#. So, any tool used to measure F# code is essentially usable for other programming languages on .NET CLR as well.

Again, the easiest way to objectively measure performance is by using quantitative measurements. The following are some common ways of measuring running codes:

- Using .NET timers
- Using native Win32 timer
- Using Visual Studio Diagnostic
- Running functions inside unit tests

The previous numbers are ordered from the subtlest and difficult to the quickest way of having statistical timing as performance measurements.

Using .NET timers

There are many timer classes in the .NET Framework but not all of them have a general purpose from the perspective of implementation details and in the context of execution environments.

In the context of execution environments, .NET timers are divided as follows:

- UI timers (timers that are run on an UI thread)
- Non-UI timer (timers that are run on the common CPU thread)

All UI timers are not always synchronized with a non-UI thread, so they are not guaranteed to have high precision. An example of this is when using `System.Windows.Forms.Timer`, while at the same time having a background thread run. In the internal implementation of `System.Windows.Forms.Timer`, this object uses the `Win32 WM_TIMER` message and processes it in a message loop.

In addition, the behavior of `System.Windows.Forms.Timer` is synchronous relative to the other UI thread, and therefore the UI thread processes this message loop of `WM_TIMER` as long as it is not processing other Windows messages that come in the middle.

Therefore, an elapsed event of this timer may slip as the timer has no lock on the current UI thread of Windows message loops, especially when there are blocking threads running, such as when downloading from the Internet or printing to a printer.

For the sake of objective measurement and also calculating with as high precision as possible, we are not going to use UI timers and will instead focus on non-UI timers.

The following non-UI timers are available:

- `System.Timers.Timer`
- `System.Threading.Timer`
- `System.Diagnostic.Stopwatch`

The `System.Timers.Timer` is a special case of timers. It may run indirectly on a UI thread, not just on a system worker thread. `System.Threading.Timer` always runs on a worker thread, and we cannot mix worker threads and UI threads easily. This condition is raised because the nature of `System.Threading.Timer` is asynchronous. But this is also a nice feature to use as it will not lock the running UI thread, since the thread has to be explicitly treated or handled in a different manner.

Using `System.Timer.Timer` is easier to use than `System.Threading.Timer` as it uses an event model instead of forcing to use callbacks. It's also easier to understand because we can control the number of ticks for triggering the elapsed event.

Let's create a separate project to test the timer of `System.Timers.Timer` to measure our function.

Create a new F# console project and name it `FSTimer01`. A window editor that shows the opened `Program.fs` is now open.

Change the code of `Program.cs` as follows:

```
open System
let rec fact x =
    match x with
    | 1 -> 1
    | a when a < 1 -> 1
    | _ -> x * fact (x-1)

[<EntryPoint>]
let main argv =
    let timer1 = new System.Timers.Timer(1.0)
    let mutable timeElapsed = 0
    timer1.Enabled <- true
    timer1.AutoReset <- true
    timer1.Elapsed.Add (fun _ -> timeElapsed <- timeElapsed + 1)
    timer1.Start()
    for cnt = 1 to 3000000 do
        fact 5 |> ignore
    timer1.Stop()
    Console.WriteLine(String.Concat("time elapsed for ", timeElapsed))
    0 // return an integer exit code
```

Run the code by means of running without debugging, and the time elapsed will kick for every 1 millisecond.

On my machine, it shows `time elapsed for 6`, meaning the code takes roughly about 6 milliseconds to execute. Again, this may vary on different machines with different configurations.

The previous sample code is not quite accurate in terms of precision because it relies heavily on the elapsed event when it triggered. There might be something that comes before and after the timer has elapsed, and this might block the current thread before the elapsed event and even after the elapsed event is triggered. To use `System.Timers.Timer` more accurately, we should not use timer mixed with another blocking thread, such as I/O, or another thread that might change the system state, such as querying or updating operating system settings.

For more details of comparison on these timers (other than Stopwatch), we can see the timers in action in this archived article in MSDN Magazine February 2004 edition (in CHM format):

```
http://download.microsoft.com/download/3/a/7/3a7fa450-1f33-41f7-9e6d-3aa95b5a6a
ea/MSDNMagazineFebruary2004en-us.chm
```

Next, we use `System.Diagnostic.Stopwatch`, which is often called Stopwatch. Although this timer is quite similar to `System.Timers.Timer`, Stopwatch has its own algorithm flow, and it is clever enough to use a performance counter, as defined in the MSDN Library:

> *The Stopwatch measures elapsed time by counting timer ticks in the underlying timer mechanism. If the installed hardware and operating system support a high-resolution performance counter, then the Stopwatch class uses that counter to measure elapsed time. Otherwise, the Stopwatch class uses the system timer to measure elapsed time.*

A high resolution performance counter is obtained by calling the native (unmanaged) Win32 API of `QueryPerformanceCounter`. But this Win32 API should not be used directly as it may require some privileges. particularly elevated privileges. To safely determine that we have a high resolution performance counter available, we should use the properties of Stopwatch, `Frequency` and `IsHighResolution`.

For more information about `System.Diagnostics.Stopwatch`, have a look at the official MSDN documentation:

```
https://msdn.microsoft.com/en-us/library/system.diagnostics.stopwatch(v=vs.110)
.aspx
```

It is quite easy to use Stopwatch as we do not need to pay attention to any time-elapsed event, because there is no specific elapsed event to handle manually. Stopwatch also uses .NET `TimeSpan` to measure how much time has passed from beginning to end.

Using the solution as a timer beforehand, we can test Stopwatch by creating a new project on top of the current solution.

Create a new console project called `FSTimer02`. A default `Program.fs` editor appears, so then copy the codes from the previous `Program.fs` that has the `System.Timers.Timer` example, as we are reusing the `fact` function.

Change the function body into the following code:

```
[<EntryPoint>]
let main argv =
    let stopwatch1 = new System.Diagnostics.Stopwatch()
    stopwatch1.Reset()
```

```
stopwatch1.Start()
for cnt = 1 to 3000000 do
    fact 5 |> ignore
stopwatch1.Stop()
let timeDuration = stopwatch1.ElapsedMilliseconds
Console.WriteLine(String.Concat("time elapsed in milliseconds:",
timeDuration))
    0 // return an integer exit code
```

This time it will show the time duration at a point after the execution of `Stopwatch.Start` until the point before `Stopwatch.Stop` is executed. The number of milliseconds of the `ElapsedMilliseconds` property is actually the same result of `Elapsed` as `TimeSpan`. Both properties call the same `private` method of Stopwatch: the `GetElapsedDateTimeTicks` method.

Set the `FSTimer02` project as a startup project and then run it. The time shown has a tendency to be higher than the time shown by `System.Timers.Timer`. This is as expected because Stopwatch queries to the system performance counter first and then tries to decide whether a performance counter with a higher resolution is available. If it is available, it will try to use it; otherwise, it will use the existing system CPU ticks.

We have experienced how to use .NET timers to measure the duration of the running code. The data available is very useful for comparison, especially when testing different functions, language constructs, and when performing optimizations on inline functions.

But using these timers is not always the best practice, as they may be subject to the Windows' thread scheduler, and other running background Windows processes with the most administrative privileges may interfere, although, it is somehow possible.

Running functions inside unit tests

One of the most common ways to measure is by running and testing our code inside a unit test. It is recommended because you are forced to think about all of the possible scenarios for errors or exceptions that might occur, not just successful scenarios. Here, the term *scenario* means considering various inputs to be tested (including having incorrect or undesirable inputs) that are taken as parameters.

A quick introduction to unit tests

There are many definitions of a unit test, but a unit test is simply a test that focuses on testing the smallest testable part of a program; this might be a simple function or a complex function that has calls to other functions. To cover the objectivity of the unit test, the test must also cover any scenario of having various inputs to test the results and the possibility of exceptions that may occur.

It is known that unit tests are closely related to **Test-Driven Development** (TDD), where developers focus on possible scenarios that may produce different results or even errors as exceptions. By thinking of the possible scenarios upfront, the chance of having bugs in the implementation is minimized or even close to zero. You can also identify the failing scenarios, particularly when you consider an invalid input for certain functions that contain any operation with potential exceptions, such as division operations, square roots, or even out of memory situations. This is why unit test is one of the examples of TDD in action, as testing scenarios are being thought out before the implementation of the function.

Unit test support in Visual Studio

There are many unit test frameworks in .NET ecosystems, the most popular and widely used being xUnit and NUnit. These two have their own integration with Visual Studio through a test runner UI. Visual Studio itself has built-in support for unit tests; it is a Microsoft Test Framework often called **MS Test**. MS Test provides tooling, classes, and attributes for use to support unit tests, and in conjunction with Visual Studio, the unit test has its own test runner UI support as well.

All of the test frameworks, such as MS Test, xUnit, and NUnit, have integration support as part of the Visual Studio SDK. This extension of test runners inside Visual Studio has been available since Visual Studio 2010. The extensibility is done to extend the base test runner, and the available tests are displayed at Visual Studio **Test Explorer**. The Visual Studio test runner extensibility runs on .NET 4 CLR, so it is language agnostic. We could also create our own extensions in F#, not just by using C# and VB.

For documentation on the Visual Studio Testing Tool API, please visit MSDN at
`https://msdn.microsoft.com/en-us/library/dd465178(v=vs.120).aspx`.

For more information about the Visual Studio test runner, this is the official starting documentation of Visual Studio SDK:

`https://msdn.microsoft.com/en-us/library/bb166441.aspx`

Unfortunately, F# in Visual Studio has no inherent or template support in the form of a unit test project template, unlike C# and VB. However, we can still leverage MS Test by using the open source library of FsUnit for MS Test. The best part of this FsUnit for the MS Test library is how easy it is to install as a NuGet package.

 It is recommended to use F# code files (.fs), instead of F# scripting, to implement and run F# unit tests. Running a unit test in script mode will yield undesirable results, including runtime exceptions, as the Visual Studio test runner is not meant to run integrated with F# FSI.

Using FSIUnit is better than using xUnit, NUnit, or MS Test directly because FsUnit is created with the functional programming style at the beginning instead of using the common `Assert` method to test the result of a function.

Let's set up FsUnit and use it to implement a unit test in F#.

Using FsUnit to implement a unit test in F#

FsUnit itself has support not just for MS Test but also for xUnit and NUnit. FsUnit is part of many F# open source projects under the governance umbrella of the F# Software Foundation (FSSF). All of the F# open source projects have a landing page at this GitHub page, http://fsprojects.github.io/.

For more information about FsUnit, visit the official landing page at https://fsprojects.github.io/FsUnit/index.html.

Let's import FsUnit for the MS Test NuGet package. First, right-click the project name of FSConsole01, then choose the **Manage NuGet packages..** menu item. Then, a tab of **NuGet Package Manager** for the FSConsole01 project appears as shown in the following screenshot:

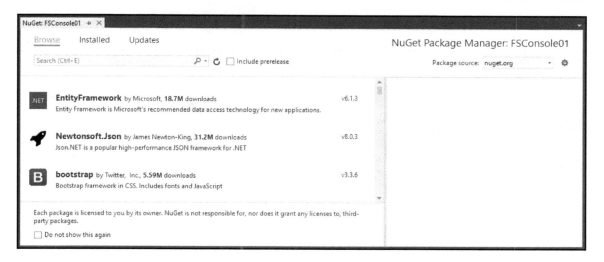

Let's do the following steps to add FsUnit NuGet package into our sample project:

1. In the search text box, type FsUnit and press *Enter*. A list of FsUnit related NuGet packages is shown:

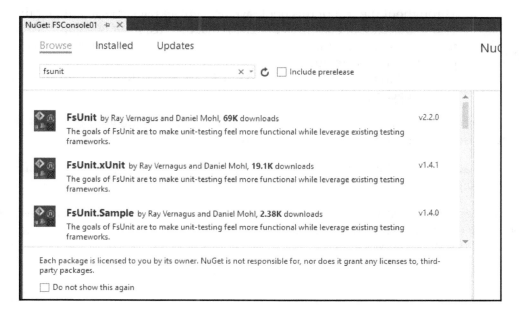

2. Scroll down and choose **FSUnit30Unit.MSTest**:

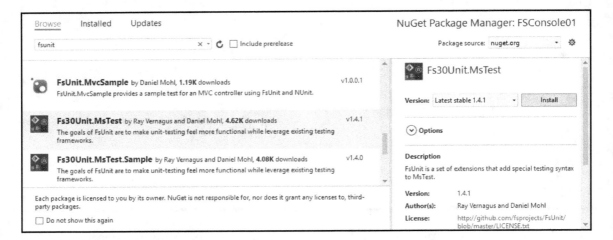

3. Then, click the **Install** button to download and install this package. Note that the **Package source** is pointing to **nuget.org**.

Throughout the rest of this book, we use NuGet packages to enrich our base experience of coding in F#. The NuGet source itself is not just from **nuget.org**; there are many other NuGet package sources. These NuGet package sources are often called NuGet feeds as these sources are displayed in actual RSS feeds before being listed in the Visual Studio NuGet package manager.

For more information on NuGet, including how to host and to create your own NuGet packages, visit the NuGet official website at `https://www.nuget.org/`.

The download and installation process is always projected at the **Output** window of the NuGet package manager.

If the package already exists (hence, installed), then NuGet will check the existing version of the NuGet package. If the version is older, by default it will try to update the existing version and install the newer version.

The successful NuGet installation is shown in the **Output** window of **Package Manager** as **Finished**:

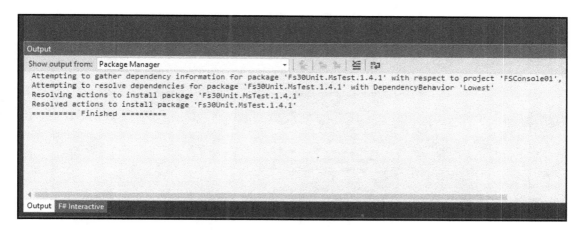

We can now be sure that `FS30Unit.MsTest` is available to use to perform a unit test in F#. However, the main MS Test framework is not yet installed. We have to add this library manually.

The name of the MS Test framework library is `Microsoft.VisualStudio.QualityTools.UnitTestFramework`.

This library is available as an extension library in the .NET project. It is also in the existing .NET **global assembly cache** (**GAC**) in Windows, installed by default by Visual Studio 2015 Community Edition and above.

In previous versions of Visual Studio before Visual Studio 2010, the name of the library was different, and it was named `Microsoft.VisualStudio.TestTools.UnitTesting`. The change of the name reflects that the Visual Studio Unit Test Framework has been part of Microsoft Visual's Studio Quality Tools since the release of Visual Studio 2010, including Microsoft Coded UI Test, Web Test, and Windows Store Test.

The documentation of the classes and attributes of Visual Studio Unit Test Framework in Visual Studio 2015 is available at `https://msdn.microsoft.com/en-us/library/microsoft.visualstudio.testtools.unittesting(v=vs.140).aspx`.

Add this `Microsoft.VisualStudio.QualityTools.UnitTestFramework` by adding references to the project, and then choose the **Extensions** tab:

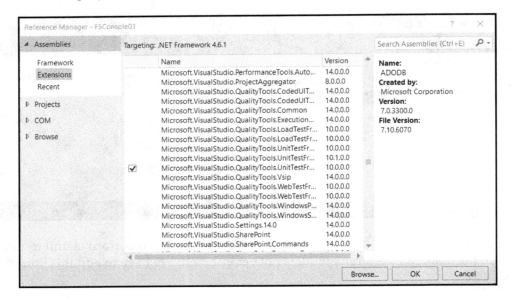

Now that we have that set up, and it is available for use, we can now code the unit test. We can also combine our entrypoint for the F# console with the factorial function and the unit test. It is also recommended to separate the factorial function from the main module that has an entrypoint as the concern of the module that has the entrypoint is actually different from the factorial function.

Always pay attention to the indentation inside the modules, types, and the functions. F# always relies on the indentation to mark wrong indentation as that will always result in compiling errors.

This is the official guideline on code indentation in F#:

```
https://msdn.microsoft.com/en-us/visualfsharpdocs/conceptual/code-formatting-gu
idelines-%5Bfsharp%5D
```

First, we have to set multiple module files to be compiled correctly for this console project. The entrypoint of `Program.fs` needs to be modified to be included in an explicit module under the namespace, `FSConsole01`.

In `Program.fs` in the code window, type the following code:

```
namespace FSConsole01
```

```
module Program =

    [<EntryPoint>]
    let main argv =
        printfn "Hello F# world"
        0 // return an integer exit code
```

Build it, and an error warning will show the following message:

```
A function labeled with the 'EntryPointAttribute' attribute must be the
last declaration in the last file in the compilation sequence, and can only
be used when compiling to a .exe
```

Ignore this error for now, as we will fix this later.

Let's move our factorial function into the unit test.

Create a new F# source file and name it FSConsoleUnitTest.

Type the following in the code window:

```
namespace FSConsole01
    open Microsoft.VisualStudio.TestTools.UnitTesting
    open FsUnit.MsTest

module MathFunc =
        let rec fact x =
            match x with
            | 1 -> 1
            | a when a < 1 -> 1
            | _ -> x * fact (x-1)

module FSConsoleUnitTest =

    [<TestClass>]
    type FactTest() =
        class
            [<TestMethod>]
            member this.FactTest01() =
                MathFunc.fact 3 |> should equal 6
        end
```

The code in the FSConsoleUnitTest module shows that we now have a class of FactTest and the method to be our unit test.

The TestClass attribute on FactTest means that this class will be used by the test runner as the starting class to hold the unit test. The TestMethod attribute on FactTest01 means that this method is our unit test under the FactTest class.

This is a common convention as the class to be used for a unit test cannot be a static class. The nature of a unit test is instantiating the class that has the attribute of `TestClass` before running the tests inside the methods with the `TestMethod` attribute.

For more information on creating, running, and debugging unit tests using MS Test (and also for other test frameworks) in Visual Studio 2015, visit this MSDN Library:

`https://msdn.microsoft.com/library/dd264975`

Let's fix the previous error by reordering `Program.fs` to be the last order of the file order. We do this by right-clicking `Program.fs` and moving down `Program.fs`:

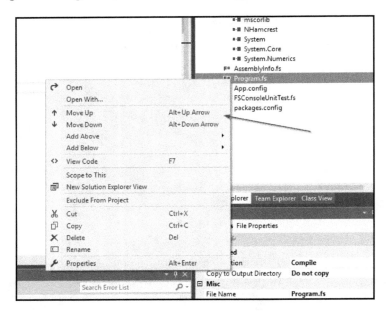

Ensure that `Program.fs` is the last file.

 Note that file ordering in F# is very important.

Build the project. Then, display the **Test Explorer** window if it's not open. On the General collection default setting, the **Test Explorer** menu item is available under the main menu **Test**.

The `FactTest01` test will be shown in the **Test Explorer** as follows:

Let's run the test by clicking **Run All** on the **Test Explorer**. **Test Explorer** will display the number of milliseconds it takes to run the unit test on the right of the test method name:

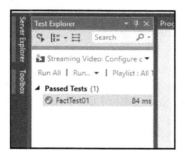

The number of milliseconds may vary depending on different hardware, because it is influenced by the speed of the CPU and the number of CPU cores. The function we have tested is a simple function, but we can have a function that has parallel calls by utilizing .NET Task Parallel Library (TPL). The consequences of the usage of .NET TPL are that numbers can vary greatly across different systems with different configurations, such as the operating system used (in this context, the Windows version and edition) and different CPU specifications.

For example, testing using a machine that has a 4th generation core i7 2.4 Ghz CPU might be a little bit faster than a machine that has a 6th generation core i5 2.2 Ghz CPU. The number of cores may have some influence as well, as the number of cores in a modern CPU is always increasing.

In our code, there is no direct use of MS Test's Assert at all. This is actually available under the cover of FsUnit. We can look at FsUnit source codes in the GitHub repository of FsUnit, in particular, FsUnit code to support MS Test. All the code related to MS Test is under the folder named `FsUnit.MsTestUnit`.

To recap again, FsUnit has support for the NUnit and xUnit test frameworks, and both of them use the same context of implementing `Assert` methods under the cover of a functional FsUnit. You may use test frameworks other than MS Test, as long as they are supported by FsUnit. It is recommended to participate with or contribute to FsUnit as this project is encouraging contributors to support other test frameworks such as MbUnit.

At the time of writing, FsUnit supports both F# 3.1 and F# 4.0. But it is recommended to use FsUnit with F# 4.0 because this will provide you with the highest compatibility with the .NET 4.5 and .NET 4.6 frameworks. In addition, F# 4.0 is the closest work in progress to the future release of F#, which will provide support for .NET Core.

The FsUnit GitHub repository is available at `https://github.com/fsprojects/FsUnit`.

Summary

You learned that you can measure performance quantitatively and qualitatively. Although it is easier to have quantitative measurement than qualitative measurement, it is quite straightforward and common to have quantified data as a foundation to have qualitative analysis.

With the help of .NET tooling ecosystem and libraries available at our disposal, we can ensure the objectiveness of our performance measurement. It is also recommended to have a basic understanding of .NET CLR memory management as our foundation to have performance measurement from the perspective of qualitative analysis.

We will start exploring the aspects of performance optimizations with the knowledge and concept in this chapter, starting from F# data structures in `Chapter 3`, *Optimizing Data Structures*.

3
Optimizing Data Structures

It is common in many applications to leverage all kind of objects that are used as data. The types of data can be primitive, object reference, and collection types. F# itself has its own unique types, especially collection types.

These types, especially when doing many computing-intensive operations, are crucial. Optimizations need not only relate to the location of the value of data stored according to the types, but also how we access them can have a big impact on overall performance.

The deciding factors determining the best types to use, besides the memory locations, can vary. This is why it is quite hard to measure qualitatively. Measuring quantitatively can be tricky, although the statistical numbers may be informative.

We shall use the knowledge gained in Chapter 2, *Performance Measurement* relating to the qualitative understanding of the internals of running F# code (the IL, tooling, and the GC) and have quantitative measures (the execution durations using timers and unit tests) as a gentle requirement for this chapter and the rest of this book.

The knowledge of IL assembly and the fundamentals of .NET GC will help us to understand the internal working of .NET and F#'s unique data structures. Then we can optimize them by deciding the best use cases and the best types to choose for our specific needs.

 A basic knowledge of .NET 4 BCL types and collections (including those that shipped out of band/OOB, such as immutable collections) is needed. There should be no easy way of thinking or taking shortcuts when using a type/collection for all cases, for example, using .NET advanced collection such as BindingList<T> explicitly for all collections that are only meant to be read and forwarded instead of IEnumerable<T> or List<T>.

This chapter provides an overview of the available types in F# and the best practices to choose, use, and optimize. The data structure optimization is covered in the following topics:

- Overview of the types to store specific data in F# and their best usages (including structs, classes, and records)
- Best practices in using F# collections, with a comparison to .NET collections
- Best practices in choosing an evaluation strategy (lazy or eager)

Overview and best practices of types in F#

To store a value as data, every value needs to have a type, especially for static typed languages such as F#, C#, and VB. Many modern programming languages after the year 2000 put emphasis on types as the type of value of the data, instead of using the simple term of *data structure*. The types here also mean the types that are not just concrete types, but also generic types when used in conjunction with concrete types.

Static typing versus dynamic typing

F# by default has no built-in support for defining and optimizing types to store data as dynamic types on top of **Dynamic Language Runtime** (**DLR**). This dynamic type support is available in the form of a library from the F# FSSF open source project communities, the *FSharp.Interop.Dynamic*. This is available at https://github.com/fsprojects/FSharp.Interop.Dynamic.

This library is also available as a NuGet package as well.

DLR is basically an extension that runs on top of CLR to provide an infrastructure for dynamically typed languages such as Python, Ruby, and JavaScript that have no restriction on type definition. This means that any type is typed as dynamic in the beginning at the compile time, and the type resolution is resolved at the runtime.

The impact of this dynamic type resolution has decreased performance at the initial runtime, as the type has to be resolved at runtime instead of compile time. Therefore, the use of dynamic types is not recommended, although F# can support dynamic type interoperability by having interop with DLR as demonstrated by *FSharp.Interop.Dynamic* library..

Since .NET Framework 4.0 (and CLR 4.0), DLR is included in the framework, and not as a separate download anymore. The original DLR repository is hosted in CodePlex, but the rest of the DLR development in .NET 4.0 is continued in Microsoft's .NET GitHub repo of .NET CLR.

For more information about DLR, visit the following landing page of MSDN at `https://msdn.microsoft.com/en-us/library/dd233052(v=vs.110).aspx`.

In functional programming languages, it is also implicitly required to have static typing because it's also part of the requirements of having a type inference feature. Having type inference is very crucial, as functional programming needs to be as concise and as close as possible to mathematical function syntaxes.

The use of dynamic type is against the common best practices of functional programming languages. Types are inferred statically and therefore resolved at compile time. Inferring type statically also gives us the ability to compose functions and values intuitively without worrying about casting and boxing at runtime. The nature of easily composing functions (operations in OOP) is one of the *main traits* (or required features) of functional programming languages.

Static typing has these following advantages over dynamic typing:

- Type resolutions are solved at compile time. All of the inconsistencies of invalid value assignments or casts always give compile errors. A compile error is easier to fix than a runtime error.
- Because of the type resolution at the compile time, the compile time is slower than the compile time of the dynamic type. Because the type resolution may add overheads when compiling, a slower performance is to be expected. Because the type resolution itself is in action, this is closely related to the F# compile phases of lexing and parsing. The compiler can perform more optimization by having incremental compilation as the background process under the infrastructure of Visual Studio tooling.
- Static type is also more reasonable to reason about the code, since all of the variables and functions have types that flow nicely.
- Having the knowledge of static type gives innovative and useful features such as code completion when accessing F# modules and functions, including the function parameter's type resolutions and XML summary documentation.

The term *code completion* is also called statement completion in Microsoft's MSDN Library. It means that when we code in the IDE, the language service will provide richer information about the type and its members (properties, function/methods, and events) and display it to us.

Visual Studio since Visual Studio 5.0 has a robust feature called **Intellisense** that shows automatically the information about the type as we type . (dot) after the variable name.

This picture of F# code being edited shows Intellisense in action:

```
 2    // See the 'F# Tutorial' project for more help.
 3    open System.Threading
 4
 5    type TestClass =
 6        class
 7
 8            member this.Property1 : string = "Readonly"
 9        end
10
11    [<EntryPoint>]
12    let main argv =
13        printfn "Hello %A" argv
14        0 // return an integer e
```

⊙ Clone	
⊙ CopyTo	
⊙ Equals	System.Object.Equals(obj: obj) : bool
⊙ GetEnumerator	
⊙ GetHashCode	Determines whether the specified object is equal to the current object.
⊙ GetLength	
⊙ GetLongLength	
⊙ GetLowerBound	
⊙ GetType	

Intellisense is active by default, and it is highly recommended to keep the setting as active. It adds little overhead on loading type information in the background as the compiler runs in the background, but it definitely increases productivity.

Although called statement completion by Microsoft, its use is not just for the code's statement completion. It is used in a broader sense in statements, class/module members including functions/methods, and public/protected/internal properties. Intellisense is also helpful in decreasing compiler errors because the full metadata becomes available at the frontend, minimizing compiler errors because of incorrect type names or syntax errors.

The technique of having type resolution at compile time is often called **early bound**, compared to the **late bound** nature of dynamic typing solved at runtime.

This is related to one of the main traits of functional programming: function and data are the same first-class citizens of the functional programming language itself. To maintain this inseparable concept as a function and data, type inference must flow nicely. And type inference explicitly requires that the type must have a definition and must have strong type support as well.

For more details about the traits of functional programming languages, we can check out F#'s documentation from MSDN. MSDN has simple but concise definitions of the required features of functional programming in F#:

```
https://msdn.microsoft.com/en-us/visualfsharpdocs/conceptual/functions-as-first
-class-values-%5bfsharp%5d
```

Therefore, we will not discuss further the dynamic type support in F# because it's not recommended in the sense of the functional programming perspective and the performance at runtime. Throughout the rest of this book, we will only focus on the static typing of F#.

Quick introduction to types in F#

Types in F# are basically categorized as two types: types in .NET BCL and types that are only available in F#. Although there are types specific to F#, these F# types can be used in C#/VB because basically all F# types are implemented on top of .NET CLR.

Based on .NET CLI standard partition I section I.8.2 about value types and reference types, the documentation is divided into two kinds of types:

- **Value type**: The values described by a value type are self-contained (each can be understood without reference to other values). It is using one of the basic, built-in data types or a user-defined structure. The exception of this built-in type is a string; it is reference type. In F#/C#/VB, this value type is also known as a structure or struct.
- **Reference type**: The value denotes the location of another value. The location is actually a pointer to a location of a value.

There are four kinds of reference type:

- An object type is a reference type of a self-describing value. Some object types (for example, abstract classes) are only a partial description of a value.
- An interface type is always a partial description of a value, potentially supported by many object types.
- A pointer type is a compile-time description of a value whose representation is a machine address of a location. Pointers are divided into managed and unmanaged.
- Built-in reference types.

There is also support for generic parameterized types built in the fabric of CIL/CLR. The notation of a generic type in CIL/CLR is also enriched with covariance/contravariance support. It is mandatory for all of static programming languages run on top of CIL/CLR to have at least support for basic generic type, although covariance/contravariance may not be supported at language level.

By further looking at the CLS rule of CIL/CLR, we shall see that covariance/contravariance support is not mandatory. For further information, we can check the CLS rule starting at section I.7.3 of CIL/CLR ECMA-335 standard.

Quick overview of generic type support in F#

F# has generic type as the parameterized type support, just as in C#/VB, and all have the same concept and similar semantics, although F# goes further by allowing type generalizations.

For example, in F#, to declare a type that has a generic type parameter in use:

```
List<'t>
```

If the parameter is used in code, the parameter of the generic type must be filled in, such as in this example:

```
List<int>
```

In our last example, the generic type becomes specialized as int. The List is a sample of a concrete type that has a generic type as the type parameter. This concept is also similar to the semantics in C#/VB.

> Throughout this book, the types in F# that support the generic type such as F# List, Map, Set, and Array will use the same notation as F# types in the MSDN Library, although the complete compilation name may differ. For example, F# Map type is known as FSharpMap from outside of F#'s scope (when used in other languages such as C#/VB).

There is also a unique way in F# to treat generics: the statically resolved generic. According to the F# documentation in the MSDN Library:

> *"Statically resolved generic is a type parameter that is replaced with an actual type at compile time instead of at run time. They are preceded by a caret (^) symbol."*

Using a statically resolved generic type parameter is more efficient than the normal generic type, but there is one caveat: it cannot be used on functions or methods that are not inline. It is also orthogonal at the normal generic type: normal generic type cannot be used on inline functions. The usage of statically resolved generics is discussed further in `Chapter 7`, *Language Features and Constructs Optimizations*.

For official information on the F# statically resolved type, please consult the MSDN Library:

```
https://msdn.microsoft.com/en-us/visualfsharpdocs/conceptual/statically-resolve
d-type-parameters-%5Bfsharp%5D
```

F# can use the available types in .NET and the types specific to F#. F# has its own types because F# has supports for functional programming related types, including DU.

The documentation of types in F# is available from MSDN at the following URL:

```
https://msdn.microsoft.com/en-us/visualfsharpdocs/conceptual/fsharp-types
```

The basic summary and syntaxes of F# types are also available at the MSDN Library. We are now focusing on the type itself as the data structure.

These are the types in F#:

- **Primitive types**: These are the same as .NET primitive types such as `Int32`, `Boolean`, `Single`, `Double`.
- **Unit type**: This is equal to `void` in C# and `Nothing` in Visual Basic
- **Options**: These are special types in F# that describe a type that may contain a value or empty.
- **Structures**: These are the same concept and semantics as `struct` in C#/VB.
- **Classes**: These are the same concept as `class` in C#/VB.
- **Records**: These are unique in F#.
- **Discriminated unions**: These are unique in F#.
- **F# collections**: such as `Array`, `List`, and `Sequence`. All of F# collections are immutable by default, but the implementations of these collections are different in semantics from the BCL in .NET as used in C#/VB.
- **Functions**: These are specific to the F# function. The F# function is also implemented as `FSharpFunc` delegate.
- **Delegates**: These delegates support include F#'s own delegates and .NET delegates. F# delegates have the same concept as delegate in .NET, but the semantic is implemented differently due to F# particular `FSharpFunc` implementation.

- **Attributes**: These are the same as attributes in .NET BCL, therefore they are the same as attributes in C#/VB.

Throughout this chapter, we will focus on types that are specific to F#, such as options, structures (because of the difference in semantics), records, discriminated unions, F#'s specific collections, and functions. Class will be discussed as well because it's also a F# OOP feature but we are going to focus on the semantic differences and the way F# treats classes.

Discriminated union (DU) is one of F#'s unique types and a feature that is also part of the functional programming language's commonly used types. It is also available in Haskell and Scala, among others.

 DU is one of the unique feature of types in a functional programming language. In fact, DU is quite similar in Haskell's algebraic data types, although Haskell's algebraic data types are richer than F#'s DU. Scala uses combinations of traits and case classes and is more verbose. But the concept is the same in Scala.

Overall runtime strategy of handling data types

Before diving further into the optimization of types to store specific data structures, we need to know the basic understanding of how the F# types are implemented in the resulting (compiled) generated code. The compiler may handle different types differently, although there could be compiler-specific optimizations later on.

Introduction to memory storage allocation

The type of storage in memory to store the data value according to the CLI standard specification basically falls into these three storage categories (from fastest to slowest):

- Register
- Stack
- Heap

Register

Register is the fastest to access, because it does not have memory allocation overheads compared to stack and heap. The concept of register is similar to the processor's register.

This register is not the same as stack and heap; it is related to how the value is stored in the code. Usage of register in CLR is translated into any of the processor's registers, and depends on the platform used. For example, when running on x86/x64 processors, Intel's general purpose register of EAX, EBX, ECX, EDX will be used.

Stack

The nature of stack is **LIFO**, abbreviated from **last in first out**. It means that data is stored not in a first come, first served basis, but the last one stored is the first one that can be read, as data is stored from the bottom to the highest layer of stacked fixed locations. This is why it is simply called stack. The analogy can be seen when we wash dishes:

- The first dish is the first stack on the lowest stack.
- The second dish is put onto the first stack.
- The next one is put on the second stack, and this process is the same for the following dishes.
- To wash the dishes, we have to take the highest stack on the top of the stack first before we go to the first one. So the last stack is the first one to be washed because the last stack is located at the highest layer. This mechanism is the main reason why it is called LIFO.

In the world of computer science, the act of storing or putting the data onto a stack is called *push*, and the act of taking the data out from a stack is called *pop*.

The terms push and pop on stack are also the same concept in .NET CLR, and they are quite similar in semantics although the implementation detail is *virtualized* by the .NET CLR. The actual machine assembly code after AOT or JIT in the Debug mode is translated into the related processor's PUSH and POP instructions. In the context of .NET CLR on the x86 (32-bit) or x64 (64-bit) platform, these PUSH and POP instructions will be translated into a one or more calls to machine assembly of PUSH and POP.

The virtualization of data and the operations are important, as .NET CLR has its own isolations to help to prevent intentional manual memory allocation of pointers, subroutines, and data to be mixed. It is quite common for the virtualization to have its own mechanism of disposing unused objects (for example, out of scope when a method/function has finished executing) or an object that is explicitly disposed. Modern virtualization often has its own garbage collector for these unused/disposed objects. The isolations, garbage collections, and the sequence of garbage collections (Gen-0, Gen-1, Gen-2) are actually part of the .NET CLR memory management, and this is called *managed memory management*. This is the reason why the code running on top of CLR is called managed code.

The concept of virtualization in CLR is quite similar to the concept of virtualization in *Java Virtual Machine* (JVM). The concept of having garbage collection is also part of the virtualized environment nature of CLR and JVM.

Details on the raw flow of machine assembly of PUSH and POP are out of the scope of this book, as we are not dealing with machine assembly instructions directly. For more information on assembly language, please consult Intel's landing page of the software developer manual on Intel processors at http://www.intel.com/content/www/us/en/processors/architectures-software-developer-manuals.html.

The following diagram illustrates storing or pushing data:

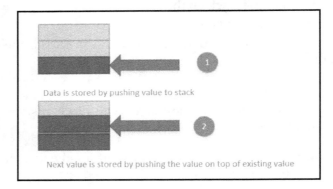

Getting out or popping data from stack is done by accessing the last of the data pushed. The operation goes from top (the last pushed) to bottom.

The advantages of using stack are as follows:

- Stacks are fast to store, the act of pushing data onto stack is just adding data consecutively. It does not require a pointer allocation.
- There is no fragmentation, because the order of filling stack is always contiguous.

These are the disadvantages:

- Stacks take a predefined length of the number of data stored and cannot be allocated dynamically. This is intentional, as stack is allocated up front and it is also bound to the limits imposed by the processor and the size of memory (RAM).
- Each stack has a predefined length for each slot of data. Therefore, stack is not ideally suited for variable lengths of data such as strings.

- Stacks are often quickly exhausted as most stack size is limited and always less than the allocated heap. For example, stack is often used to store the initial pointer of recursive function calls, which is why every recursive call means pushing a pointer of the location of the initial call. After a function finishes its operations, it pops the last pointer to go to the caller. If the recursive calls are too deep, the stack is exhausted and this condition is often called *stack overflow*.

The stack overflow is usually thrown as a `System.StackOverflowException`. Starting with .NET Framework 2.0, we can't catch `StackOverflowException` directly as this is not allowed. The CLR/CIL 2.0 also implies this as well. For more information, please consult the `StackOverflowException` documentation at MSDN Library:

```
https://msdn.microsoft.com/en-us/library/system.stackoverflowexception(v=vs.110).aspx
```

For the case of recursive function calls, F# has optimized most recursive function calls by translating them into a loop in the IL. This loop optimization guarantees that the function will not take lots of stack allocations and therefore prevents stack overflow caused by deeply nested recursive function calls.

To allocate storage dynamically, the only way is to use heap.

 The term heap is not to be confused with *heap as data structure*. Heap in a data structure is rarely used, as it's actually a specialized tree.

Heap

Heap is simply a pool of large memory; usually it's in a form of virtual memory space. It can be allocated and deallocated dynamically on demand. The term allocate means the act of reserving a portion of memory. The term deallocate means freeing the resource (portion of memory) that was previously allocated.

Heap is used to allocate memory for storing these kind of variables:

- Reference types
- Unsafe methods
- Weak reference methods
- Reference unsafe pointers and managed pointers

Best practices of types for storing and accessing data

When discussing best practices of types to use to store data, we must consider these conditions:

- The form of the value of the data. We can simply define this as the form of the data, or the semantics of the data value as the type of the value. The precision of the data is also part of the form of the data.
- The use of the data is manipulated in the code. Is the data manipulated inside a function lambda or not as part of a function lambda? It is also important as this is implementation-specific in F# and .NET CLR.
- The nature of the lifetime of the data. This later will define where and how the data is stored in the memory, and we will discuss this in detail.
- The final decision regarding implementation in the generated IL may vary as well. This is compiler-specific but it is still closely related to the first point about the form and the second point about the lifetime of the data.

Let's discuss each of the previous points and the relations between them.

The easiest one to understand is the form of the value of the data. To understand more about the form of the value, it is common to approach the form as the type of the value. For example, the numeric value, the `Boolean` value, and the `String` value. A type must be attached to each value, as this is a basic requirement of a static typed language such as F#.

CLR itself implies that all values *must* have defined types, because there are explicit type declarations in the IL which must be easily seen. The types are usually declared in the return type of the method, the method parameter signatures, and the `.locals` section in the IL.

Let's look at some sample cases of these in the generated IL from F# compiler.

For example, the `fact` function in the FSConsole01 in Chapter 2, *Performance Measurement* has these type declarations for return type, parameter, and each variable used in the function body:

```
.method public static int32  fact(int32 x) cil managed
{
  // Code size       44 (0x2c)
  .maxstack  5
  .locals init ([0] int32 V_0,
           [1] int32 a,
           [2] int32 V_2)
```

The variables are given a local name as `v_0`, `a`, and `v_2` respectively.

In this IL, the `.maxstack` directive defines how much the stack is allocated. The stack is allocated to use five slots of stack to store five values for this function to operate.

There are the stack operations beginning with `IL_0001` to `IL_0004` line segment:

```
IL_0001:    ldarg.0
IL_0002:    stloc.0
IL_0003:    ldloc.0
IL_0004:    ldc.i4.1
```

The operations for those four lines of IL are:

1. The IL `ldarg.0` means load argument with index 0 (the first argument/parameter of the fact function) onto stack. This means pushing the value of the parameter onto stack.
2. The IL `stloc.0` means the pops value from stack to the local variable. The popped value is the value from the previous IL, the `ldarg.0` instruction.
3. The IL `ldloc.0` means load the local variable onto stack. This means pushing the value of the local variable to stack. The local variable is the index 0, the first local variable declared in the `.locals` section.
4. The IL `ldc.i4.1` means push value 1 onto stack with the type as `Int32`. All of the IL of `ldc.x` means pushing a numerical constant with the desired type, whereas the `i4` means `Int32`.

For more information about these ILs, please consult partition III of ECMA-335 about the CIL standard. The availability of `ldc.i4.1` IL also means that the value must have the type declared explicitly. This is further proof that .NET CLR implies static typed, even at the IL level.

There are two kinds of types that are used in F# from the perspective of programming language features: primitive types and non-primitive types.

Primitive types are types that are available built-in as language features, and they are often types that are the easiest to construct (initialize) and manipulate. To maintain a higher compatibility with CLR and .NET BCL, the primitive types of F# support all of the primitive types in .NET BCL with the additional F# unique primitive type, `unit`.

The priority order of feature support from the base to the top on F# is:

1. .NET CLR (runtime) support
2. .NET BCL support (including `BigInteger`, as this is not explicitly supported in CLR)
3. F# unique types

CLR type support must come first, as all of the primitive types must support CLR types first, especially all of the value types in CLR. This mandatory requirement is also part of official F# 4.0 Language Specification.

For an official list of F# primitive types, visit the MSDN Library at `https://msdn.microsoft.com/en-us/visualfsharpdocs/conceptual/primitive-types-%5bfsharp%5d`.

Let's start by using the .NET original type name instead of using F# keyword, as it's also easier to understand based on the list of primitive types. For example, it's easier to use `Int32` as F# int because we might misunderstand *int* as `Int16` instead of `Int32`. This is quite common in programming languages, because of different implementations of how a language specification defines basic integer length. Fortunately, F# int is the same as C# `int` and VB Integer, as they both have the same length of 32 bits (4 bytes). But this symmetry might not be the same for C++ and other languages, although they may have support running on .NET CLR.

If the value is a primitive type that has fixed length and it is also directly related to IL types such as `Char`, `SByte`, `Int16`, `Int32`, `Int64`, `Boolean`, `Single`, `Double`, or even an unsigned numeric such as `Byte`, `UInt32`, then the compiler will mostly store this on stack. `Char`, although it's not a numeric, is stored as a numeric.

String does not have a fixed length, and it is also a composite type, because it is not a type that is standalone (it is not a type that contains other types). It is a type that contains other types as a collection. This is obvious because the declaration of `String` class in .NET BCL implements an object that implements `IEnumerable<Char>`. Therefore, string is composed as collection of `Char`.

Because of the nature of a collection, the length may vary. It is also quite normal to assume that a string literal will always vary in length. Therefore, string is treated differently from other primitive types.

To push a string constant value onto stack, the IL instruction is `ldstr`. To illustrate this, let's revisit our `FSConsole01` project. It has as its entry point the `main` method. Let's see the IL of `main`: (`IL_0006` and `IL_000b` are omitted):

```
.method public static int32  main(string[] argv) cil managed
{
  .entrypoint
  .custom instance void
[FSharp.Core]Microsoft.FSharp.Core.EntryPointAttribute::.ctor() = ( 01 00
00 00 )
  // Code size       19 (0x13)
  .maxstack  8
  IL_0000:  nop
  IL_0001:  ldstr       "Hello F# world"
...
  IL_0010:  pop
  IL_0011:  ldc.i4.0
  IL_0012:  ret
} // end of method Program::main
```

The `Hello F# world` string is treated as a string constant value, and it is pushed by `ldstr` at the beginning. At the end of `main`, before returning 0 as the successful running code, it removes the string value from stack using the `pop` IL.

This shows that string has its representative in CIL as well. It is typed as `string`, mapped to `System.String` in .NET BCL.

For more information, please see partition I section I.8.2.2 of the CIL standard (ECMA-335) to check all of the CIL types of .NET BCL primitive type mappings.

Any primitive types, by default are stored in the memory using stack as its container storage. It is a bad practice to always assume that all of the uses of value typed will always be stored on stack, especially when the code that uses the data is implemented.

This is subjective to the internal implementation of F# compiler, but this technique is quite common in C#/VB compiler as well. F# has to conform to Common Language Specification rules as governed by the CIL standard, not just C#/VB. Therefore, it is intuitive by default in the normal code (without any closure that is common in lambda functions) that all of the primitive types of CIL will be stored onto stack.

Any constant string value is always pushed on stack, as shown in the sample `main` method.

Other than that, string can be stored in stack or heap, depending on the actual implementation of the code and the use of data manipulated in the code. Any variable used in the code can be implemented differently, according to the code. The storage location depends on the location of the closure as well.

A *closure* is simply a technique to capture a variable that is scoped outside a lambda function. Closure is a very useful feature in many programming languages, although it is mostly used when we use lambda functions. The way closure works in F# is the same as in C#/VB.

F# can be used to treat the function scoped variable to be the reference type for the inner function, although the type of the variable is the struct/value type. This is also a rule of the restriction of the F#: variable used for the closure that is going to be mutated/changed; it must have a reference type on its value, whether the type of the variable is a struct or not.

For example consider:

```
let Counter =
    let count = ref 0
    // *Return a function that carries the current context* (ie. "count",
on
    // the heap). Each time it is called, it will reference, and increment,
    // the same location
    (fun () -> incr count; !count)
```

The line that declares the `count` variable uses the `ref` keyword to define that it is not just a passing value; it is also passing references as well.

The use of immutable data captured as closure will be stored on stack, but this is actually an implementation detail of F# compiler.

The point regarding the lifetime of the data concerns how long the data in a variable is used throughout the flow of the code. It is also related to closure implementation.

To fully recap and understand the relations of the form of the data and the lifetime of the data, these are the rules of treating the data based on the lifetime of the data used:

- If the data is used many times as a closure but it is immutable, this can be defined as having a short lifetime. The data is stored on stack.
- The string constant value is always considered as short-lived data. Therefore, it is stored on stack and this is also the main implementation detail of the CIL/CLR `ldstr` instruction.

- All of the mutable/immutable variables that are scoped locally in a function/method that are not used as a closure will always be stored on stack, because this function/method scoped variable is defined to be short-lived. It is only used within the scope of the function/method.

- All the value type (struct) is by default stored on stack. There are some special cases that the value type will be stored on stack. When the value type is referenced within `System.WeakReference<T>`, the value will be stored on heap along with the `System.WeakReference<T>` container. Also the use of `ref` when assigning the function scoped variable will mostly put the value on heap.

- If the data as closure is intended as a mutable reference type, it will be stored on heap.

- If the data is part of public properties of a class/record, the data is stored on the heap of the container class/record. For example, a `public` property member of a class is stored on heap.

- Long-lived data is always stored on heap.

`WeakReference` is useful because we can use it to enforce GC not to do garbage collection on the data upon which the type is parameterized. The data is contained in this `WeakReference`. Any other type of reference will always be garbage collected at any Gen-0 or Gen-1 phase.

For more information about `WeakReference` usage, consult the MSDN Library at `https://msdn.microsoft.com/en-us/library/gg712738(v=vs.110).aspx`.

Based on the rules, it is recommended to use immutable closure instead of mutable, especially when it is marked to be a reference type.

The most common best practice still holds: allocating stack is faster than allocating data on heap. It is quite obvious that the immutable closure is recommended and better than reference typed closure.

To simply recap, the choice is often choosing between struct and class (including record, DU) in F#. All of record, DU are implemented as classes in the IL, and therefore they are basically specialized types of classes.

The strategy is as follows:

- Always know the difference of value type and reference type. But never assume that the value type is always stored on stack.

- Prefer value types instead of classes.

- Use object pool to contain the most used types and put them in a collection. This will prevent GC from always automatically performing garbage collection each time the variable is used. But this strategy is not recommended if the variable used is mostly short-lived and the intention is mostly for a quick calculation that is repeated in parallel.

- Run garbage collection when the code is running idly after processing inputs or after ending all of the long running processes. This will increase the efficiency of garbage collection to minimize overheads instead of doing GC when the code is busy doing computations or even side-effect computations. Although the overhead of Gen-0, Gen-1 may impact the memory deallocation and allocation process, having garbage collection run on idle times will minimize overheads when the collection happens on heavy computations (especially when performing recursive operations in parallel).

- Use `WeakReference` for an object that has a tendency to be long lived but used frequently to decrease the GC overhead.

- Use an immutable value when capturing the value inside a function lambda. Immutable values when captured in lambda are always stored on stack.

The distinction details of the value type and the reference type, and how they behave in memory, especially in the stages of garbage collection, are described in detail in the CIL/CLR ECMA-335 standard.

Actually, these F# rules are also applied for C#/VB. Eric Lippert (former developer of the C# compiler) has discussed this in a detailed explanation on his MSDN blog:

```
https://blogs.msdn.microsoft.com/ericlippert/2010/09/30/the-truth-about-value-t
ypes/
```

Again, although this is mostly hidden from us as F# developers, these implementation details will help us to understand and avoid misconceptions.

The current discussion has different semantics depending on whether or not a collection of data is used in the implementation.

Best practices in using F# collections

The F# types are mostly describing types that are not collection types. F# has its own unique collection types as well.

The F# collection features are mostly implemented as modules, with the namespace of `Microsoft.FSharp.Collections`. The following are the F# collection modules:

- Module `Array`: Basic operations on arrays
- Module `Array2D`: Basic operations on two-dimensional arrays
- Module `Array3D`: Basic operations on rank 3 arrays
- Module `Array4D`: Basic operations on rank 4 arrays
- Module `ComparisonIdentity`: Common notions of comparison identity used with sorted data structures
- Module `HashIdentity`: Common notions of value identity used with hash tables
- Module `List`: Basic operations on lists
- Module `Map`: Functional programming operators related to the `Map` type
- Module `Seq`: Basic operations on enumerable collections
- Module `Set`: Functional programming operators related to the `Set` type

`List`, `Map`, and `Set` are unique to F#.

For more information about F# collections, please consult the MSDN Library at: `https://msdn.microsoft.com/en-us/visualfsharpdocs/conceptual/fsharp-collection-types`.

The page shows the list of types and also the computation complexity or algorithmic speed (*big O notation*) of each function of the collection. It is recommended that you should pay close attention to the number of computation complexities of each function and use them carefully.

Big O notation is originally coming from the realm of basic computer science. It is almost non-trivial in the programming world. But it's crucial to understanding the abstract performance in the terms of computation complexity, as it is always having has a direct relation on the overall performance. Simpler computation complexity such as *O(1)* or *O(log n)* is always better than *O(n)*.

For example consider:

The function `tryPick` in `Array`, `List`, and `Seq` is *O(n)* and in `Map` it is *O(log N)*. This means the `tryPick` in `Map` is faster when the number of elements are very large, such as more than `1000`:

```
O(log 1000) = 3
```

Whereas *O(n)* for `1000` elements means:

```
O(1000) = 1000
```

Some concrete operations are often quite trivial to spot or to deduce quickly; for example, loops that run a definite n number of times are always at least *O(n)*.

There's no simple way to reduce running times further, unless the loop is executed within a parallel flow of a parallel loop. Parallelism is actually also one way to have optimization as part of the concurrency support/features of F#. We will discuss concurrency further in `Chapter 4`, *Introduction to Concurrency in F#* and `Chapter 5`, *Advanced Concurrency Support in F#*.

For more information about big O, please refer to the MIT computer science course overview at `http://web.mit.edu/16.070/www/lecture/big_o.pdf`.

The complexity scales value in terms of big O is better in `Map` than in `Array`, `List`, and `Seq`.

The big O notation may break or may not be valid anymore when the code runs in parallel because there's no exact guarantee of the number of executions that actually happen when the code runs in parallel.

 Starting from this chapter, we will enrich our perspective on measuring performance by the quantitative and qualitative methods we learned in `Chapter 2`, *Performance Measurement* combined with the necessary big O notation, to understand performance optimization in the perspective of computation complexity. The use of big O should come after having quantitative and qualitative measurements first, as big O often shows no real quantitative data when measuring concurrency in action.

But the use of `Map` is not always the best option for all cases. `Map` behaves like the .NET `Dictionary`, as it stores elements that have pairs of keys and values in it. The semantics of `Map` are different from `Dictionary`, as will be explained later.

These are the conceptual mappings of the F# collection to .NET BCL:

F#	.NET BCL	Notes
Seq (sequence)	IEnumerable<T>	F# Seq is an alias of IEnumerable<'T>. Therefore it is also valid and safe to use Seq for all operations that leverage IEnumerable and IEnumerable<'T>, and they are eagerly evaluated by default.

List	List<T>	F# `List` is implemented as single linked list. To have only immutability parity, .NET BCL has `ReadOnlyCollection<T>` type that is equal to the immutability feature. F# `List` is also thread safe. The equivalent of `List<T>` that has a thread safe feature in .NET BCL is the `SynchronizedCollection<T>` in the System.Collections.Generic namespace, and this collection is not immutable. So currently there is no equivalent type of F# `List` in .NET 4/4.5.4.6.1 BCL that is both immutable and thread safe.
Array	Implicitly implemented as implementation of `IEnumerable<T>` but it is restricted to being a single variant, not a covariant.	F# `Array` is a single variant. Both the F# `Array` and .NET BCL `Array` have a fixed length.
Map	Dictionary<TKey, TValue>	Both `Map` and `Dictionary<TKey, TValue>` implement the `IDictionary<TKey, TValue>` interface. Therefore, in the conceptual perspective, it is the same but not in the semantic perspective. F# `Map` is just immutable by default.
Set	No equal type.	There's no equal type of `Set` in .NET BCL. The `Set` is actually a container of items but the item in the elements of the set must be unique.

For more information about the .NET BCL collection types, please consult the starting page of `System.Collections` at `https://msdn.microsoft.com/en-us/library/mt481475(v=vs.110).aspx`.

The F# sequence can create an infinite collection by initializing `Seq` using the `seq.initInfinite` function. A sequence will always be evaluated lazily. The consequence of this is the efficiency: the operation is applied as necessary to regenerate the elements of the sequence.

There is no compiler or runtime trick for this infinite sequence. The F# infinite sequence is also available for use in C#/VB.

Comparing F# List to .NET List<T>

The `List` is similar to .NET `List`, because they both have indexes and the same methods as well, although the semantics are different.

The `List` is implemented as a single linked list, not as the `List<T>` in .NET BCL. This linked list implementation is faster than `List<T>`. The `List` can be stored recursively by easily using F# `head::tail` syntax.

A single linked list means that each element of the list contains a portion of property that points to the next element of the list, as illustrated here:

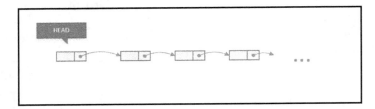

F# `List` is efficient and faster than `List<T>` in a sense that a single linked list always guarantees that any operations that access only the head of the list are *O(1)*, and element access is *O(n)*. It is ordered that each element can have a pointer to the next element.

The apparent advantages of F# `List` over .NET `List<T>` are as follows:

- F# `List` is immutable. It can be considered as a persistent data structure when combining with `List`.
- The nature of a linked list of the F# `List` means that it is efficient when combining lists using concatenation, as explained later.
- It has efficient access to the recursive nature of `head::tail`, which can then be used in recursive functions. This is common in functional programming languages, as the recursive nature is deeply implemented not just on functions, but on data structures as well.

For an example of a recursive `head::tail` in a recursive function, let's look at the following sample code from F# MSDN of the F# `List` documentation:

```
let rec sum list =
    match list with
    | head :: tail -> head + sum tail
    | [] -> 0
```

The `sum` function will call the `sum` function again with the parameter of the rest of the elements (`tail`) after the first element (`head`).

The recursive nature of `head::tail` will continue automatically on the next recursive call as the next `head::tail` will contain the list of the resulting previous `head::tail`.

The `head::tail` syntax in the previous code sample can be leveraged to recursively access the head and the rest of data on the tail. There is no comparable feature for this in C#/VB. If there is any, the implementation would be less efficient when `List<T>` is used.

As linked lists, concatenating F# `Lists` are also faster than concatenating a .NET `List<T>`. Concatenating between two or more `List` items is done in the following way:

1. Create a new `List` that has the total capacity of all `List` items.
2. Copy the source `List` structurally (not referentially).
3. The tail link of the source is linked to the head of the destination list, and the rest of the destination lists are copied structurally.
4. The process is repeated until all the participant lists have been copied and linked.
5. The operations do not (visibly) update the structure in place, but instead always yield a new updated structure.

F# has a convenient operator to concatenate `List`, using the `@` operator.

For example consider:

```
let list3 = list1 @ list2
```

The `list3` will contain the concatenation of `list1` and `list2`.

Comparing F# Map to Dictionary<TKey,TValue>

F# Map is equal to .NET BCL Dictionary<TKey, TValue> conceptually because they both implement .NET IDictionary<TKey, TValue>. But F# Map is semantically different from Dictionary<TKey, TValue>.

 Please do not confuse F# Map as type with F# Map as a module. F# Map as a module is called Map. From outside, it is called by referencing to the namespace of FSharp.Collection.Map module. The F# Map as a type is available from outside F#. The name is called FSharpMap.

From the performance perspective, it is still faster because of its immutability behavior.

From the correctness perspective, F# Map is enforcing us to be more correct because of the constrained key and value of the generic type parameter.

Let's look at the type definition signature of F# Map:

```
type Map<[<EqualityConditionalOn>]''Key,
[<EqualityConditionalOn;ComparisonConditionalOn>]'Value when 'Key :
comparison >(comparer: IComparer<''Key>, tree: MapTree<'Key,'Value>)
```

It is actually translated into this:

- Map has two generic type parameters: Key and Value
- Key is marked with EqualityConditionalOnAttribute
- Key is constrained to be derived from the comparison
- Value is marked with EqualityConditionalOnAttribute and ComparisonConditionalOnAttribute

 The ComparisonConditionalOnAttribute means that the generic parameter type satisfies the generic comparison constraint if and only if the type satisfies this constraint.

The EqualityConditionalOnAttribute means the generic parameter type satisfies the F# equality constraint only if a generic argument also satisfies this constraint.

Map has the default constructor that accepts parameter of the comparer and the tree is the base collection for bespoke comparison.

The comparer parameter is constrained implementing IComparer.

Although F# has no support for covariance/contravariance, implementing

`IComparer` for the comparer parameter means that it is also implicitly covariant. This is quite obvious because `IComparer` has the signature of `IComparer<in T>`.

These additional attributes might add a little overhead when doing comparisons and equality checks, but are necessary because of these correctness rules:

- The `Key` must be able to be checked for equality, because the key must be unique.
- The `Value` must be able to be checked for equality and comparison. This is also important, as the value must be able to be sorted later (having a sorting operation is optional).

The deciding considerations in choosing `Map` or `Dictionary` are:

- If you just want to have a collection that has keys and values but needs immutability, use `Map`. The net effect of checking the equality of the values is not bigger than the usefulness of immutability.
- If you just want to have a collection that has keys and values without worrying about the order of the values and need immutability, use `Map`.
- If you just want to have an immutable implementation of `Dictionary` with sorted `Keys`, use `Map` with `Keys` that have been sorted by sorting the map's keys.
- If you need a mutable `Dictionary`, use `Dictionary<TKey, TValue>` instead of `Map`. It is better to use `Dictionary<TKey, TValue>` directly for mutable purposes than marking a `Map` instance as *mutable*. Marking a `Map` instance value as mutable means we are using `Map` but treating it as mutable. This simple hack may break interoperability with other languages such as C#/VB, because `Map` is supposed to be kept as immutable but the integrity is broken as mutable. The intention of correctness is also broken.
- If you want to have a mutable `Dictionary` sorted by keys, use `SortedDictionary` instead. It is thread safe, unless you inherit `SortedDictionary` and implement your own sorted `Dictionary` because there is no further guarantee that on your own custom sorted dictionary, the thread safety will not be violated or overridden. Furthermore, referential transparency is not guaranteed to be the same or not broken.

By considering these scenarios, we should use F# `Map` as the main consideration. Marking `Map` as mutable to cheat on the mutability is not recommended. This applies also to the other collection types such as F#'s `List` and `Set`.

Choosing a value evaluation strategy

We know that F# collections have support for lazy evaluation, not just eager evaluation. Almost all of F# collections are lazy, except the operations that require modifications on the order of the elements. The collections in F# that do not have a lazy feature are F# `Array` and `Set`, as the semantics are similar to the .NET BCL array.

Collection modules on F# are not all lazily evaluated. The same behavior is applied on these modules: `Array`, `List`, and `Sequence`. The F# developer team is working hard to end the feature disparity by making relevant functions to be available for all modules.

For a more complete list of F#'s progress on narrowing feature disparity (focusing on what's new in F# releases) visit:

`https://msdn.microsoft.com/en-us/visualfsharpdocs/conceptual/whats-new-in-visual-fsharp`

For example, `map` and `filter` do not require modification of the order of the elements; sort (`orderby` in LINQ) and `groupby` require modifications.

The real reasons why we could deduce that all of the operations of the functions that modify or reorder the content of a collection make it lazy is almost impossible because of the way these operations work, especially when considering operations that relate to category theory and relational algebra, subjects borrowed from the realm of mathematics. All of the function implementation of map, filter, fold, and unfold are actually based on relational algebra.

Category theory deals with how the function compositions work, especially when the chaining of functions has to be composable. Relational algebra deals with operations of map, reduce, filter, fold, and unfold on a collection of elements. Relational algebra and category theory are the foundations of how F# collection operations work, and they are quite commonly known in other functional programming languages as basic features.

The topics of category theory and relational algebra are beyond the scope of this book, although it is recommended to understand the basics of these mathematical disciplines.

To learn more about relational algebra, please check one of this sample course from MIT:

`http://ocw.mit.edu/courses/electrical-engineering-and-computer-science/6-830-database-systems-fall-2010/`

Category theory is the foundation knowledge of functional constructs composition such as Monad and Monoid, and it is also the base theory behind lambda calculus and higher order functions. Lambda calculus and higher order functions are part of the common functional programming features.

The terms lazy or eager evaluation are based on the evaluation strategies of the programming language.

Lazy evaluation means expressions are only evaluated once and then only if the evaluation is actually needed. It is also called on-demand evaluation or deferred execution (the operation is deferred to be executed later).

Eager evaluation means expressions are evaluated as soon as the computation expression is bound to a variable. F# by default is using eager evaluation for any variable assignment, unless the assignment has explicit lazy expressions.

As a consequence of having lazy evaluation, the type must be aligned and well defined before being lazily evaluated. Otherwise, type casting or invalid argument exceptions may occur. This is one of the main reasons why static typing is mandatory in functional programming languages such as F#.

In F#, lazy evaluation can be applied on a type and can also be implemented as functions on collections such as `Seq` and `List`.

On collection, the resulting collection from the operations that have lazy evaluation are executed when the collection is going to be read in iteration, including evaluating `head::tail`.

When applied on a type, F# has a `lazy` keyword to denote lazy computation to enclose the operation to be lazy. The result is a variable that has an operation to be executed and evaluated later when the evaluation to read is needed.

This is an example of lazy computation in action when used as standalone type (not a collection):

```
let x = 10
let result = lazy (x + 10)
printfn "%d" (result.Force())
do()
```

If we put a debugger breakpoint on the second line, the result is not yet having a value and stepping over the line will not execute the x + 10 operation. After stepping over line 3, the result will have a value. This will ensure on-demand execution or computation.

By default, when operating on a type, F# will always do eager evaluation unless a lazy computation is applied. Using a lazy evaluation on all of operations or expressions will increase stack allocation overheads, and these overheads will exhaust stacks as well.

It is recommended to only apply lazy computation on a type if the expression is reused at in many methods, because applying lazy means the operation within the lazy computation will only be executed once and then the result will be used many times.

For more information about lazy computation on types, visit the following MSDN documentation:

```
https://msdn.microsoft.com/en-us/visualfsharpdocs/conceptual/lazy-computations-%5Bfsharp%5D
```

There is also a language construct that implements lazy evaluation implicitly as a state machine: using `yield` as an iterator efficiently on a F# `Sequence`.

For example consider:

```
seq { for i in 1 .. 10 do yield i * i }
```

Another sample that saves `yield` into a variable is:

```
let multiplicationTable =
    seq { for i in 1..9 do
             for j in 1..9 do
                 yield (i, j, i*j) }
```

Internally, `yield` is implemented as a state machine, which lazily computes the operation if the sequence is read or iterated. The F# `yield` is similar to the C#/VB `yield` although the actual semantics are different. It is similar in terms of the state machine based on a common design pattern of iterator.

For more internal details of how an iterator works, check Microsoft's developer blog entry written by Raymond Chen:

```
https://blogs.msdn.microsoft.com/oldnewthing/20080812-00/?p=21273
```

His blog has a series to describe iterators from an abstract as syntactic sugar to the raw implementation, although he describes the yield iterator from the perspective of the C# yield iterator specific implementation.

The use of yield in F# is actually a syntactic sugar that translates into a complex state machine as described in Raymond Chen's article. We should not worry about the implementation detail of this yield, because next releases of F# may change the implementation details of yield.

The yield and lazy are sample features of F# that hide the implementation details of the complex machinery of state machine. This will let us focus on what we are going to have as the result, instead of worrying about how we compute the result. This is often called a declarative instead of purely imperative. The declarative aspect of F# does not stop here; many concurrency constructs such as the async computation are declarative as well.

Most performance characteristics of lazy evaluation are better than eager evaluation, especially when the expression captured and evaluated lazily is used many times. The total net effect of using a lazy expression is noticeable, because of the execution on demand.

From the perspective of the F# unique approach as a functional programming language is not pure. F# is not doing all the aspects of language constructs lazily. For example, not all operations of Seq implement lazy evaluation. If we compare F# to other pure functional programming languages such as Haskell, Haskell has emphasized lazy evaluation on almost all cases, including comprehensive type resolutions, collection iterators, and even encapsulating side effects such as I/O lazily.

There are some disadvantages of having all expressions and functions to be lazy:

- Compile times will always slower than eager evaluation.
- If all operations are having lazy evaluation implemented, all of the complex state machines must be implemented for each case for all operations. This will result in a long compile time, including translating to state machines at the IL level.
- There is no guarantee that having all expressions and functions as lazily evaluated will not exhaust stack.

The detail of the possibility of scenarios for lazy evaluations is described in the next section.

Scenarios involving evaluation strategy and memory allocations

Lazy evaluation always consumes stack to allocate the metadata, the pointer to the expression. The expression evaluated may also be stored on stack if the expression is simple and no reference type (for example, usage of string or having a value captured in WeakReference) is used.

We must consider these scenarios:

- Always use lazy evaluation whenever possible when doing operations on collections, especially when using a collection that only does forward-only features such as `Sequence` or `IEnumerable`, including `IEnumerable<T>` as well.

- For more complex recursive expressions or computation, lazy evaluation will consume stack rapidly, especially when combining complex lazy evaluation within recursive functions. Eager evaluation is preferred for this scenario, as the result of recursive functions always stored on stack as a stack frame with the last pointer of the previous same function call. If the lazy operation inside a recursive function is guaranteed to be simple and only calculating value types, then we can use lazy evaluation quite safely without consuming too much stack.

- When the lazy operation involves a reference type, an overhead of going back and forth between allocating stack and heap will always occur and this will result in having poor performance in terms of memory consumptions and time consumed during roundtrips of memory allocation between stack and heap. GC overhead will always occur during this heavy round trip, because GC cannot be guaranteed to collect at the right time after a recursive call function is finished and returned to its previous recursive function call. At first, stack will always be garbage collected first but mixed stack and heap will make GC slower to collect as stack needs to detach any references to heap allocation before being popped and garbage collected.

- If our function is used in parallel, any atomic expression inside the function should be implemented lazily, as this is more efficient especially when the function will be running many times. Unless the function is implemented as a recursive function that has lazy operations in parallel it is also consuming stack quite rapidly, as described in the second scenario.

- Avoid side effects whenever possible. If the lazy evaluation or yield expression contains side effects such as I/O, an exception may occur and this is expensive in terms of stack trace and stack frame allocation overhead. CPU bound calculation is a side effect but this kind of side effect can be ignored, as long as it is combined with other concurrency techniques such as parallelism.

- It is recommended to avoid lazy evaluation on UI threads. F# and CIL/CLR do not allow cross-threads.

- Having implementation of async computation workflow inside of a function that has lazy evaluation is fine, but we should avoid mixing lazy evaluation with side effects based on the fifth point, as usually async may deal with async I/O operations. Therefore, the use of eager evaluation when dealing with side effects within async computation is recommended. This scenario is one of the subtle scenarios that is often not observed well or is badly ignored.

- Always pay attention to side effects that may occur, even any subtle side effects such as having calls to Windows API invocation. Not just exception needs to be handled, but there are some dangers of thread blockings or even deadlock when side effect computation is in effect.

- Lazy evaluation inside a computation workflow or quotation has to be treated carefully. There is a possibility that lazy evaluation might decrease performance of certain computation workflows such as async, as async itself is a complex state machine.

- Any cancellation being handled during async computation that has lazy evaluation is fine, because a cancellation handles a side effect computation of the context switching of an asynchronous operation in a graceful manner as recommended by common pattern in .NET TPL.

- Do not perform synchronized lock within a lazy computation, as the execution context may behave unexpected side effects. A chance of deadlock may occur if the lazy computation contains a lock that locks a complex object. Lock is also not recommended within normal running F# code.

These scenarios may not cover all of the cases of choosing evaluation strategy, but they are quite common in implementing functions that combine lazy and eager evaluations. Therefore, lazy evaluation is not a single bullet for all kinds of performance optimizations in the value evaluation strategy.

More detailed scenarios that may cause unexpected behavior or unexpected results when dealing with concurrency, are discussed in Chapter 4, *Introduction to Concurrency in F#*.

Summary

Data structures are not just a crucial feature of any programming language, they play very important part in our codes, regardless whatever programming language we use. Understanding data structures in .NET are also the foundation of any programming language that runs on .NET CLR, including F# data structures.

We now not just have enough understanding of F# data structures, but we can leverage F# data structures by applying and combining with best practices. The best practices that we have covered in this chapter are not just best practices of using the existing F# data structures, but we also have best practices of optimizing the data structures.

This data structure optimization understanding can be brought into deeper understanding of concurrency in F# in Chapter 4, *Introduction to concurrency in F#*.

4
Introduction to Concurrency in F#

Performance optimizations are not just about understanding the underlying platform, profiling, toolings and measurements, and data structures. Now, with the rising trend of multicore processors and at the same time, the increasing needs of responsive applications to be achieved as and when required, concurrency is not just becoming more relevant but also a necessary requirement across all kinds of enterprise applications, especially applications across all full stacks of layers of multi-tier architecture applications.

It is also evident that concurrency is one of those performance optimizations that are often misunderstood. Some common misunderstood samples have already been described in Chapter 1, *Performing Common Optimizations in F#*. In this chapter, we will focus on concurrency features in F# and also get to know the basic strategy behind the deciding factor of the actual implementation.

To understand the background reasoning for the chosen strategy, first we must get to know the features of concurrency in F# especially in F# 4.0. There is no noticeable difference between F# 3.0 and F# 4.0 in terms of the existing concurrency features. There are F# 4.0 additional features to have interop with .NET Task Parallel Library, as these interop features will be explained in this chapter.

Having a knowledge of measurement tooling, covered in Chapter 2, *Performance Measurement*, qualitative knowledge of the mechanism of running F# code (the IL, tooling, and the GC), and having quantitative measures (the execution durations using timers and unit tests) are requirements in order to easily understand the importance of concurrency and the decisive factor of choosing the right concurrent model.

Throughout this chapter, we will see that there is no silver bullet for all kinds of concurrency problems. For example, using only parallel computation to handle I/O operations is not recommended because I/O operation is a good sample of a blocking thread. However, it is also important to identify which threads or processes are blocking threads. Combining this with asynchronous computation is recommended. Also, there is not a single concurrency feature that cannot be combined with other kinds of concurrency features, as will be introduced in this chapter.

This chapter gives a gentle overview of the concurrency features of F#, focusing on F# 4.0. We will also provide an overview of the best practices to implement and optimize it. Advanced topics of concurrency optimizations in F#, such as combining asynchrony and parallelism, the F# message passing agent, `MailboxProcessor`, and further interop with .NET TPL, will be described in `Chapter 5`, *Advanced Concurrency Support in F#*.

This chapter covers the following topics:

- Introducing concurrency support in F# 4.0
- Identifying blocking threads
- Introducing asynchronous workflow

Introducing concurrency support in F# 4

It is important to have concurrency support from the programming language perspective, especially as built-in language features. In F#, concurrency support in F# was available before F# 4.0. Two of the concurrency features: the asynchronous workflow and `MailboxProcessor` have been available since F# 1.9.

In a quick overview, F# has the following concurrency features:

- Asynchronous workflow
- Asynchronous message passing using actor model and an F# special class that functions as an agent for message passing, `MailboxProcessor`
- Parallel programming support for asynchronous workflow
- Interop with .NET Task Parallel Library (TPL)

Asynchronous workflow is actually an implementation of a computation expression that is escalated as syntactic sugar. It is escalated within a block of asynchronous code that has calls to asynchronous functions, marked in the beginning with `async` as keyword.

From the perspective of conceptual concurrency, it is quite intuitive and easier to understand that F# has support for the following:

- **Asynchronous concurrency**: in `async` and `MailboxProcessor`
- **Parallel concurrency**: parallel supports in asynchronous workflow and interop with .NET TPL

Each of the supports is not a static solution for a single problem; for example, `MailboxProcessor` can be combined with parallel concurrency as well. It is also quite common to combine `MailboxProcessor` with async workflow, and then execute it in parallel as well.

There is no comparable built-in asynchronous message passing support in other languages such as C#/VB in the release of Visual Studio 2015. Even in .NET BCL, there is no message passing agent implementation at all. Some known message passing agents are available from outside .NET BCL, in the form of message passing combined with the actor model. Usually, they come in the form of a NuGet package available for download or in the form of a commercialized class library.

The discussion on the best practices and usage of `MailboxProcessor` will be discussed in `Chapter 5`, *Advanced Concurrency Support in F#*.

There is a known actor-based library of concurrency that comes from Microsoft Research; it is called Orleans. It is open source but it is unfortunately only optimized for cloud development and deployment especially in Azure. For more information about Orleans, visit:

`https://www.microsoft.com/en-us/research/project/orleans-virtual-actors/`

Fortunately, F# concurrency can be used and implemented in accordance with the other languages as well, as long as it's based on a common version of .NET CLR. We could also leverage the async-await model of C#/VB into the F# async workflow.

To use and to have interop with asynchronous methods in the .NET Framework that are designed for other asynchronous models with the F# asynchronous programming model, you create a function that returns an F# `async` object. The F# library has functions that make this easy to do.

On the implementation detail, F# concurrency support has the following building blocks:

1. **Control.Async<'T>**: This is a type in the `Microsoft.FSharp.Control` namespace to contain asynchronous operation.

2. **The Control.Async**: This is a class in the `Microsoft.FSharp.Control` namespace that contains all of the supports for asynchronous operations, support for .NET TPL, and for executing asynchronous workflow in parallel.

3. **Control.AsyncBuilder**: This is a builder class in `Microsoft.FSharp.Control`, to construct F# asynchronous workflow, including the implementation of `let!` and `use!` for containing the result of asynchronous operations.

4. **F# asynchronous primitives**: These are classes that may extend the existing .NET BCL with methods that implement F# asynchronous workflow, such as the `Control.WebExtension` and `Control.CommonExtension` modules. Both of them are in the `Microsoft.FSharp.Control` namespace.

To further illustrate the relations, all of the asynchronous types, parallel types, and builders for asynchronous workflow are concentrated under the `Microsoft.FSharp.Control` namespace.

The hierarchical illustration is as shown in the following diagram:

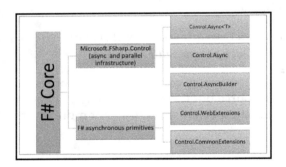

F# asynchronous primitives are called **asynchronous primitives** because they perform a single asynchronous task and return the result.

It is quite common that asynchronous workflow is often used to handle blocking threads. Whether we are aware of the existence of blocking threads or not, it is very important to know the traits or characteristics the blocking threads have and not just to understand the definitions of a blocking thread.

Identifying blocking threads

A thread, from the perspective of interactions with other threads, is divided into two kinds: *non-blocking thread* and *blocking thread*. A non-blocking thread is usually a thread that does not block any other thread.

A blocking thread means a thread that does operations that often force the execution context to wait for other *operations*. By nature, in this context of operations, there can be many kinds of operations and interactions with other kinds of subsystem components such as I/O and CPU thread counter such as the operation performed in `System.Threading.Thread.Sleep`.

Overview of the background technical reasons for the blocking nature of I/O

I/O is never separated from the implementation and usage of our application, especially applications that deal with networking and sending commands to an output device outside the scope of the subsystem, such as printers. It is often ignored, but it is becoming relevant that as a running application is expected to be as responsive as possible, the nature of any I/O operation cannot be ignored.

I/O operations have a tendency to force us to wait, although this wait should be treated as being placed in a different execution context rather than in the current thread. This is why the concept of having asynchronous operations is more relevant as the wait should not be synchronous.

Then why are I/O operations really *blocking threads*?

Consider the following sample facts/scenarios:

- You send I/O commands to a printer (with the data) to print some data (usually, any kind of data formats supported by the underlying OS). There is no guarantee that the printer is always turned ON or that the printer is not busy. There can also be some forms of latency that we cannot control directly, such as network latency when transferring commands and data to be printed. Even when you are connecting your machine directly to the printer, there is no guarantee that the printer is always on and ready to process your commands. For example, your machine might have other running background processes that deal with other I/O, such as hard disks, especially when performing virus scans.
- You send HTTP requests on a host that you have tested with a ping before. There is no guarantee that at the time of sending the HTTP requests, the destination host is still available or that the host is even ready to process your requests and return responses. If the host is available and ready to process your requests, you cannot control exactly how quickly the destination host would reply with responses and how responsive it would be. Again, network latency also plays a huge role in dealing with roundtrips of HTTP request-response.

- A simple ping to any other host is also an I/O operation in action. Again, there is no guarantee that the destination host will respond to your ping (usually in ICMP packets).
- You are performing defragmentation on your local hard disk and expecting to do something else. Even with most of the Windows or other modern OSes such as Linux's distributions with latest kernel, there is no guarantee that you won't have to wait for the defragmentation to finish completely or that you can do other operations without interruptions from the defragmentation operations. Normally, you should not interrupt or even interfere with the current intentional I/O operations such as storage defragmentation. This is often misunderstood by a common computer user as bugs, although it is defragmentation that is obviously impacting storage as I/O. Therefore, it should not be considered as a bug in our code.

Based on the preceding common facts, these I/O operations all have one thing in common: *we have to wait*. It also clearly defines that I/O operation is one sample of a side-effect because we cannot control it fully and it is out of the scope of the current execution thread of our code.

The conclusion is obvious and quite clear: any I/O operation must be considered as a blocking thread.

These side effects should not be considered as bugs based on the nature of the operations running out of the scope boundary of the execution, but any errors, especially exceptions that might have occurred, must be handled. In other terms, these side effects must not be ignored and cannot be treated in a normal synchronous way because we have to wait for them to complete.

The best practices of exception handling (including the details when dealing with concurrency problems) will be discussed in detail in `Chapter 7`, *Language Features and Constructs Optimization*.

It is easier to summarize blocking threads as part of operations that are also considered as blocking threads, such as I/O operations described previously.

Obvious trait of a blocking thread

In a simple definition, a blocking thread is part of any operation or function that *waits for an event to occur or a time period to elapse*. While a blocking call is waiting, the operating system can often remove that thread from the scheduler, so it takes no CPU time until the event has occurred or the time has elapsed. Once the event has occurred, then the thread is placed back in the scheduler and can run when allocated a time slice.

It seems quite difficult to relate with I/O, but all I/O operations again always have a waitable behavior and can always be considered as blocking operations. This is not just a strong sample of a side effect. The operations that require us to wait are also available in other kinds of operations, especially if the operations are doing many things either in a definite amount of time or indefinite amount of time. We can parallelize this, but there is always a limited amount of computations available as opposed to the nature of most applications that usually do not care about this.

The context of waitable operations is the source of inspiration for the introduction of TPL in .NET 4.0, especially to define any task that is waitable as identified by the async-await pattern and the `TaskAwaiter` implementation. All of these waitable tasks can be used in asynchronous blocks.

 It is also in sync with the C# 4 and VB 10 releases: the async models leverage these waitable patterns by enforcing all the tasks to be awaitable, wrapped in an awaiter of `TaskAwaiter`.

For example, you cannot always consider that your application will always run using the fastest CPU with many cores. Any assumption that your application will run successfully in many cores without paying attention to how you treat the concurrent running of your application can slow down your application performance.

Any successful enterprise application must be able to scale itself in a sense that it must consider that the number of users of the application can grow and that the operations they will engage when they use the applications can be arbitrarily complex. Therefore, paying attention to how the code will run across many CPU cores and also paying attention to the responsiveness of the application, especially paying attention to any blocking operations, are requirements, not just recommendations.

It also brings a more interesting fact that it is easier to get used to identifying blocking threads by identifying blocking operations first. Identifying blocking threads first is also a good practice to have a best practice mindset because we often misunderstand blocking threads as non-blocking threads due to common assumptions that applications usually running in modern CPUs are always fast by default.

The context of *does not block any other thread* is often misunderstood. A thread can block other threads even if it was considered a non-blocking thread. For example, a very intensive computation that requires CPU-intensive operations, such as complex number-related calculations that are targeted for a specific CPU core, can block other threads that want to use any available core if the other core might be busy processing other calculations or processes.

Consider this sample illustrated scenario running on the 4th generation of Intel core i5 that has two physical cores:

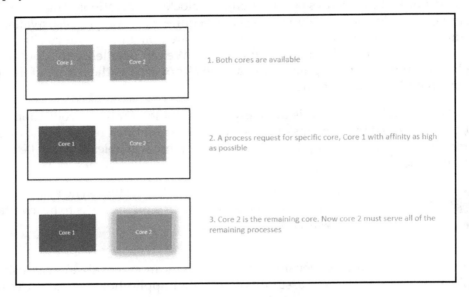

The details of the scenario are as follows:

1. The running code runs on a machine that has the 4th generation of Intel core i5 processor. This processor has two physical cores and each core has two hyper-threading units.
2. The running code (it acts as a process under the runtime context) asks to run on the 1st core explicitly, so it assumes that the remaining core (in this case, only one core) should be available for others.
3. Then the other process suddenly runs in the background, and it needs a high thread affinity, for example, processes by antivirus software. Most antivirus software always try to ask for a higher thread affinity when they are scheduled to run a full scan at a scheduled time. Another sample is when a Windows update is performing a background installation update after it has finished downloading all of the updates available at the time the code runs.

4. All of these other processes, therefore, are cramped into only one core, and they can interfere with each other so that one process may take over the entire CPU core cycle.

Based on this scenario, a blocking thread can be caused by non I/O operations as well.

It is quite important to know or to keep up with the latest of x86/x64 processors as we should never assume that our code runs automatically in parallel, although we must not rely on the number of actual physical cores. It is also closely related to paying more attention to concurrency because the trends for the last 6 years have been leaning toward having more cores instead of having a higher speed of CPU clock. The intention here is clear: *the awareness that concurrency is increasingly more relevant as the age of multicores outweigh the free increase of higher-speed CPUs.*

It is also a strong evidence that *free lunch is over*, stated by Herb Sutter (we first mentioned this article in `Chapter 1`, *Performing Common Optimizations in F#*), is correct.

Therefore, this book is not going to describe the full characteristic details of Intel or AMD processors because it is outside the scope of this F# book.

For more information on the full specifications of Intel processors, please consult `http://ark.intel.com/`.

For more information on the specifications of AMD, please consult `http://www.amd.com/en-us/products/processors/desktop`.

 There are other processors supported by .NET, but most processors today are dominated by Intel and AMD. A sample of this is ARM, powering some WinRT machines for Windows 8 and Windows 8.1 tablets and Microsoft's own tablet, Surface. The ARM architecture is different from that of Intel and AMD, although it has multiple cores as well, and the market share for these processor-based devices is also very small. It can be safely assumed that since the introduction of Visual Studio 2015, the target processor architecture is for x86 and x64 only, unless you are targeting other kind of devices, such as mobile phones.

Now that we have a basic knowledge of what a blocking thread is, the next challenge is whether we have to wait and not do anything else or whether *we can do other things while waiting*. Doing other things while waiting is actually an implementation of the asynchronous way. It is conceptually the same as the restaurant waiting problem we had visited in `Chapter 1`, *Performing Common Optimizations in F#*.

F# provides support for implementing asynchronous operations using asynchronous workflow without any complexity of having callback implementation.

Introducing asynchronous workflow

Asynchronous support in F# is implemented nicely using async workflow computations.

The initial release of F# 1.0 did not have it. Asynchronous workflow was introduced in F# 1.9.2.9, and it is categorized as a workflow because it is actually an implementation of a computation expression (builder) that is escalated as a language block of `async`. It is also a good sample of a best practice in implementing function compositions and in expressively implementing **Monad**. Monad is one of the functional composition implementations, an idea taken from or inspired by the category theory knowledge domain.

Function composition is actually a composition of computation operations; they can be functions or composite statements such as for loop constructs. It is also quite intuitive, and it's also easier to use as the necessary detailed composition operations are hidden. Usually, there is a `bind` operator to compose two functions (or computations).

The foundational theory of this is quite common, back to the world of set theory. Set theory is further extended in Category theory where composition is more emphasized between functions. For example, consider the following:

$f => f(x)$

$g => g(x)$

$f \circ g = f(g(x))$

Here, the $f \circ g$ is read as *f circle g* where *circle* is the composition between the functions *f* and *g*.

Usually the composition in a Monad is expressed by the `bind` operator, symbolized as >>= in many other functional programming languages such as Haskell. This composition of a function also implies that the return type of *g* must be the same as the type of the parameter of *f*. From the perspective of real-world functional programming, type safety is always enforced even though the type is not mentioned. Everything will always be inferred based on the type inference of the function's return type and the result of the currying functions.

The built-in workflows in F# are not just limited to the asynchronous workflow; there are Sequence and LINQ query workflows as well.

In asynchronous workflow, there is a `bind` builder (it is conceptually similar to bind in Monad) implemented to compose operations, but the implementation is hidden by the syntax of the `let!` keyword.

The implementation and optimization of a builder in F# to compose a workflow will be further discussed in `Chapter 7`, *Language Features and Constructs Optimization*.

The implementation of F# computation expressions is also called a workflow because it usually defines the compositions of functions as the results of binding (`bind`) operations and control flows.

The goals of F# asynchronous workflow are as follows:

- Increase responsiveness by not blocking the running thread and get the other process done first.
- Ease programming in asynchronous concurrency without worrying about callback and explicit continuations.
- Intuitively, the code flows more naturally because the flow is not looking like going back and forth between a function that contains an asynchronous call and callback since callback is not called explicitly in the code.
- Compositional nature of asynchronous workflow means that it can be composed with other concurrencies such as parallelization.
- The asynchronous block implies that some basic I/O operations on the web usually have their own *begin* and *end* web operations. It is further supported and wrapped into F# Async primitives to ease interoperability with asynchronous models such as .NET Asynchronous Programming Model.
- The asynchronous block also provides exception handling in a compositional way and also in a safe manner without losing too much referential transparency.

Asynchronous workflow is nicely wrapped in the following common syntax:

```
async { <expression>... }
```

The term `expression` is not only a single line of expression but can also be a compound expression. This means it can contain more than one statement as well.

Getting to know asynchronous workflow

We can start looking at the first sample of `async` from MSDN Library. I have added the necessary detail on handling specific exceptions that may occur when we are dealing with HTTP request/response operations.

This is the code:

```
open System
open System.Net
open System.IO
open Microsoft.FSharp.Control.WebExtensions

let urlList = [ "Microsoft.com", "http://www.microsoft.com/"
                "MSDN", "http://msdn.microsoft.com/"
                "Bing", "http://www.bing.com"
              ]

let fetchAsync(name, url:string) =
    async {
        try
            let uri = new System.Uri(url)
            let webClient = new WebClient()
            let! html = webClient.AsyncDownloadString(uri)
            printfn "Read %d characters for %s" html.Length name
        with
            | :? IOException as ex -> printfn "IO Exception: %s"
(ex.Message);
            | :? System.Net.HttpListenerException as httplistenerexn ->
printfn "IO Exception: %s" (httplistenerexn.Message);
            | genex -> printfn "General Exception: %s" (genex.Message);
    }

let runAll() =
    urlList
    |> Seq.map fetchAsync
    |> Async.Parallel
    |> Async.RunSynchronously
    |> ignore

runAll()
```

Let's visit the details of this sample.

The intention of this sample code is to download the content of a web page from a collection of URLs asynchronously while also executing the download of the web page of all URLs in parallel.

The `urlList` variable contains all URLs as a collection. F# will infer this collection as a list of tuple of *string * string*. Then, this list is passed as a parameter to the `fetchAsync` function, which is then continued to be passed to the next sequence in the pipeline of the `|>` pipeline operator. The `fetchAsync` function returns an `async` block, implying that it returns an `async` function.

In a simplified flow, the entire chain of function compositions is composed nicely using the pipelines of `|>` within the `runAll` function as follows:

1. The `urlList` is passed to the `Seq.map` function.
2. The `Seq.map` function still needs one more parameter: the `map` function. The `map` function takes `fetchAsync` as a parameter. The result of `map` returns a sequence of functions.
3. The sequence of functions is executed in parallel by `Async.Parallel`, which then returns an array of `async` functions. The executions are not yet run.
4. The `async` block includes exception handlings. The difference from the code in MSDN Library is the way the handling of the exceptions. In our sample code, exception handling is more specific than the original code in MSDN Library. This specific exception handling model is very important, because the exception occurred might have resulted as different types of exceptions caused by any errors in HTTP request/response operations and the specific exception should be handled differently.
5. The array of functions is then executed immediately by `Async.RunSynchronously`.
6. The ignore construct ignores the returning result. It will be inferred further as a unit.

Execute the code in F# scripting/interactive; then, within the interactive window, we will see the types inferred for `urlList`, `fetchAsync`, and `runAll` functions as follows:

```
For help type #help;;

>
val urlList : (string * string) list =
  [("Microsoft.com", "http://www.microsoft.com/");
   ("MSDN", "http://msdn.microsoft.com/"); ("Bing", "http://www.bing.com")]

>
val fetchAsync : name:string * url:string -> Async<unit>

>
Read 82679 characters for Bing
Read 1020 characters for Microsoft.com
Read 47277 characters for MSDN

val runAll : unit -> unit
val it : unit = ()

>
```

The declaration of let for asynchronous workflow can be written in two ways, using `let` and `let!` (pronounced *let bang*).

The sample uses `let!`; it means that the computation is focusing on returning a result. It means that the intention of the `async` operation is to execute the `download` function, `webClient.AsyncDownloadString(uri)`, and return the result, not the operation. Then, the thread on the `fetchAsync` scope is suspended. In other words, it is blocked because it waits for an event to be raised to notify that the process being waited for is completed. The outer thread (outside the `fetchAsync`) is not blocked.

All the code after the line of `webClient.AsyncDownloadString(uri)` is executed later, after the download is finished. However, the execution will not have to wait for the download to be completed; instead it will go outside the `async` block and execute the code after `fetchAsync` is called. In this sample, it will execute the code after the call to `fetchAsync`.

After the download is completed, the execution context returns to the code within the `async` block; it will point to the execution point of code after the call to `webClient.AsyncDownloadString(uri)`. The code at this point will be executed.

Because there is `Async.Parallel`, which executes all of the `fetchAsync` in parallel, the execution looks sequential, although the execution of the `AsyncDownloadString` calls is parallel.

In the sample, the execution is triggered by the call to the `Async.RunSynchronously` function.

The `let` means that the execution is not performed immediately; it is stored in a variable to be executed later. It does not return the result immediately.

Consider the following sample of `let` and `let!`:

```
// let just stores the result as an asynchronous operation.
let (result1 : Async<byte[]>) = stream.AsyncRead(bufferSize)
// let! completes the asynchronous operation and returns the data.
let! (result2 : byte[])  = stream.AsyncRead(bufferSize)
```

`let!` is conceptually equal to await in C# and VB as it awaits the actual result of `Task<T>`. It is still semantically different in its implementation.

Using asynchronous with Dispose pattern

There is another equivalent declaration to define the result of an asynchronous workflow using the use! keyword as compared to let!. The difference between let! and use/use! is in the usage: use! is used to handle asynchronous calls that will later dispose the object.

The use! keyword is the asynchronous counterpart of F#'s synchronous use and using keywords. In C#/VB, the concept of disposable is equal to the using keyword in C# and the Using keyword in VB, except that there is no comparable using model for disposable to be used in an asynchronous way.

The capture of a pattern, which is going to be disposed when not in use anymore before going out of scope, is called the Dispose pattern. It is also a sample of a coding design pattern. In today's programming language terms, the Dispose pattern is often escalated to have syntactic sugar, which is then translated as try...finally or (something else with similar semantics). Many programming languages have leveraged this Disposable pattern, not just C#, VB, and F#. It is also used in C++, Java, and other modern programming languages.

The following are the requirements for wrapping an object or type for usage in use/use!:

1. The result object must implement the IDisposable interface; therefore it must explicitly implement the Dispose method. However, in the real semantic of the Disposable pattern, it only looks for the implementation of the Dispose() method that has a void Dispose() signature.

2. An unmanaged resource is highly recommended to implement IDisposable. The main reason for why it must explicitly implement the Dispose method is because the object with an explicit Dispose method is usually an unmanaged resource wrapped as a CLR object, such as File, network Socket, and database connection object.

A managed object, if it is guaranteed to have no side effects, is also welcome to implement IDisposable.

The advantages of implementing the IDisposable interface and, at the same time, implementing our own Dispose method is that it minimizes the garbage collection overhead because implementing the Dispose method means that we decide the lifetime of the object before disposed.

Basically, the use and use! constructs in F# involve wrapping the try...finally pattern in the generated IL.

For example, consider the following scenario:

We are going to implement code that has usage of use!.

In the following sample, we are going to use the SqlDataReader class because it implements the IDisposable interface. This instance of SqlDataReader, the dataReader object, will be disposed after the execution of the asynchronous call is completed.

Here is the sample code:

```
open System.Data
open System.Data.SqlClient

let UseBangSample (dbconstring: string) =
    async {
        use dbCon = new SqlConnection(dbconstring)
        use sqlCommand = new SqlCommand("SELECT * FROM
INFORMATION_SCHEMA.TABLES")
        use! dataReader =
Async.AwaitTask(sqlCommand.ExecuteReaderAsync(CommandBehavior.Default))
        printfn "Finished querying"
    }
```

Let's dive deeper into the previous sample code.

The code will only refer to System.Data and System.Data.SqlClient. Any references to System, System.Data, and System.Data.Common do not need the external reference to the library outside of BCL. Some of the classes (especially .NET primitive types) used in the code have namespace prefix of System are available at mscorlib.dll and System.dll. The F# compiler will automatically know the location of mscorelib.dll and System.dll. For SQL server-related database connections, we have to add reference to System.Data.SqlCient.dll in our project. This is the same for another library such as System.Web.dll. If you want to use other libraries such as System.Web.dll, you have to add a reference to it.

For normal F# code, you can add reference by adding library references to the project reference.

For F# scripting, you have to inform the compiler about the location of the DLL that you want to use by registering it manually before using it. It is recommended that you register it before any open statement so as to ensure that you have registered the necessary DLL at the first section of the script. The registration is done by using the compiler directive of #r.

For more information about the `#r` compiler directive of F#, please visit the MSDN Library at
`https://msdn.microsoft.com/en-us/visualfsharpdocs/conceptual/compiler-directive`
`s-%5bfsharp%5d`.

The `use!` keyword (called *use bang*) will treat the `WebResponse` result from `req.AsyncGetResponse`.

We can examine the compiler result of the code sample by copying and pasting the code into any `.fs` code, or we can simply put the source code into the F# console project of a default file containing the main `EntryPoint, Program.fs`.

Compile it and open the executable file of the EXE using ILDASM. We will roughly see the following layout in the disassembled view:

Let's dive into the IL of the `async` block, starting from the `UseBangSample` method:

```
.method public static class
[FSharp.Core]Microsoft.FSharp.Control.FSharpAsync`1<class
[FSharp.Core]Microsoft.FSharp.Core.Unit>
        UseBangSample(string dbconstring) cil managed
{
  // Code size       21 (0x15)
  .maxstack  5
  .locals init ([0] class
[FSharp.Core]Microsoft.FSharp.Control.FSharpAsyncBuilder builder@)
  IL_0000:  nop
  IL_0001:  call        class
[FSharp.Core]Microsoft.FSharp.Control.FSharpAsyncBuilder
[FSharp.Core]Microsoft.FSharp.Core.ExtraTopLevelOperators::get_DefaultAsync
Builder()
  IL_0006:  stloc.0
  IL_0007:  ldloc.0
  IL_0008:  ldarg.0
  IL_0009:  ldloc.0
  IL_000a:  newobj      instance void Program/UseBangSample@10::.ctor(string,
                                                                      class
[FSharp.Core]Microsoft.FSharp.Control.FSharpAsyncBuilder)
  IL_000f:  callvirt    instance class
[FSharp.Core]Microsoft.FSharp.Control.FSharpAsync`1<!!0>
[FSharp.Core]Microsoft.FSharp.Control.FSharpAsyncBuilder::Delay<class
[FSharp.Core]Microsoft.FSharp.Core.Unit>(class
[FSharp.Core]Microsoft.FSharp.Core.FSharpFunc`2<class
[FSharp.Core]Microsoft.FSharp.Core.Unit,class
[FSharp.Core]Microsoft.FSharp.Control.FSharpAsync`1<!!0>>)
  IL_0014:  ret
} // end of method Program::UseBangSample
```

The method calls `UseBangSample@10` by instantiating it, and then it calls the `Invoke` method. It is quite common in the generated IL as the class is treated as an executable operation like a delegate.

Ignore the cryptic names of the generated type and method of the IL. If you compile the code on your own, the resulting type and method might have different names. The source code and the related IL from ILDASM for this chapter is already set up and available for us to examine the IL assembly code with the related F# code.

The common flow is actually the execution of the `Invoke` method. In this context, the `Invoke` method of `UseBangSample@10` will be executed.

Let's dive into the IL of `UseBangSample@10.Invoke`:

```
.method public strict virtual instance class
[FSharp.Core]Microsoft.FSharp.Control.FSharpAsync`1<class
[FSharp.Core]Microsoft.FSharp.Core.Unit>
        Invoke(class [FSharp.Core]Microsoft.FSharp.Core.Unit unitVar) cil
managed
{
  // Code size        35 (0x23)
  .maxstack   8
  IL_0000:  nop
IL_0001:  ldarg.0
  IL_0002:  ldfld        class
[FSharp.Core]Microsoft.FSharp.Control.FSharpAsyncBuilder
Program/UseBangSample@10::builder@
IL_0007:  ldarg.0
  IL_0008:  ldfld        string Program/UseBangSample@10::dbconstring
IL_000d:  newobj       instance void
[System.Data]System.Data.SqlClient.SqlConnection::.ctor(string)
  IL_0012:  ldarg.0
  IL_0013:  ldfld        class
[FSharp.Core]Microsoft.FSharp.Control.FSharpAsyncBuilder
Program/UseBangSample@10::builder@
  IL_0018:  newobj       instance void
Program/'UseBangSample@11-1'::.ctor(class
[FSharp.Core]Microsoft.FSharp.Control.FSharpAsyncBuilder)
  IL_001d:  callvirt     instance class
[FSharp.Core]Microsoft.FSharp.Control.FSharpAsync`1<!!1>
[FSharp.Core]Microsoft.FSharp.Control.FSharpAsyncBuilder::Using<class
[System.Data]System.Data.SqlClient.SqlConnection,class
[FSharp.Core]Microsoft.FSharp.Core.Unit>(!!0,
class [FSharp.Core]Microsoft.FSharp.Core.FSharpFunc`2<!!0,class
[FSharp.Core]Microsoft.FSharp.Control.FSharpAsync`1<!!1>>)
  IL_0022:  ret
} // end of method UseBangSample@10::Invoke
```

The line `IL_001d` explains the correlation between the IL and the corresponding code, the use! declaration. This `use!` will actually call the `FSharpAsyncBuilder.Using` builder to do the actual dispose pattern by instantiating `FSharp.AsyncBuilder` first.

All of these complex details are nicely hidden in the implementation detail of builders, in the implementations of the following three related Async types:

* `Control.Async` for the `Async.*` methods
* `Control.AsyncBuilder` for the builder implementation of asynchronous workflow

- `Control.Async<'T>` type to contain the implementation result of asynchronous workflow

Again, never mind the cryptic name of the generated code. As long as the name alias of the method and the classes is correct, we can simply deduce the use of `AsyncBuilder.Using` to handle the `use!` declaration in order to implement the Disposable pattern.

F# also comes with built-in asynchronous support for HTTP requests. This additional asynchronous operation is available in the `WebRequest` type, and it has been available under the `Microsoft.FSharp.Control.WebExtensions` namespace since F# 3.0. In F# version 2.0, it is available under the `Microsoft.FSharp.Control.CommonExtensions` namespace.

There has been a namespace reorganization in F# 3.0 and above as it is more aligned to the purpose or intent of the types and operations inside the namespace. For example, `WebRequest` related operations, now inside `Microsoft.FSharp.Control.WebExtensions`, were previously available under `Microsoft.FSharp.Control.CommonExtensions`.

 The main reason for this reorganization is the stabilization and standardization of intents because F#, since F# 2.0 in Visual Studio 2010, is not just a research product anymore, it is becoming a commercial product or being productized. Again, the reorganization is also a working result of responding to developer feedbacks.

Always consult MSDN Library documentation for F# 4 and above. It is highly recommended to focus on F# 4 and the later versions. Further namespace changes are very unlikely in the next version, unless the feedback from the F# community is crucial and is agreed upon by the F# developer and designer team at Microsoft.

For more information on the starting guide to F# asynchronous workflow as computation expressions, please consult MSDN Library:

```
https://msdn.microsoft.com/en-us/visualfsharpdocs/conceptual/asynchronous-workf
lows-%5bfsharp%5d
```

The details of computation expressions themselves and optimizing computation expressions will be discussed in Chapter 7, *Language Features and Constructs Optimization*.

Operations in asynchronous workflow

The first sample in this chapter shows `Async.Parallel` and `Async.RunSynchronously` in action. These two belong to the F# `Control.Async` class with other functions as well.

The `Control.Async` class is available in the `Microsoft.FSharp.Control` namespace as we have witnessed by disassembling the code demonstrated in the *Using asynchronous with Dispose pattern* section covered earlier. `Control.Async` cannot function alone when used in an asynchronous workflow block; it depends on the builders in the `Control.AsyncBuilder` type.

A complete starting point of reference for `Control.Async` as a type is available at `https://msdn.microsoft.com/en-us/visualfsharpdocs/conceptual/control.async%5b't%5d-type-%5bfsharp%5d`.

All operations of the async workflow in F# are available at `https://msdn.microsoft.com/en-us/visualfsharpdocs/conceptual/control.async-class-%5bfsharp%5d`.

The following is a table of interesting operations (commonly used) in F# `async`:

Function	Quick Remark
`AsBeginEnd`	Creates three functions that can be used to implement the .NET Framework **Asynchronous Programming Model (APM)** for the supplied asynchronous computation.
`AwaitEvent`	Creates an asynchronous computation that waits for a single invocation of a CLI event by adding a handler to the event. Once the computation completes or is cancelled, the handler is removed from the event. `AwaitEvent` is the best fit to handle .NET EAP model.
`AwaitIAsyncResult`	Creates an asynchronous computation that will wait on the `IAsyncResult`. It is used for the .NET APM model.
`AwaitTask`	Returns an asynchronous computation that waits for the given task (.NET TPL `Task`) to complete and returns its result.
`CancellationToken`	Creates an asynchronous computation that returns the `System.Threading.CancellationToken` that manages the execution of the computation.

DefaultCancellationToken	Gets the default cancellation token to run asynchronous computations.
FromBeginEnd	Creates an asynchronous computation in terms of a Begin/End pair of actions in the style used in CLI APIs.
FromContinuations	Creates an asynchronous computation that includes the current success, exception, and cancellation continuations. The callback function must eventually call exactly one of the given continuations. This exact map of one cancellation for one continuation is also the same concept as .NET APM.
Ignore	Creates an asynchronous computation that runs the given computation and ignores its result.
Parallel	Creates an asynchronous computation that executes all the given asynchronous computations, initially queueing each as work items and using a fork/join pattern.
RunSynchronously	Runs the provided asynchronous computation and awaits its result. When RunSynchronously is used to run an async block, it will run the code in the async block immediately in a separate runtime context as long as the code in the async block follows the pattern as defined in asynchronous workflow.
Sleep	Creates an asynchronous computation that will sleep for the given time. This is scheduled using a System.Threading.Timer object. The operation will not block operating system threads for the waiting duration.
Start	Starts the asynchronous computation in the thread pool but does not await its result.
StartAsTask	Executes a computation in the thread pool. Returns a Task that will be completed in the corresponding state once the computation terminates (produces the result, throws an exception, or gets canceled). If no cancellation token is provided, then the default cancellation token is used.

StartChild	Starts a child computation within an asynchronous workflow. This allows multiple asynchronous computations to be executed simultaneously (in parallel). The child computation can be composed to start in parallel with other child computations using `Async.Parallel`.
StartChildAsTask	Creates an asynchronous computation that starts the given computation as a `Task`.
StartImmediately	Runs an asynchronous computation, starting immediately on the current operating system thread. The main difference between `Start` and `StartImmediately` is quite subtle but important: `StartImmediately` uses `ThreadPool`.

The operations in `ControlAsync` are not all targeted at working with .NET TPL. From the perspective of the available asynchronous model in .NET, the operations of `Control.Async` provide supports for the following:

- .NET Asynchronous Programming Model (APM)
- .NET Event-based Asynchronous Pattern (EAP)
- .NET Task Parallel Library (TPL), only available for .NET 4 with added asynchrony operations or programming support in .NET 4.5 and later. The Task asynchrony is called Task-based Asynchrony Pattern or TAP.

Let's dive into the supports.

It is worth assessing that .NET TPL (including TAP) is considered to be a modern concurrency model. The legacy .NET asynchronous models are as follows:

- Asynchronous Programming Model, often abbreviated as APM
- Event-based Asynchronous Programming pattern (EAP)

You might wonder why they are called **legacy models**. They are legacy models in the sense that they are not supposed to be used anymore. Since .NET 4.0, the preferred model to be used is the .NET Task Parallel Library (TPL) model.

Using .NET TPL is recommended, not just because it is easier to use and more intuitive but also because every operation is wrapped as `Task` or `Task<T>` and it is easier to reason about your code. In F#, APM and EAP are usually handled using asynchronous-related operation methods but it is quite difficult to do in a real APM or EAP way.

It is recommended that APM and EAP should not be used anymore although they are still available in .NET 4.6. EAP is harder to implement than APM because it focuses on event handling, which usually happens on any action or operation that has event handling; otherwise, we have to handle the completed event on our own by implementing custom completed action's event handler.

Creating child asynchronous workflow

In F#, it is possible to create a nested asynchronous operation within an `async` block as the child or children of the current asynchronous workflow.

These children asynchronous workflows are executed in a sequence at first (based on the sequence of creation) but they do not have to finish simultaneously. They can run or start in parallel.

There are two operations to create a child asynchronous workflow: `Async.StartChild` and `Async.StartChildAsTask`. The `Async.StartChildAsTask` will return the resulting asynchronous workflow as `Task<T>` based asynchrony of Task-based Asynchronous Pattern or TAP.

This method is generally used with `let!` because it is supposed to return the result of a child asynchronous process, and this is why it is supposed to be bound to a process that returns a result, which is then to be observed or used by the parent asynchronous block.

The returning result of `Async.StartChild` is usually called **completor** because it is typed as a computation that has to wait for completion. This is also described by the MSDN Library as follows:

> *"When used in this way, each use of StartChild starts an instance of childComputation and returns a completor object representing a computation to wait for the completion of the operation. When executed, the completor awaits the completion of childComputation."*

Putting it simply, the completor is an object to contain the operation of the asynchronous process and wait for it to be completed. This is why the returning value of `Async.StartChild` is typed as `Async<Async<'T>>` instead of just `Async<'T>`.

WARNING: The use of `use!` is not allowed to capture an asynchronous child; it will yield an unpredictable result. Future releases of F# will not allow this to be used. It is required to use `let!` instead. The main reason is that the nature of the asynchronous child is not for disposable objects as it is focused on the process, not on the object that is part of the result to be awaited, although the process contains an asynchronous function that may have a result as denoted by the `Async<Async<'T>>` type.

The following is a simple example from MSDN Library:

```
open System.Windows.Forms

let bufferData = Array.zeroCreate<byte> 100000000

let asyncChild filename =
        async {
            printfn "Child job start: %s" filename
            use outputFile = System.IO.File.Create(filename)
            do! outputFile.AsyncWrite(bufferData)
            printfn "Child job end: %s " filename
        }

let asyncParent =
        async {
            printfn "Parent job start."
            let! childAsync1 = Async.StartChild(asyncChild
"longoutput1.dat")
            let! childAsync2 = Async.StartChild(asyncChild
"longoutput2.dat")
            let! result1 = childAsync1
            let! result2 = childAsync2
            printfn "Parent job end."
        }


let form = new Form(Text = "Test Form")
let button = new Button(Text = "Start")
form.Controls.Add(button)
button.Click.Add(fun args -> Async.Start(asyncParent)
                             printfn "Completed execution." )
Application.Run(form)
```

Ensure that `System.Windows.Forms` is available on the project references to run this sample.

For more information on `Async.StartChild`, including the sample code, visit the MSDN Library at
`https://msdn.microsoft.com/visualfsharpdocs/conceptual/async.startchild%5b%27t%5d-method-%5bfsharp%5d.`

> `Async.StartChild` is not recommended to be used with the legacy .NET EAP. The result of the child asynchronous process can be placed in a different execution context and thread because EAP can be implemented during the event-driven nature of UI threads such as Windows Forms thread or WPF thread.
>
> The risk of getting unpredictable results (side effects) may outweigh the comfort and ease of creating child asynchronous processes. The side effects of cross threads are also very hard to identify and debug. The only way to avoid the risks is by simply not using `Async.StartChild` against EAP or against the possibility of operating inside a UI thread such as Windows Forms or WPF.

F# asynchronous workflow support for legacy .NET APM and EAP

The F# asynchronous workflow still provides support for legacy .NET APM and EAP model, but the support is meant *to consume* the model because it is not intended to fully implement our own custom APM and EAP models. It is called *to consume* as F# has no support for implementing our own APM and EAP model, so it is not recommended to implement a custom APM or EAP in F#.

There is another reason why these APM and EAP models are not recommended anymore, especially when implementing your own custom models in F#. The complexity of going back and forth of having callbacks with side effects computation such as crossing CPU thread and UI thread is also a very strong reason.

The following operations are targeted at any .NET Asynchronous Programming Model (APM):

- `AsBeginEnd`
- `AwaitIAsyncResult`
- `FromBeginEnd`

The .NET APM is one of the legacy asynchronous models in .NET. It has a distinct pattern of having an operation prefixed with `Begin`, an operation prefixed with `End`, and a callback function to be called. For example, .NET `System.IO.FileStream` has `BeginRead` and `EndRead` methods. Each method has a delegate parameter that functions as callback.

The preferred way to support .NET APM in F# is by using `Async.FromBeginEnd` in order to be as flexible as we can to include the `Begin` operation, the `End` operation, and the parameter for the `Begin` and `End` operations. Using `Async.FromBeginEnd` is also the easiest way to leverage the existing .NET APM, which is usually available when dealing with I/O. For example, `System.IO.FileStream` and `System.Net.Sockets.Socket` have the pattern of `BeginXXX` and `EndXXX` methods.

Let's start by consulting the documentation for `Async.FromBeginEnd` (that has no parameter) in MSDN
at https://msdn.microsoft.com/visualfsharpdocs/conceptual/async.frombeginend%5b%27t%5d-method-%5bfsharp%5d.

The link has the shortest form of `Async.FromBeginEnd` (that does not need a parameter and only returns a result) syntax:

```
static member FromBeginEnd : (AsyncCallback * obj -> IAsyncResult) *
(IAsyncResult ->'T) * ?(unit -> unit) -> Async<'T>
```

If you need parameters (from 1 to 3 parameters), the syntaxes are as follows (the `static` member modifier is the same as the previous; it is omitted for simplicity):

```
FromBeginEnd : 'Arg1 * ('Arg1 * AsyncCallback * obj -> IAsyncResult) *
(IAsyncResult ->'T) * ?(unit -> unit) -> Async<'T>
FromBeginEnd : 'Arg1 * 'Arg2 * ('Arg1 * 'Arg2 * AsyncCallback * obj ->
IAsyncResult) * (IAsyncResult ->'T) * ?(unit -> unit) -> Async<'T>
FromBeginEnd : 'Arg1 * 'Arg2 * 'Arg3 * ('Arg1 * 'Arg2 * 'Arg3 *
AsyncCallback * obj -> IAsyncResult) * (IAsyncResult ->'T) * ?(unit ->
unit) -> Async<'T>
```

Just looking at the signature might be confusing at first; fortunately, a sample usage of `Async.FromBeginEnd` is available in the MSDN Library.

The sample leverages `System.Net.Socket` by enhancing it using an implicit extension method, added on the existing `Socket` class.

Here is the code definition of the asynchronous operations sample:

```
module SocketServer =

    open System.Net
```

```
open System.Net.Sockets
open System.Collections.Generic

let toIList<'T> (data : 'T array) =
    let segment = new System.ArraySegment<'T>(data)
    let data = new List<System.ArraySegment<'T>>() :>
IList<System.ArraySegment<'T>>
    data.Add(segment)
    data

type Socket with
    member this.MyAcceptAsync() =
        Async.FromBeginEnd((fun (callback, state) ->
this.BeginAccept(callback, state)),
                            this.EndAccept)
    member this.MyConnectAsync(ipAddress : IPAddress, port : int) =
        Async.FromBeginEnd(ipAddress, port,
                            (fun (ipAddress:IPAddress, port, callback,
state) ->
                                this.BeginConnect(ipAddress, port,
callback, state)),
                            this.EndConnect)
    member this.MySendAsync(data : byte array, flags : SocketFlags) =
        Async.FromBeginEnd(toIList data, flags,
                            (fun (data :
IList<System.ArraySegment<byte>>,
                                flags : SocketFlags, callback, state)
->
                                this.BeginSend(data, flags,
callback, state)),
                            this.EndSend)
    member this.MyReceiveAsync(data : byte array, flags : SocketFlags)
=
            Async.FromBeginEnd(toIList data, flags,
                            (fun (data :
IList<System.ArraySegment<byte>>,
                                flags : SocketFlags, callback, state)
->
                                this.BeginReceive(data, flags,
callback, state)),
                            this.EndReceive)
```

The name of the method that contains an asynchronous call follows common guidelines: it has an `Async` suffix. For example, the `this.MyConnectAsync` method contains an asynchronous call to `Socket.BeginConnect` that follows the APM naming conventions.

`Async.FromBeginEnd` uses the syntax for two parameters. It is also used to wrap and simultaneously handle the following pairs of the asynchronous Socket:

- `BeginAccept` and `EndAccept` pair
- `BeginConnect` and `EndConnect` pair
- `BeginSend` and `EndSend` pair
- `BeginReceive` and `EndReceive` pair

The related syntax on the MSDN Library is `Async.FromBeginEnd<'Arg1, 'Arg2, 'T>` because it needs two parameters (or arguments in MSDN Library terms).

To test those `Socket` methods in the `async` block, consider the following partial sample:

```
let port = 11000

let socket = new Socket(AddressFamily.InterNetwork, SocketType.Stream,
ProtocolType.Tcp)
let ipHostInfo = Dns.Resolve(Dns.GetHostName())
let localIPAddress = ipHostInfo.AddressList.[0]
let localEndPoint = new IPEndPoint(localIPAddress, port)
socket.Bind(localEndPoint)

let connectSendReceive (socket : Socket) =
    async {
        do! socket.MyConnectAsync(ipHostInfo.AddressList.[0], 11000)
        let buffer1 = [| 0uy .. 255uy |]
        let buffer2 = Array.zeroCreate<byte> 255
        let flags = new SocketFlags()
        let! flag = socket.MySendAsync(buffer1, flags)
        let! result = socket.MyReceiveAsync(buffer2, flags)
        return buffer2
    }
```

For the complete documentation of `System.Net.Socket`, consult the MSDN Library at `https://msdn.microsoft.com/en-us/library/system.net.sockets.socket(v=vs.110).aspx`.

For more information, consult .NET APM on the MSDN Library at `https://msdn.microsoft.com/en-us/library/ms228963(v=vs.110).aspx`.

The EAP model simply models the implementation of asynchronous event-driven programming by using an event as the handler of the completed event. Unfortunately, it is not quite clear how the flow of waiting is implemented as the pattern focuses on what will happen when the operation is completed. It is also not clear about deciding the implementation detail of how the EAP is used to handle the I/O operations that are blocking by default.

F# supports EAP by providing one method, the `Async.AwaitEvent` operation.

Compared to APM, EAP focuses more on the completion of the action and the state of an object instead of getting the result of an operation.

For more information about the legacy .NET EAP model, consult:

```
https://msdn.microsoft.com/en-us/library/ms228969(v=vs.110).aspx
```
To illustrate F# support for EAP, we must understand and focus on the event programming model first.

The event programming model is actually not so different from the event-based approach of Windows UI programing, where a UI control has events for any kind of event happening to it, such as clicked, mouse over, focus, or lost focus. But there are some events that need to be handled with care, such as timer events. When a timer is active, it ticks on every period based on how long it takes to tick between intervals. Usually, when an interval is set, the timer implicitly makes us to wait until some time period has elapsed.

> The use of a timer is crucial as sometimes the time elapsed may vary depending on what kind of timer we use. Avoid the use of a UI timer as much as possible because the resolution (the precision of timing) of a UI timer is lower than `System.Threading.Timer` or any other non-UI timer, as highlighted in Chapter 2, *Performance Measurement*.

All of the execution is based on the sequence of events; it is also natural to call it an event-driven model. Unfortunately, this wait might take some time blocking the current thread. It is therefore recommended to handle this asynchronously.

If we look at the documentation for `Async.AwaitEvent` on the online MSDN Library, the documentation does not have a good explanation on how we relate this to .NET EAP.

The following is the sample code from the MSDN Library documentation:

```
open System.Windows.Forms
open System.IO

let filename = "longoutput.dat"
```

```
if File.Exists(filename) then File.Delete(filename)
let watcher = new FileSystemWatcher(Directory.GetCurrentDirectory(),
filename, NotifyFilter = NotifyFilters.LastWrite)
watcher.Changed.Add <| fun args -> printfn "The file %s is changed."
args.Name
watcher.EnableRaisingEvents <- true

let async2 filename =
    async {
        printfn "Waiting for file system watcher notification."
        // If you omit the call to AwaitEvent, an exception is thrown that
indicates that the
        // file is locked.
        let! _args = Async.AwaitEvent(watcher.Changed)
        printfn "Attempting to open and read file %s." filename
        use inputFile = File.OpenRead(filename)
        let! buffer = inputFile.AsyncRead(100000000)
        printfn "Successfully read file %s." filename
        return buffer
    }
```

This sample is quite simple, and at the same time, it directly shows the sample usage of
`Async.AwaitEvent`. The sample `await` construct for any file or folder changes in a folder.
If any changes occur (as a changed event), it will continue to print the file name and do
some I/O operations, such as opening the file. The file is then read asynchronously.

For more information on `Async.AwaitEvent`, check out
https://msdn.microsoft.com/visualfsharpdocs/conceptual/async.awaitevent%5b%27de
l%2c%27t%5d-method-%5bfsharp%5d.

We now have basic knowledge of how F# interops with .NET EAP, although the
interoperability is not quite as straightforward as using the async-based `Task<T>`.

Ignoring asynchronous operation asynchronously

`Async.Ignore` is essentially the same as using `ignore`. However, it is semantically
different as `Async.Ignore` must only be used to ignore asynchronous operations, not non-
asynchronous operations.

The signature of `Async.Ignore` is as follows:

```
static member Ignore : Async<'T> -> Async<unit>
```

`Async.Ignore` implies that it cannot be used independently as it needs an `async` operation as its parameter.

`Async.Ignore` has its ignore implementation asynchronously; therefore, it is guaranteed not to block the current thread synchronously. This means that it will not block the current thread of the calling function as well.

The common place of `Async.Ignore` is generally used to ignore the returning result of the following:

1. All EAP-based asynchronous operations.
2. All asynchronous operations that return nothing (`unit` in F#, `void` in C#, or the `Sub` procedure/method in VB).

Therefore, we must not use `Async.Ignore` if we want to examine or get the results from asynchronous operations. Also, `Async.Ignore` is already optimized for non-returning result of any asynchronous workflow.

 Please do not confuse the non-returning result of asynchronous operations with the F# unit. The term non-returning result should be treated as simply intuitive–not returning any result–because the main focus here is the on completion of any actions.

It is recommended that you use `Async.Ignore` on F#-specific asynchronous workflows (including F# support on EAP) and .NET TPL instead of using it on other kinds of asynchronous models, as it is more predictable and more optimized.

Using `Async.Ignore` is also fine when combining with F#'s `MailboxProcessor` because `MailboxProcessor` is designed to be compatible; it's also recommended to use `MailboxProcessor` in asynchronous workflow blocks.

Delaying asynchronous workflow

What if we delay an asynchronous implementation without blocking the outside calling thread? We could do this easily by using `Thread.Sleep`, but `Thread.Sleep` always blocks the calling thread and not just the current execution thread. Therefore, `Thread.Sleep` always enforces us to wait synchronously instead of asynchronously. It is also often misunderstood that `Thread.Sleep` would not block as it actually blocks the current thread. We can wrap `Thread.Sleep` into an `async` block, but then the outside thread still has to wait for `Thread.Sleep` to finish first.

There is the `Async.Sleep` method to support delay asynchronously. The syntax is as follows:

```
Sleep : int -> Async<unit>
```

Consider the following sample usage:

```
Async.Sleep(100)
```

It's still better to assume that any asynchronous delay implementation uses `Async.Sleep` instead of `Thread.Sleep` because `Async.Sleep` never blocks the current operating system threads.

According to a short description on MSDN Library, `Async.Sleep`:

Creates an asynchronous computation that will sleep for the given time. This is scheduled using a System.Threading.Timer object. The operation will not block operating system threads for the duration of the wait.

This is not the actual implementation detail because it depends on the current runtime. Internally, `Async.Sleep` creates an asynchronous operation that inserts the delay by calling `Task.Delay` internally if it's run under .NET Core or by using the asynchronous timer mechanism utilizing `System.Threading.Timer` for non-.NET Core, with the *trampoline* algorithm in place.

The term *actual implementation detail* means that the actual internal implementation detail will be changed in the next release of F#. We must also include the fact that F# core class libraries are open source as part of the Microsoft Visual F# open source repo on GitHub.

Therefore, there is a high possibility that the actual source code implementation of F# will change by the time this book is published. It could change based on the progress of feedbacks from Microsoft and external contributors. It is also quite common to always assume that the actual implementation will always be changed, based on the nature of open source contributions.

Starting from this chapter, we will sometimes visit the internal implementation of F# 4 core class libraries by looking at its source code. This is very important because we have to dig deeper than just using the libraries in order to fully understand what is happening behind the scenes of calling F# core functions. It is also a common best practice to increase our knowledge of the internal workings of how F# presents its features.

We can *peek* at the source code of `Async.Sleep` on the F# GitHub repo (some comments have been omitted):

```
#if FSHARP_CORE_NETCORE_PORTABLE
        static member Sleep(dueTime : int) : Async<unit> =
            // use combo protectedPrimitiveWithResync + continueWith
instead of AwaitTask so we can pass cancellation token to the Delay task
            unprotectedPrimitiveWithResync ( fun ({ aux = aux} as args) ->
                let mutable edi = null

                let task =
                    try
                        Task.Delay(dueTime, aux.token)
                    with exn ->
                        edi <- ExceptionDispatchInfo.RestoreOrCapture(exn)
                        null

                match edi with
                | null -> TaskHelpers.continueWithUnit(task, args)
                | _ -> aux.econt edi
            )
#else
        static member Sleep(dueTime) : Async<unit> =
unprotectedPrimitiveWithResync (fun ({ aux = aux } as args) ->
let timer = ref (None : Timer option)
                let savedCont = args.cont
                let savedCCont = aux.ccont
                let latch = new Latch()
                let registration =
                    aux.token.Register(
                        (fun _ ->
                            if latch.Enter() then
                                match !timer with
                                | None -> ()
                                | Some t -> t.Dispose()
                                aux.trampolineHolder.Protect(fun () ->
savedCCont(new OperationCanceledException()))) |> unfake
                        ),
                        null)
                let mutable edi = null
                try
                    timer := new Timer((fun _ ->
                                        if latch.Enter() then
                                            registration.Dispose()
                                            match !timer with
                                            |  None -> ()
                                            |  Some t -> t.Dispose()
                                            aux.trampolineHolder.Protect
```

```
(fun () -> savedCont ()) |> unfake),
                                    null, dueTime=dueTime, period = -1) |>
Some
                with exn ->
                    if latch.Enter() then
                        edi <- ExceptionDispatchInfo.RestoreOrCapture(exn)
// post exception to econt only if we successfully enter the latch (no
other continuations were called)

                match edi with
                | null ->
                    FakeUnit
                | _ ->
                    aux.econt edi
                )
#endif
```

The full source code is available at
https://github.com/Microsoft/visualfsharp/blob/master/src/fsharp/FSharp.Core/control.fs.

For more information about `Async.Sleep` visit the MSDN Library, at
https://msdn.microsoft.com/visualfsharpdocs/conceptual/async.sleep-method-%5bfsharp%5d.

So far, we have covered how to declare an `async` block and delay it. Now, we need to know how to cancel it.

Handling cancellation in asynchronous workflow

It is quite possible that the user may cancel the ongoing asynchronous process even in the middle of an asynchronous operation.

In F#, the common way to have support for cancellation that can be done in the middle of any running asynchronous operation is as follows:

1. Requesting a token in the form of the `CancellationToken` type structure.
2. This `CancellationToken` instance is obtained from `System.Threading.CancellationTokenSource`. Internally, `CancellationToken` will always be loaded and pushed onto a stack, which is later popped after use when the ongoing asynchronous operation is canceled.

3. `CancellationToken` needs to know which one of the asynchronous operations to have cancellation support for. This can be done by linking `CancellationToken` with the asynchronous function by calling `Async.Start` or `Async.StartImmediate` with an override that has `CancellationToken` as a parameter.

Before using `CancellationToken` and `CancellationTokenSource`, you need to ensure that references to the `System.Threading.dll` assembly are available on the project reference setting when the code is in an FS file or that you have registered the assembly manually when the code is in an FSX file and executed in scripting mode (in F# Interactive mode).

To add cancellation support as mentioned in Step 3, the linking of the asynchronous operation (usually wrapped as an `async` block) is done by linking the `async` function with `CancellationToken`, and this linking must be done carefully. This `CancellationToken` instance is a *value typed object, so the instance of this CancellationToken must not be derived, and it must not be used and linked to other async functions*. It is also implicitly immutable, including the referential transparency of the initial design of `CancellationToken`.

This linking of the asynchronous operation is crucial; if the same value is linked to more than one `async` block, it will cancel each of the linked functions unpredictably because the same object value may interfere with other linked `async` blocks as well. This will violate the referential transparency and may therefore raise many unwanted side effects. Such multiple function linking is a bad practice as it will cause side effects such as unpredictable cancellation.

Because of the nature of `CancellationToken` as a structure (value type), multiple instances of different tokens of `CancellationToken` will always be stored and pushed into stacks, which is fast to store and retrieve (pop) as well.

Therefore, multiple linking to multiple `async` blocks from the same `CancellationToken` is not recommended and should not be allowed.

To see the usage sample of `CancellationToken`, we can revisit our existing `use!` sample and leverage the overloaded method of `ExecuteReaderAsync` with an additional `CancellationToken` parameter.

The existing code sample now looks as follows:

```
open System
open System.Data
open System.Data.SqlClient
open System.Threading
```

```
open System.Threading.Tasks

let UseBangCancellationSample (dbconstring: string,
tokenSource:CancellationTokenSource) =
    async {
        use dbCon = new SqlConnection(dbconstring)
        use sqlCommand = new SqlCommand("SELECT * FROM
INFORMATION_SCHEMA.TABLES")
        use! dataReader =
Async.AwaitTask(sqlCommand.ExecuteReaderAsync(CommandBehavior.Default,
tokenSource.Token))
        printfn "Finished querying"
    }
```

The preceding sample code highlights the following steps to add cancellation support:

1. The `UseBangCancellationSample` function shows that it takes a parameter, `tokenSource` typed as `CancellationTokenSource`. Then `CancellationToken` is taken from the `CancellationTokenSource.Token` property.

2. To cancel the ongoing asynchronous operation, call the `Cancel` method of the `CancellationToken` instance, which is passed into the related asynchronous operation started.

3. It is important that the instance of `CancellationToken` knows which asynchronous process it needs to cancel. In the preceding sample, `CancellationToken` is linked to `ExecuteReaderAsync` by setting it as a parameter.

We now know how to utilize `CancellationToken` and `CancellationTokenSource` by leveraging the `System.Threading.Tasks` namespace. This also serves as a warm starter to the introduction to interoperability with the Task library and .NET TPL.

Common conventions when implementing asynchronous operations

We have seen samples of implementing calling asynchronous operations and wrapping them in asynchronous blocks. There are some patterns and best practices that we must follow in accordance with the F# implementation and .NET standards.

There are certain guidelines or standards that must be followed not only to enhance the code's readability but also because it will become easier to understand the code and reason about what it will do.

The following are some common conventions of implementing asynchronous workflow:

1. A method that has an asynchronous call inside it should be suffixed with Async, to define that this function or method contains an asynchronous call and must be called inside the asynchronous block.

2. Any kind of event handling that has an asynchronous call should not be suffixed with Async, for example, the `Button1_Click` method to handle the Click event that has a call to `DownloadWebAsync`.

3. An `async` block that needs to delay some operations should use `Async.Sleep` instead of `Thread.Sleep`. Otherwise, the current thread will be blocked; the execution will be observed as synchronous and will be executed synchronously instead of asynchronously.

4. All I/O operations must be treated asynchronously. This includes I/O operations to send commands to other output devices such as printers, not just I/O in network or I/O to storage devices.

Now that we know the basic usage of the `Control.Async` operations in F#, we will dive into the basic interop of asynchronous workflow with .NET TPL.

Introduction to interop with .NET TPL

F# has a high compatibility support for .NET TPL; it can nicely use the .NET TPL objects of `Task` and `Task<T>` back and forth. This means that F# can also use the `Task/Task<T>` results from other languages as well and not just from F#.

In .NET TPL, the concurrency support is not just for parallel programming, but also for the awaiter of the async-await model that has currently started in C# 5.0 and VB 11, as related in .NET 4.5 and later.

In this chapter, we will start from the overview of .NET TPL support in F# in terms of leveraging `Task` and `Task<T>`. We will discuss the interop perspective from outside of F#, such as interop with F# asynchronous workflow, in `Chapter 5`, *Advanced Concurrency Support in F#*.

A quick overview of asynchronous programming in .NET TPL

For asynchronous operations (or asynchronous programming, as is mostly mentioned in C#/VB documentation in MSDN) the async-await model relies heavily on the `Task` and `Task<T>` classes.

The `Task` class is for asynchronous operations that have no result; `Task<T>` is for asynchronous operations that have results. The generic parameter `T` is the type of the result.

`Task<T>` contains the result in a property called `result`.

The `Task` and `Task<T>` classes are available under the `System.Threading.Tasks` namespace. For more information, consult the landing page of `System.Threading.Tasks` in .NET 4.6 on the MSDN Library at
`https://msdn.microsoft.com/en-us/library/system.threading.tasks(v=vs.110).aspx`.

In F#, the following are the operations that support `Task/Task<T>`:

- `Async.AwaitTask`
- `Async.StartAsTask`
- `Async.StartChildAsTask`

All these methods have two overrides in common, one for dealing with `Task` with no result and the other for dealing with `Task<T>` that will return a `Task` with a result typed `T`. Dealing in this context means having interoperability with the Task-based Asynchrony Pattern (TAP) of .NET TPL.

We are not going to reintroduce the detail of .NET TAP because we are focusing on best practices. For more information on .NET TAP in .NET 4.5 and 4.6 on MSDN Library, visit
`https://msdn.microsoft.com/en-us/library/hh873175(v=vs.110).aspx`.

The documentation for `Async.AwaitTask` and `Async.StartChildAsTask` does not provide a sample code for us at all. Only `Async.StartAsTask` has a very simple sample code.

Work to address these shortcomings in the Visual F# documentation repository is still in progress, and all of us are welcome to participate.

The following is the sample code in the `Async.StartAsTask` documentation, and we have to modify it to successfully run it under the UI thread:

```
let async1 =
async {
    use outputFile = System.IO.File.Create("longoutput.dat")
    do! outputFile.AsyncWrite(bufferData)
}

[<EntryPoint>]
[<STAThread>]
let main argv =
    let form = new Form(Text = "Test Form")
    let button = new Button(Text = "Start")
    form.Controls.Add(button)
    button.Click.Add(fun args -> let task = Async.StartAsTask(async1)
printfn "Do some other work..."
task.Wait()
printfn "done")
    form.Show()
    Application.Run(form)
```

The code is explained as follows:

1. The asynchronous code is running within the UI thread of Windows Forms. Therefore, it is advisable that the main method be marked with the `System.STAThread` attribute.
2. The `async` block is contained in the `async1` function. It is then executed using `Async.StartAsTask` with no result. It will then return a `Task` instead of `Task<T>`.
3. `Async.StartAsTask` is written inside an inline event handler of the Click event, `button.Click`, by using addition to the current event handler of event Click. It is the same as `AddHandler` in VB or the syntactic sugar of the += operator in C#.

The original sample code in the MSDN Library does not have this `STAThread` attribute and it will yield an exception because `System.InvalidOperationException` has occurred due to the invalid cross thread, although the error message is quite confusing:

```
F# Interactive                                                                                  ▼ ₽ ×
  val form : Form = System.Windows.Forms.Form, Text: Test Form
  val button : Button = System.Windows.Forms.Button, Text: Start
  val it : unit = ()

>
> System.InvalidOperationException: Starting a second message loop on a single thread is not a valid operation. Use Form.ShowDialog instead.
   at System.Windows.Forms.Application.ThreadContext.RunMessageLoopInner(Int32 reason, ApplicationContext context)
   at System.Windows.Forms.Application.ThreadContext.RunMessageLoop(Int32 reason, ApplicationContext context)
   at System.Windows.Forms.Application.Run(Form mainForm)
   at <StartupCode$FSI_0005>.$FSI_0005.main@() in F:\PACKT\PACKT_CHAPTER4\FSBook_HiPerf\Chapter4.IntroConcurrency\Async.SampleStartAsTask.fs
Stopped due to error
```

It literally gives the following as the reason:

```
System.InvalidOperationException: Starting a second message loop on a
single thread is not a valid operation. Use Form.ShowDialog instead.
```

This is not the real error. The real error is in the code where we put the code/function that calls `Application.Run` marked with `STAThreadAttribute`. It is also quite common as it is often demonstrated by C#/VB samples in the default project template of Windows Forms.

Not just Windows Forms, the terms of operating under `STAThread` are also valid for WPF as well.

For a detailed explanation of `STAThread`, visit:

```
https://msdn.microsoft.com/en-us/library/system.stathreadattribute(v=vs.110).as
px
```

And for more information about the Thread apartment model (including STA and MTA with respect to COM), visit the MSDN Library at
`https://msdn.microsoft.com/library/ms809971.aspx`.

> By default, F# and C# use MTA; VB uses STA. For a Windows Forms application, the default is using STA. STA and MTA have nothing to do with how you create `System.Threading.Thread`. It is a threading apartment model, not a general multithreading model.

For the other `Async.AwaitTask` and `Async.StartChildAsTask` samples, let's revisit the sample of `UseBangSample`: (with `Async.AwaitTask` highlighted):

```
open System.Data
open System.Data.SqlClient

let UseBangSample (dbconstring: string) =
    async {
        use dbCon = new SqlConnection(dbconstring)
        use sqlCommand = new SqlCommand("SELECT * FROM
INFORMATION_SCHEMA.TABLES")
        use! dataReader =
Async.AwaitTask(sqlCommand.ExecuteReaderAsync(CommandBehavior.Default))
```

```
        printfn "Finished querying"
}
```

The preceding code demonstrates how to await a result from an asynchronous operation by awaiting `Task<T>`. The `T` in this context is typed as `SqlDataReader`, inferred by the return builder of asynchronous workflow. The return builder is coded implicitly in the `use!` construct/keyword as nicely captured from the execution of the `ExecuteReaderAsync` method.

Summary

When we are developing any applications, starting from small mobile applications to a large-scale enterprise application, concurrency is becoming very relevant, not just because of the trend of multi-core CPUs but also because having optimizations on concurrency gives us many advantages as described in this chapter. Although there is no single solution for all concurrency problems and optimizations, we know that we could leverage concurrency support in F# and .NET.

In *Chapter 5*, *Advanced Concurrency Support in F#*, we will discuss the advanced topic of concurrency in F#, including one of F#'s unique features: the message-passing agent, `MailboxProcessor`.

5
Advanced Concurrency Support in F#

We now have a basic understanding of F# concurrency features, including using and implementing the best practices of F# asynchronous workflow, and combining the asynchronous workflow with .NET APM, EAP, and TAP.

We have seen that `Control.Async` is the basic building block of all related asynchronous workflows, in terms of using it and also carefully deciding the best practices of using a returned object, especially when we have a nice construct of Disposable pattern in the asynchronous workflow.

Know only that the asynchronous workflow features in F# are not unique, in that C#/VB already has them, and C#/VB's `async` construct is actually inspired by F#. We can further harness the F# advanced asynchronous workflow implementation of `MailboxProcessor`, as part of learning and leveraging the advanced concurrency support in F#.

Again, we will see that there are no silver bullets for all kinds of concurrency problems. We shall see this fact applies to `MailboxProcessor` usage and implementation as well.

This chapter describes the advanced concurrency features of F#, focusing on F# 4.0. We are also introducing an overview of best practices to implement and optimize, such as combining asynchronous and parallelism, the F# message passing agent of `MailboxProcessor`, and further interoperability with .NET TPL.

The introduction to concurrency in F# is covered in the following topics:

- Using F# `MailboxProcessor`
- Interoperability with .NET Task Parallel Library (TPL)
- Introduction to asynchronous workflows

Using F# MailboxProcessor

F# has extensive features of asynchronous operations such as the way it uniquely separates and differentiates from other .NET-managed languages, such as C#/VB, Managed C++, Nemerle, IronPython, and IronRuby. But at the same time, it runs on top of .NET CLR, providing high compatibility with other languages.

F#'s own unique asynchronous features are not just the asynchronous workflows; it has a class that acts as a message passing agent or actor, `MailboxProcessor`. The `MailboxProcessor` feature was introduced at the same time as asynchronous workflow was released, and the implementation of `MailboxProcessor` itself is actually an implementation of a set of asynchronous workflows.

Background case of having message agent

The advantage of having an asynchronous model is the fact that we don't have to wait for the operation or task to be completely finished before doing something else, especially the next operations. The advantage that we don't have to wait for the completion of a task is related to the illustrations of blocking operations that we mentioned in `Chapter 4`, *Introduction to Concurrency in F#*.

Introducing fire and forget pattern

The most common example of blocking operations is the I/O operation. This may include any network operation, including any data transfer-either incoming or outgoing. These data transfers take in many forms, ranging from a simple PING call (ICMP packets) to complex operations such as uploading files and sending emails. The operations, in most cases, are not guaranteed to have responses immediately and in many cases *don't need to have replies* as well. Some of the obvious cases need responses as soon as possible since most cases have operations that need real-time responses when the operations are in session.

We can simply conclude that it is intuitive that asynchronous operations can be categorized further in terms of the necessity for responses:

1. Operations that are invoked by an external party and that don't need to have a response/reply back. In many cases, we can simply ignore the status of the completion; this is often called the *fire and forget* pattern or model. Once it is fired, we can simply forget about waiting for the reply, for example, when sending emails or sending commands as messages to an external party or agents expected to execute actions based on the commands.

2. Operations that are invoked by an external party or an internal process on your machine that needs a reply after the operations are completed, for example, when uploading files or downloading web content, the calling execution needs to be notified if the operation is completed. Another example is waiting for an elapsed event on a timer in the .NET EAP model. This is often (generally) called **Promises model**, in the form of callbacks. We have already covered this in `Chapter 4`, *Introduction to Concurrency in F#*.

Both of these are still categorized as asynchronous because of the simplicity of not having to wait, and it's also highly predicted to have a non-blocking behavior.

Examples of fire and forget pattern (from simple to complex) are as follows:

- Sending emails through SMTP.
- Sending network broadcast messages.
- Sending commands to a network printer queue server. This is different from sending a command directly to a connected network printer that has to reply, at least giving status updates of the out-of-paper status to print job completion.

Not all commands sent to a printer are always fire and forget. There are many cases where sending commands to a printer, especially sending commands to a printer directly connected to our machine, are not fire and forget.

The operation of sending this command is usually asynchronous, with callbacks to notify the status of the finished/completed job.

On an OS such as Windows, sending a command to devices directly connected to our machine always requires replies or responses because it is expected that we have a response at least showing the status of the device in real time. It is normal to have this assumption as a requirement as the printer is directly connected to our machine and is also not shared. This is the reason why it is not part of fire and forget.

For example, on Windows, all printing operations are handled by the Windows Printing API on top of the printer's device driver. In the implementation of the Printing API, the commands sent to the printer have the requirement of the availability of any printing device installed. It does not care about how many printers are installed; it only cares about the status of any printing device available, by always querying the availability of a printing device using a Windows Message (the `WM_XXX` API) in an event of *message loop*.

The term *message* in this message loop is different from the message in a message queue: the message is an encapsulation of a known system event to ease communication of system events. It always happens in loops and can be in the form of a looping queue (circular queue), instead of a queue in a message agent that does not operate in a loop (open ended queue).

For more information about the Windows message loop of Windows API, consult the MSDN Library at:

https://msdn.microsoft.com/en-us/library/windows/desktop/ms644927(v=vs.85).aspx

It is common in Windows API to have this message loop of calling GetMessage, coded like this (this code is in C++):

```
while(GetMessage( &msg, hWnd, 0, 0) != 0)
{
    if (bRet == -1)
    {
        // handle the error and possibly exit
    }
    else
    {
        TranslateMessage(&msg);
        DispatchMessage(&msg);
    }
}
```

The preceding code will always loop by examining any incoming Windows WM_XXX messages. It will end the loop if there are implied errors, especially system errors. This common practice is also used in built-in Windows applets, such as the applets in the Control Panel (compiled as .cpl).

We can also implement the code of handling Win32 message loops in F#, but then, we have to hook into Win32 API calls by defining the entry point to Win32 API using P/Invoke. The P/Invoke declaration is required, but then, F# may lose HWND context if the message loop is handled within a non-UI thread. It is highly recommended to handle the Win32 message loop in a separate UI thread by explicitly executing it as invoking delegates. But interoperatibility with Win32 message API is beyond the scope of this book.

The queue used in this context can be a combination of an ordinary queue and the usage of round-robin, or it can be a simple queue, such as first come first served, and the incoming message is queued at the last line of the queue but the queue line itself always *moves forward*.

Round-robin is one of the examples of queue handlings. But round-robin has its own overhead: it moves the pointer of the queue and also the data within the queue line. If this overhead pointer movement is executed in memory, the overhead cost might be deferred by high speed access to memory. This is why round-robin is also popular in the operating system world, from the use of the message loop to the scheduling of running processes, threads, and *coroutines*.

The coroutine is quite common in many platforms, including .NET, Windows, and UNIX. In .NET, a sample coroutine is the yield iterator's implementation detail in C#/VB and F#. In Windows, a sample of a coroutine is the implementation of *fibers* in Windows (since Windows 2000). However, fiber in Windows and coroutine in .NET are different in semantics.

What is coroutine? There are many definitions of coroutines but not all of them are correct in the sense of the concurrency and runtime of any managed language/platform. The cleanest and simplest definition is available from the MSDN Library. Coroutine is defined as:

> *Coroutine is a method that can stop in mid-execution and provide a value to the caller without returning program flow.*

This definition is taken from this MSDN Magazine on the MSDN Library:

```
http://download.microsoft.com/download/3/a/7/3a7fa450-1f33-41f7-9e6d-3aa95b5a6a
ea/MSDNMagazineSeptember2003en-us.chm
```

It is quite the same as yield, where yield can stop in the middle of the execution and will continue as needed. C#/VB/F# yield and Windows fibers are very good sample implementations of coroutine that can have multiple entries and exits, depending on the state we are handling.

For more information about fiber in Windows API, visit:

```
https://msdn.microsoft.com/en-us/library/windows/desktop/ms682661(v=vs.85).aspx
```

 NOTE: We are not going to dive further into the implementation detail of coroutine in .NET, especially on yield. The implementation detail of the yield iterator may change in the future .NET versions after .NET 4.6. However, it is important to at least have a basic understanding of coroutine.

A simple evidence of this message loop in action, always querying printing devices, can be seen in how Windows displays the current status of a print job in the Print Management applet in Windows 8/8.1 and Windows 10.

The Print Management applet in the legacy Control Panel always displays the current status of any available installed and connected printers:

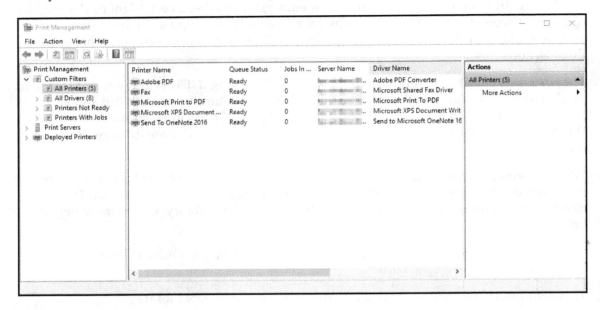

The Printing API is also a good sample of Promises in action because a reply to notify that a print job is completed; it is a promise to at least give response that a print job is either completed or failed.

Other samples of Promises are the same as those of TPL, .NET EAP and APM. Basically, the semantics are mostly in the form of a notification when the action is completed.

There is a mixture of the *fire and forget* model and the *Promises* model, although the promise in this mix may not be a true promise in the implementation details.

For example, we want to have an asynchronous way of processing any of the incoming transactions against savings accounts, and the transactions are expected to have commenced across many kinds of savings accounts. Even in the same bank, a person can have multiple accounts that may have traffic of incoming and outgoing transfers, either scheduled or manual.

It is optional to notify that the incoming transfer is successfully credited to the account. And this is also a promise, although it is not mandatory to be enforced to notify back a successful transaction. If it is mandatory, then a reply will be sent back later. But this reply can be made using an event triggered when the incoming transfer has been calculated as credited into the account. At the implementation detail, the notification on the receiving agent is not mandatory after all; the customization may be added as an event trigger.

In the case of online e-commerce, the response is mandatory, as the transactions of any purchase must have a reply immediately, as close to real time as possible. Then the promise is enforced, although it is not a pure promise after all, as the receiver is using an event trigger for any incoming successful transaction that it will send a notification back to inform a failed/successful transaction. The wait for any incoming transaction is continuous. It is similar to always listening to any incoming signal of an incoming operation. Therefore it is also often simply called a *listener*, to always listen for any incoming transactions.

This difference of having a promise is illustrated in the following simplified flow:

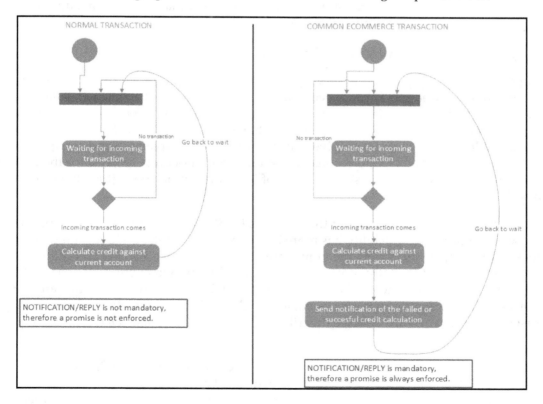

In the previous illustration, the wait for an incoming transaction usually happens on an agent. In the case of a standalone message queue manager, it is also a sophisticated or standalone listener.

This is also a good sample of an agent to handle the transaction in the form of messages that contain the operation request to withdraw, transfer, or even receive a money transfer.

Consider this sample scenario of this agent:

- A data wrapper with the necessary information about the operations (any related bank account transactions) to be carried out that is then processed by a centralized process that is to be sent while waiting for any incoming data to be consumed. Usually, all of the data sent and received is stored and processed with first come first served or **first in first out** (FIFO) in a data structure: a queue.
- The agent must be as scalable as possible. It means it must be able to serve a large number of requests per second. The initial website is usually assumed to be able to serve 500 to 1,000 requests per second, so the initial projected maximum requests to be served is 1,000 requests.

In the preceding scenario, why does it have to be a queue?

The agent was initially planned to serve more than 1,000+ requests at a time. There is no guarantee that the web server can serve more than 1,000 requests *at a time and at the same time*. In order to do this precisely, we have to be sure that at least 1,000 requests are sent and received at the same time. This means we must have parallel I/O at the heart of the hardware side, which is very expensive and very difficult to implement and set up. Therefore, having parallel I/O to enforce this simulation is not quite scalable for the current needs, and it's also not quite feasible in terms of implementation speed (time to implement) and scalability.

If we are relying on the scalability of the available I/O throughput, this is not an option because pure hardware scalability has more initial expensive costs. If we rely on serving the requests optimally by increasing the number of CPU cores, this is also not an optimal solution. Web requests usually consume less on CPU and more on network (hence I/O) bandwidth. On the consumer of the requests, there can be a wait on the I/O side, and this can block the next request to be processed, although handling this can be optimized using the asynchronous workflow that we described in `Chapter 4`, *Introduction to Concurrency in F#*.

The number of requests to be processed must be processed as first come first served. This fits into the FIFO model, and the best data structure to handle this is queue. The use of queues will always ensure that the first request is always to be processed first and then there are some actions processed afterwards.

The process of inserting new data is called *enqueue,* while removing the first item of the data is called *dequeue.*

The following is an illustration of the incoming of requests and processing in a queue:

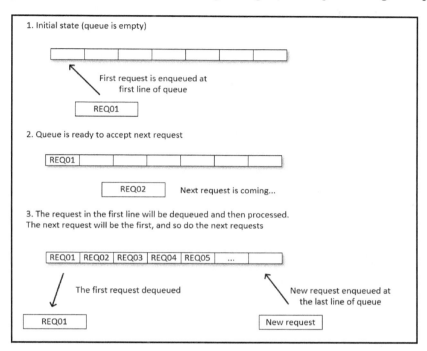

The queue of requests is usually seen as a block of data to be sent and received, and this is often called as message, because of the conceptual similarity to sending and receiving emails.

The one software component that is responsible for managing incoming requests as queue and sending replies when needed is usually called a message queue manager. From F# perspective, it is called a message agent, or in MSDN terms, it is often simply called an agent. It is also called an *actor,* and this actor model is discussed in the next section.

Overview of a message agent

This agent/ manager handles every message that is sent from senders (also called *producers*) and receives each message, which is then processed. The receivers can be from one to many receivers.

The overall main focuses in terms of the agent's operations are on:

- Sending a message (including preparations before and after). Sending is simply a sending from message agent A to message agent B.
- Receiving a message (including storing, processing). Message agent B receives messages from message agent A.

The following illustration depicts the sending of the message with the queue processing:

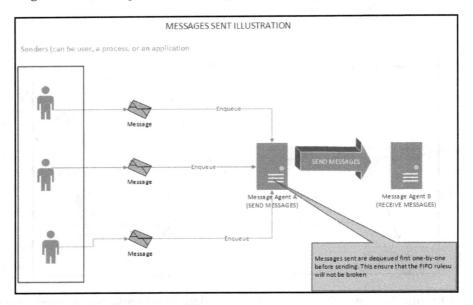

The sending and receiving operations are handled in a different context, but both sending and receiving use queues.

When a message agent is sending a message, these are the activities performed:

1. A queue is allocated. The main allocation to be considered is the available memory, then the physical storage.
2. The message to be sent is prepared with this convention first: the format of each message must have the same format, so the message will be processed in a predictable manner.
3. The message to be processed before sending usually comes in many forms. In the case of F# or any other lightweight agent, the message can be in the form of any object.
4. The object is then serialized as raw strings.

5. Serialization of the objects is then to be wrapped in a certain format. For example, the message can have headers and footers with additional information on how to process the message further.

6. The end result of the wrapped message is ready to be sent. At this time, any additional checks may be run, such as checking the availability of the network.

7. The agent sends the message. The transfer protocol used by the agent is the same protocol as the receiver.

The receiving side is illustrated as shown:

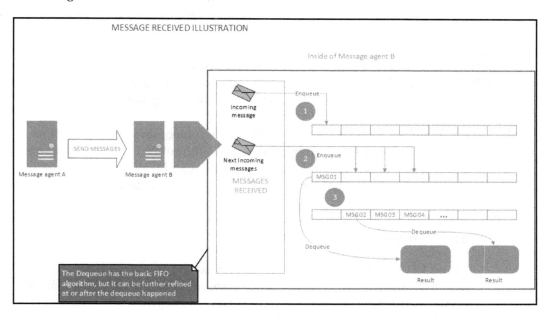

As illustrated, a queue on the agent that receives the messages is needed because:

1. The incoming messages may come in close intervals; therefore, a minimum waiting time or minimal latency is expected. Also, incoming messages need to be stored before being processed, and the order of receiving is very important, as implied by FIFO.

2. The queue can be optimized further by processing it in memory as needed, and as much as possible, as long as it matches the available memory allocation with respect to the maximum available memory of the running agent. For example, a machine with 32 GB of RAM will of course process the queue more efficiently than a machine with 16 GB of RAM.

By default, a queue is stored on heap but using a predefined size; therefore, there is minimal overhead in accessing a queue on heap. This is also the same for the queue when it comes to sending messages as well.

These are the activities that happen when receiving a message:

1. A queue is allocated. This step is actually the same as step 1 in the sending message previously.
2. The incoming message is checked for deserialization problems according to the agreed format from message agent A. This validation is necessary because there is no guarantee that all incoming messages are valid. This is the first difference in handling messages between sending and receiving.
3. The receiving messages are not guaranteed to always arrive in the same sequence as they were sent. For example, it is not guaranteed that the first message sent will be received first. It is quite normal/common for the order of the message sent not to be the same as the message received. This is the second of the differences between sending and receiving messages.
4. A valid incoming message is enqueued. The first incoming message will be processed first. This first incoming message might not be the first message sent.
5. When it is ready to be dequeued (after a certain wait for the previous incoming message to be dequeued), the message content is waiting to be deserialized further.
6. The content of the message is deserialized from `String` to an object, and can be processed further as resulting data.

It is up to the implementer to further process the queue to be ordered by certain conditions before being dequeued and this may vary. This can be the subject of evidence of being falsely treated as synchronous because the ordering of the queue will yield some process overhead and the consumer of the message will have to wait. The handling of received messages may vary in a sense that the queues may have raw FIFO without considering the order of the time the message was sent or will try to process the received messages in time order as long as it is guaranteed to proceed using certain configurations. However, using this sequence of enforcing the order of the message received by the time they were sent will defeat the nature of the message queue agent since the message received will be forced to wait for the earlier messages to arrive.

This is not the same as the era of the legacy modem as the full connection on both sides is required to ensure continuous synchronous communication. If a message agent is supposed to have full real-time processing while always waiting for the result immediately, then a message agent will always be forced to wait indefinitely for incoming replies, and this will defeat the main purpose of a message agent itself: processing message asynchronously. Anything waitable, concerns (usually processes) is mostly blocking, and if the waiting is executed explicitly, then it will block the next operation or process to be executed.

 The synchronous operations on a modem are not related to how the communication channels the transfer, either half duplex or full duplex. Many of us are mixing synchronous with half duplex/full duplex, and it is wrong. These concepts are not related at all.

The receiving of the message handling can also use a temporary storage to hold received messages if necessary. This is crucial if each message may contain certain operations or instructions to be processed heavily, for example, instructions to calculate the current positions of a pricing forecast.

The handling of the messages to be sent is processed in queues, the first message to be sent being processed first. This is the same as handling the received messages where the first message received is processed first. One of the important factors in handling the messages is **serialization**. There might be overhead on the serialization and deserialization of the object in the message.

Overview of serialization

Serialization and deserialization are often described as simply serialization. It is defined as how an object is flattened to a string of properties and values and the reverse: the construction of an object from a string of properties and values. The serialization part is actually an operation of flattening an object (or class in the type system), which is also called deconstruction of an object because the semantics of an object are translated into a string that describes the class, property, and values. The value of the properties must be serialized successfully too because we have to be able to deserialize back into the original object representation without changing the semantic value.

Serialization and deserialization are illustrated (simplified) in the following image:

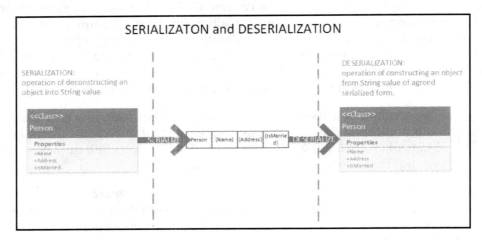

The simplest example of a working serialization is available in how we create our own custom serialization to translate an object's properties and its value's implementation using a basic override of the ToString method, which is available in System.Object. This System.Object class is inherited by all classes in .NET because System.Object is the parent object of all types in .NET. We can override the ToString() method to represent the content of the class.

For example, we have a Person class, defined as follows:

```
open System
open System.Text

type Person() =
    member val Name: String = "" with get, set
    member val Address: String = "" with get, set
    member val IsMarried = false with get, set
    override this.ToString() =
        let mutable sb = new StringBuilder()
        sb <-
sb.Append("Person{").Append(this.Name).Append("|").Append(this.Address).App
end("|")
        sb <- sb.Append(this.IsMarried).Append("}")
        sb.ToString()
```

The following are the explanations for the preceding code:

1. The `Person` class overrides the `ToString()` method with the necessary `StringBuilder.Append` operations to construct a string representation of `Person`.

2. The `StringBuilder` of sb is used as mutable because it is fine to have mutability in a locally scoped function/method because this symbol is not used outside the scope of the function and the side effect is still transparent. The property values are separated with `|`.

3. The code uses the `val` keyword in the property member declaration because the property is using the auto setter and getter.

A semantic description of the auto properties of setter-getter syntaxes for F# is beyond the scope of this book. For more information on the auto properties of F#, consult this MSDN Library page:

```
https://docs.microsoft.com/en-us/dotnet/articles/fsharp/language-reference/memb
ers/properties
```

 The semantics of F# auto properties (auto setter and getter with backing fields automatically generated by compiler) are same as C#/VB auto properties. Only the internal naming of the backing properties has different implementation details, but this should not be our concern at all since we do not care about the backing field.

We then add the code to display the serialization representation:

```
[<EntryPoint>]
let main argv =
    let anyPerson1 = new Person(Name = "John Doe", Address="Baker Street",
IsMarried = false)
    let anyPerson2 = new Person(Name="Jane Doe", Address ="Arlington
Street", IsMarried = true)
    Console.WriteLine(anyPerson1.ToString())
    Console.WriteLine(anyPerson2.ToString())
```

Let's run the code, and we will see that it will display the output:

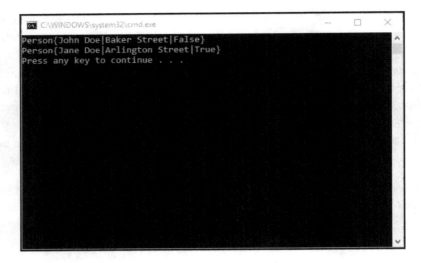

The cost of serialization is usually cheaper than deserialization, as it tries to flatten the object (the attributes or properties of the object) into strings that define the property name and the values. The property value is then converted to String by implicitly or explicitly calling the ToString() method. This is actually a simplified sample that we can also write our own serializer to further optimize or to fully streamline the process.

Deserialization is more expensive because it tries to construct a type based on the string value, because we must maintain the semantics of the properties and the properties values from the serialized String.

The following is a simplified sample of deserialization (add this code below the Person type declaration):

```
static member Deserialize (serializedString:String) =
    let mutable deserializedPerson = new Person()
    let mutable strippedString = serializedString.Substring(7)
    strippedString <-
strippedString.Substring(0,strippedString.Length-1)
    let splitString = strippedString.Split([| "|" |],
StringSplitOptions.None)
    deserializedPerson.Name <- splitString.[0]
    deserializedPerson.Address <- splitString.[1]
    deserializedPerson.IsMarried <- Boolean.Parse(splitString.[2])
    deserializedPerson
```

To test this function, we now modify the `EntryPoint` code to test `Deserialize`:

```
[<EntryPoint>]
let main argv =
    let anyPerson1 = new Person(Name = "John Doe", Address="Baker Street",
IsMarried = false)
    let anyPerson2 = new Person(Name="Jane Doe", Address ="Arlington
Street", IsMarried = true)
    Console.WriteLine(anyPerson1.ToString())
    Console.WriteLine(anyPerson2.ToString())
    let anyperson3 = Person.Deserialize(anyPerson1.ToString())
    Console.WriteLine(anyperson3.ToString())
    0 // return an integer exit code
```

We mark `Deserialize` as `static` because the main intention is to deserialize, not depend on the object that does the deserialization. We can test this deserialization by calling `Deserialize` with the existing serialized `ToString()` result with its parameter as demonstrated.

The following is the display output of the result of `anyperson3.ToString()` combined with the previous `anyPerson1` and `anyPerson2`:

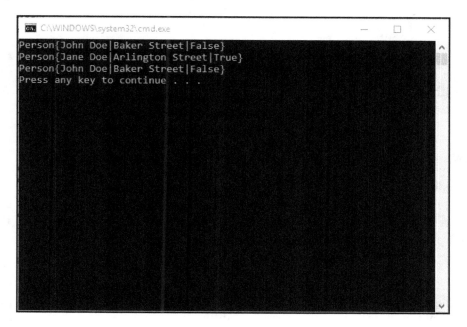

The resulting display output now has proven that we have successfully constructed the object from the serialized `String` by checking the same value of `anyPerson1` with `anyperson3`. This sample is too simple for this demonstration, but it truly demonstrates that there are certain requirements that have to be met before having successful deserializations.

These are the mandatory requirements for successful deserializations:

1. The serialized format must be agreed upon and must have the same structure format as the serializer. In terms of implementation, the type of serialization object must be the same type.
2. The serialization and deserialization must have as simple type as possible; otherwise, complex serialization and deserialization will occur. For example, serializing the object that implements the COM object, whereas implicit marshalling will always occur and crossing the thread boundary across *STA* and *MTA* threads will always yield unpredictable results, often yielding errors not in the form of a thrown exception.
3. The serialization of an object has to be a concrete object (a class); otherwise, an overhead of type check casting will occur. For example, serializing an interface is not recommended as the deserialization will always try to create an instance of a concrete class, and a runtime error will occur.

In common/daily practice, it is recommended to use an existing serializer with an already commonly-used format such as JSON, for example, `DataContractJsonSerializer` in the WCF class libraries, under the namespace of `System.Runtime.Serialization.Json`, and the commonly used third party serializer, NewtonSoft JSON serializer.

Introduction to F# MailboxProcessor

Now, we have the basic knowledge of what a message agent is, and we have also highlighted how this agent operates as to how it sends and receive messages. It is time to find out more about the F# message agent, F# `MailboxProcessor`. For the rest of this book, we will simply use `MailboxProcessor` as a class and as an agent.

The `MailboxProcessor` is actor based. It may have multiple threads spawned or just a single thread. In a sense it is an actor because as an actor, it can have its own role. In their implementation detail, the actors can act on their own without depending on other actors (although they might have the same responsibilities or same behaviors). Actors can be implemented to have the same responsibilities, such as an actor/agent to process incoming requests or to process sending requests.

The writer of `MailboxProcessor` can also be seen as a producer while the reader can be seen as a consumer.

The lightweight aspects of `MailboxProcessor` are unique. It is not just lightweight in terms of being standalone and built-in to the core F#, but also:

- It is quite easy to start using it because it operates without dependency on how the underlying operating system does asynchronous operations.
- It will not store the messages, so they are not persistent
- It can be further combined with F# asynchronous workflow
- It does not have an advanced infrastructure that has many configurable environment settings such as IBM Websphere MQ and MSMQ

Other than those unique traits, the concept of F# `MailboxProcessor` queue agent is similar to famous message queue manager software such as IBM Websphere MQ (formerly IBM MQ Series) and Microsoft MQ (also called MSMQ). It is used to handle asynchronous message transfers.

For more information about IBM Websphere MQ, visit:

`http://www-03.ibm.com/software/products/en/ibm-mq`

For more information about MSMQ, visit:

`https://msdn.microsoft.com/en-us/library/ms711472(v=vs.85).aspx`

F# `MailboxProcessor` as agent is not completely standalone (not external) because `MailboxProcessor` is part of F# core libraries, so we can use and leverage it quickly instead of having an assessment and installation setup activities before using it.

The disadvantages are:

- If many messages are sent or received, we must implement our own storage to store them. This means we maintain our own storage of a queue of messages as, by default, `MailboxProcessor` messages are not persistent.
- We must manage how we further optimize the queue operations as `MailboxProcessor`, by default, relies on operating at runtime with no offline storage feature to hold the queues.
- If the order of prioritization is critical, we cannot further customize how `MailboxProcessor` is going to use the thread affinity of the underlying machine on Windows because there is no way to do this. This is intentional, as the lightweight of `MailboxProcessor` always hides the implementation details of the synchronization of prioritization on the thread executions.

In the realm of F#, `MailboxProcessor` has the ability to write messages to send (*writer*) and to read incoming messages (*reader*).

The writer-reader model is often mentioned in the MSDN Library on the MSDN landing page of `Control.MailboxProcessor`:

```
https://msdn.microsoft.com/visualfsharpdocs/conceptual/control.mailboxprocessor
%5b%27msg%5d-class-%5bfsharp%5d
```

This reader-writer model shows that `MailboxProcessor` only focuses as an agent on writing a message and then sending it, and reading incoming messages. It may focus on one responsibility to only send, receive, or both.

If we set `MailboxProcessor` to have both send and receive, the sending and receiving processes cannot both be guaranteed to be at the same time.

Let's look at a simplified sample of `MailboxProcessor` by constructing and simulating an email message. The sample code in the landing page of F# `Control.MailboxProcessor` is actually a script file instead of a common code file because we need to evaluate and test the result immediately, a good practice for REPL interactive of F# interactive:

```
open System
open Microsoft.FSharp.Control

type EmailMessage() =
    member val From : String = "" with get, set
    member val To : String = "" with get, set
    member val Cc : String = "" with get, set
    member val DateSent : DateTime = (DateTime.Now) with get
    member val Subject : String = "" with get, set
    member val Content : String = "" with get, set

let mailbox = new MailboxProcessor<EmailMessage>(fun mailprocess ->
    let rec loop =
        async { printfn "Incoming message!"
                let! msg = mailprocess.Receive()
                printfn "Message received. \r\nFrom: %s, \r\nDate received:
%s" msg.From (msg.DateSent.ToString())
                printfn "Subject: %s" msg.Subject
                printfn "Content: \r\n %s" msg.Content
                return! loop }
    loop)
```

Start evaluating the previous code by pressing *Alt + Enter*.

The F# Interactive will evaluate the code sequentially, and this is the walkthrough of the semantics:

1. Open the `System` namespace and `Microsoft.Fsharp.Control`. The `Microsoft.FSharp.Control` namespace is needed for `MailboxProcessor`. We are using `System` namespace because we are going to use `Console` to display the output later.

2. We create `EmailMessage` type to wrap the message we are going to use. The message is simple as it contains the sender (`From`), the destination, the optional CC, subject, and the content of the message. The properties are initialized in the default constructor.

3. All of the properties use the explicit type declaration for more clarity.

4. The mailbox symbol is inferred as a `MailboxProcessor` instance with the parameterized type of `EmailMessage` as the message type.

5. The constructor of `MailboxProcessor` is a lambda that contains the loop of receiving messages.

6. This lambda contains a recursive function of loop, and it uses `return!` to signify that the returning call of loop is within the asynchronous workflow boundary. In the implementation details, `return!` is further translated to calls to `AsyncBuilder.Return`.

7. Received messages are handled by asynchronously getting results by calling the type inferred by the parameter of the lambda, `inbox`. `inbox` is actually typed as `MailboxProcessor<Message>`.

The use of `return!` is crucial because the nature of the recursive function of a loop is contained inside an asynchronous workflow. If we use only `return` instead of `return!`, it will leak the call state outside the boundary of the `async` construct, which can then yield memory leaks in crossing the context. This `return!` is translated into calls to one of the F# asynchronous workflow builders, `AsyncBuilder.Return`, before it actually returns the call of `loop`.

The internal implementation detail is available in the IL. Compile and start ILDASM, then if we open the compiled exe, we can examine the generated classes of loop. In one of the loops, we shall see it calls the `FSharp.Control.FSharpAsyncBuilder.Return`:

```
    .method public strict virtual instance class
[FSharp.Core]Microsoft.FSharp.Control.FSharpAsync`1<class
[FSharp.Core]Microsoft.FSharp.Core.Unit>
        Invoke(class [FSharp.Core]Microsoft.FSharp.Core.Unit _arg2) cil
managed
    // SIG: 20 01 15 12 29 01 12 0D 12 0D
```

```
        {
        // Method begins at RVA 0x3450
        // Code size       16 (0x10)
        .maxstack  8
        IL_0000:  /* 00  |                        */ nop
        IL_0001:  /* 03  |                        */ ldarg.1
        IL_0002:  /* 26  |                        */ pop
        IL_0003:  /* 02  |                        */ ldarg.0
        IL_0004:  /* 7B  | (04)00002E             */ ldfld        class
[FSharp.Core]Microsoft.FSharp.Control.FSharpAsyncBuilder
MailboxSample/'Loop@81-16'::builder@
        IL_0009:  /* 14  |                        */ ldnull
        IL_000a:  /* 6F  | (2B)00000A             */ callvirt     instance class
[FSharp.Core]Microsoft.FSharp.Control.FSharpAsync`1<!!0>
[FSharp.Core]Microsoft.FSharp.Control.FSharpAsyncBuilder::Return<class
[FSharp.Core]Microsoft.FSharp.Core.Unit>(!!0)
        IL_000f:  /* 2A  |                        */ ret
    } // end of method 'Loop@81-16'::Invoke
  } // end of class 'Loop@81-16'
```

It has the `FSharpAsyncBuilder.Return` call before it actually returns to outside scope.

 All of the F# `AsyncBuilder` is compiled under the name of `FSharpAsyncBuilder`. This is also reflected in the generated IL.

Then, let's see `MailboxProcessor` in action:

```
let email1 = new EmailMessage ( From = "john@somemail.com", To =
"clark@somemail.com", Subject = "Introduction", Content = "Hello there!")
let email2 = new EmailMessage ( From = "janet@somemail.com", To =
"abby@somemail.com", Subject = "Friendly reminder", Content = "Please send
me the report today. Thanks!\r\nRegards,\r\nJanet")
mailbox.Start()
mailbox.Post(email1)
mailbox.Post(email2)
```

This is the output of the previous code:

Let's dive further into the code:

1. The mailbox symbol is in fact an instance of `MailboxProcessor` with a default constructor of one parameter and the body of the message typed as `Message`.
2. After we have the `MailboxProcessor` instance, we can begin to initialize the mailbox as an agent by calling the `Start()` method.
3. We can then send messages by calling `Post()` with the message as the parameter; each call of the `Post()` method is guaranteed to be asynchronous.

From the perspective of `MailboxProcessor`, the writer operation is represented by calling `Post()`, and this is also the sending operation; the reader is represented by calling `Receive()`, and this is also the receiving operation.

This is why the type name starts with *Mailbox* because it is quite similar to the mailbox as a starting container to send and receive letters that contain messages in everyday life.

Now let's dive into `MailboxProcessor` features.

Overview of MailboxProcesor features

`MailboxProcessor` has two constructors, the simplest constructor being the one that takes one parameter of delegate. The second one takes two parameters: a delegate and a `CancellationToken` object.

The following are the syntaxes of the constructors:

```
// Signature:
new MailboxProcessor : (MailboxProcessor<'Msg> -> Async<unit>) *
?CancellationToken -> MailboxProcessor<'Msg>

// Usage:
new MailboxProcessor (body)
new MailboxProcessor (body, cancellationToken = cancellationToken)
```

In the previous sample, we called the constructor with a delegate. This delegate is the main entry of the read loop when `MailboxProcessor` starts (as initialized by calling the `Start()` method).

Not all of the operations in `MailboxProcessor` are useful for all cases; that depends on the usage and the detail of the asynchronous operations we want to use. In fact, similar to the other message agents, `MailboxProcessor` does not guarantee that the sequence of the received messages will always be the same as the sequence of sent messages.

The following are the interesting functions/methods of `MailboxProcessor`:

Function	Quick Remark
`Post`	Posts a message to the message queue of `MailboxProcessor` asynchronously. Should not be mixed with non-F# `async` such as C#/VB `async`. The posting of a message does not mandate `MailboxProcessor` to return any success/failure status of the posting action.
`PostAndAsyncReply`	Posts a message to an agent and awaits a reply on the channel, asynchronously. Should not be confused with non-F# `async` such as C#/VB `async`. It requires us to always handle the reply of the message.
`PostAndReply`	Posts a message to an agent and awaits a reply on the channel, synchronously. The sending of the message is still asynchronous. Should not be mixed with non F# `async` such as C#/VB `async`. It requires us to always handle the reply of the message.

PostAndTryAsyncReply	Similar to `PostAndAsyncReply` but returns `None` if there is no reply within the timeout period. Should not be mixed with non-F# `async` such as C#/VB `async`. It requires us to always handle the reply of the message.
Receive	Waits for a message. This will consume the first message in the arrival order. Should not be mixed with non-F# `async` such as C#/VB `async`. This `Receive` action has the same type of object as defined by the sending action.
Scan	Scans for a message by looking through messages in arrival order until the scanner returns a `Some` value. Other messages remain in the queue. This scanning action will mostly block the message replies of `Receive` and `TryReceive`.
Start	Starts the agent. The start of the agent may be included within a parallel loop, such as `Parallel.For` or `Parallel.ForEach`.
TryPostAndReply	Similar to `PostAndReply` but returns `None` if there is no reply within the timeout period. Should not be mixed with non-F# `async` such as C#/VB `async`.
TryReceive	Waits for a message. This will consume the first message in the arrival order. It also enforces synchronicity instead of receiving asynchronously. Returns `false` if the receiving message fails. Should not be mixed with non-F# `async` such as C#/VB `async`. The `Receive` action has the same type of object as defined by the sending action
TryScan	Scans for a message by looking through the messages in the arrival order until scanner returns a `Some` value. Other messages remain in the queue. The queue is only stored in memory.

In the previous table, all of the standard posts and replies, such as `Post`, `PostAndReply`, and `PostAndAsyncReply`, should not be used within the C#/VB `async` construct. The post and reply operations implemented in F# have their own thread synchronizer. This F# synchronizer often has unpredictable results when used within C#/VB `async` construct; mixing this different asynchronous model will make the F# synchronizer have race condition when switching back and forth between different execution contexts.

Further implementations of MailboxProcessor

Based on the previous table, `MailboxProcesor` can also send messages and wait for replies, not just send (post) messages. The following operations that do the sending and waiting for reply immediately after sending:

- `PostAndAsyncReply`
- `PostAndReply`
- `PostAndTryAsyncReply`
- `TryPostAndReply`

All these send and receive operations require a handle in F#. It is called `AsyncReplyChannel`, contained in the `Control.AsyncReplyChannel` class.

These are the common steps for using `MailboxProcessor`:

1. We must plan the format of the message to be transferred and received. The format of the message has to be as simple as possible.
2. The agent is created by instantiating it. At this stage, we have to decide whether the operation of sending and receiving messages can be canceled anytime by calling the `MailboxProcessor` constructor, which has the delegate and `CancellationToken` passed.
3. The delegate may contain both the sending and receiving message operations, or just receiving operations.
4. If we require it to send and wait for replies, we must carefully construct the delegate to include `AsyncReplyChannel`. It is recommended to embed this handler inside the message itself because, then, we can enforce that the reply of the sent message is closely related.

To see this sample of sending and waiting for reply in action, we also use the F# flexible type declaration to add more flexibility when handling messages.

At the declarations of the message, `AsyncReplyChannel` is embedded in the message itself:

```
type ComplexMessage =
    | OrdinaryMessage of EmailMessage
    | ForceReplyDelay of AsyncReplyChannel<DateTime>
```

This is an excerpt of the code that creates the instance of `MailboxProcessor` and performs the receiving using handles:

```
let msgManager = new MailboxProcessor<ComplexMessage>(fun inbox ->
    let rec loop msgReceived =
```

```
async { let! msg = inbox.Receive()
            match msg with
            | OrdinaryMessage omsg ->
                printfn "Message received. \r\nFrom: %s, \r\nDate
received: %s" omsg.From (msg.DateSent.ToString())
                printfn "Subject: %s" omsg.Subject
                printfn "Content: \r\n %s" omsg.Content
                return ()
            | ForceReplyDelay replyChannel ->
                replyChannel.Reply(msgReceived)
            return! loop DateTime.Now
        }
    loop DateTime.Now
    )
```

It is also nice to know that type inference not only flows nicely not just as an inferred type declaration and inferred return type but also accommodates the *discriminated unions* that infers the constructor of the type.

For example, let's see the declaration of the `ComplexMessage` type that has discriminated unions with our own previous `EmailMessage` embedded.

We can now combine this with pattern matching that checks for any Query as its *subtype*:

```
let! message = inbox.Receive()
        match msg with
        | OrdinaryMessage omsg ->
            printfn "Message received. \r\nFrom: %s, \r\nDate
received: %s" omsg.From (msg.DateSent.ToString())
            printfn "Subject: %s" omsg.Subject
            printfn "Content: \r\n %s" omsg.Content
            return ()
        | ForceReplyDelay replyChannel ->
            replyChannel.Reply(msgReceived)
```

It is also very nice to know that again this feature is unique to F#, as the current release of C#/VB does not have this discriminated union feature yet.

 There are rough plans to have discriminated union supported in C#/VB, but it is still debated. Also pattern matching is due in the upcoming version of C# 7, and VB 15 does not have the same automatic type inferences as F#. Consult Microsoft's Roslyn repo on GitHub to keep up with the latest developments in C#/VB language design.

A detailed description of the discriminated union is beyond the scope of this book because we cannot further optimize discriminated union. For more information on F#'s discriminated union, visit:

https://docs.microsoft.com/en-us/dotnet/articles/fsharp/language-reference/discriminated-unions

The pattern matching in the sample code can be further optimized. We will describe the optimizations of pattern matching as part of the F# language constructs (beside asynchronous workflow) later in Chapter 7, *Language Features and Constructs Optimization*.

To test the sending and receiving in action simultaneously, we can send (post) the message while at the same time waiting to receive the message:

```
let email1 = new EmailMessage ( From = "john@somemail.com", To =
"clark@somemail.com", Subject = "Introduction", Content = "Hello there!")
msgManager.Start()
msgManager.Post(OrdinaryMessage email1)
msgManager.PostAndReply((fun reply -> ForceReplyDelay(reply)), 100) |>
ignore
```

Since we have embedded the channel inside the message, we can have a quick guarantee that for each message we receive, we can always try to relate the message we receive to the message we send because we are using the same AsyncReplyChannel.

Looking back at the definition of the delegate inside the constructor of marketMaker, it matches the query pattern of a Message type, which then returns the related asset based on the message posted by PostAndReply.

Now, we have extended our understanding of MailboxProcessor using the sample of an order and sell transaction. It is still similar to a bank account model transaction, but we do not care how many parts or asset balances we have.

Managing side effects inside MailboxProcessor and asynchronous workflows

We may have been tempted to use a MailboxProcessor instantiation wrapped within an asynchronous workflow. *It is not recommended to have this overly complex wrapper as MailboxProcessor already has its own asynchronous context.*

This is also applied to interoperability with the UI thread as well as asynchronous context should not be mixed with the UI thread directly. Mixing the UI thread with asynchronous contexts will yield unpredictable results.

If we must use Windows forms, it is best to have asynchronous workflow and the UI coded in F#. Using WPF, we can use WPF Dispatcher to ensure we will not have cross-thread violation.

On managing side effects, using `MailboxProcessor` to do side effects activity must be handled carefully.

Consider these scenarios and the reasons:

1. Upon receiving the messages inside the delegate parameter of a `MailboxProcessor` instantiation, we have calls to get web content asynchronously. These multiple asynchronous contexts are not recommended because there can be race conditions on which processes are to be finished and return the call back to the calling delegate. This added complexity will add overhead to the stack because there is no guarantee that `MailboxProcessor` will handle the asynchronous scheduling correctly.

2. If we still want to do this, every call to get the web content must be handled using the Disposable pattern as far as possible in order to minimize the pointer leak of the call stack.

3. The original intent of `MailboxProcessor` is to have a role as message agent. The delegate and the payload of the message should be constructed to be as simple as possible. If we want to use `AsyncReplyChannel`, it is recommended to embed it as part of the message.

4. Wrapping `MailboxProcessorPost` and `Reply` in a parallel loop such as `Parallel.ForEach()` does not really guarantee that `MailboxProcessor` will send the message fully parallel unless the instantiation of `MailboxProcessor` itself is encoded within a parallel loop. This will ensure that there will be no breach outside the context of the `MailboxProcessor` delegate when `MailboxProcessor` starts.

5. It is not recommended to have a nested recursive function of `async` calling another recursive `async` function. The level of unpredictability will increase by many orders of magnitude, especially as it will be considered as a long-lived object, but it will also put a burden on `Gen0` and `Gen1` of the CLR. Normally, long-lived objects should live on `Gen1`, but the asynchronous workflow might consider it as short-lived object; therefore, the burden will be put on both `Gen0` and `Gen1`.

We have seen from many sample cases that it's important to profile the application, especially when the code contains many asynchronous workflows, including the implied `MailboxProcessor`. The result of testing how many objects live in `Gen0` and `Gen1` will determine where and how the GC may experience unnecessary overheads of garbage collections and heap allocations.

There may happen to be unnecessary overheads because of an object being short-lived but profiled as long lived; the GC `Gen0` and `Gen1` profiling reports should be the basis for actually finding out where the `Gen0` and `Gen1` continues. However, premature GC will not definitely help increase the performance because if there is aggressive garbage collection at `Gen0`, then the cost of garbage collection will affect the initial run time of your code, especially when `GC.Collect` is called within a loop of `for` and `foreach`. Each time `GC.Collect` is called, any exception that might happen during the call of `GC.Collect` will also affect the state of the current stack frame and heap allocations.

Again, there is no single solution for uncommon implementations of your asynchronous workflow.

Parallel programming with .NET TPL

We have a basic knowledge of asynchronous, parallel asynchronous, and interoperability of asynchronous workflows with .NET EAP and APM. We have finished discussing .NET Task based Asynchronous Programming (TAP) in the form of interoperability between F# asynchronous workflows and .NET TAP. We are now discussing more about interoperability with .NET TPL.

F# does not just have its own implementations of asynchronous supports and parallel asynchronous but is fully compatible with .NET BCL hence .NET TPL.

.NET TPL is not just an infrastructure of a combination of implied asynchronous and parallelism. It focuses on these three features:

- Task-based parallelism
- Data parallelism
- PLINQ, an implementation of LINQ in parallel, also called Parallel LINQ

Let's learn more .NET TPL by visiting the MSDN Library .NET TPL landing page:

```
https://msdn.microsoft.com/en-us/library/dd460693(v=vs.110).aspx
```

According to MSDN, this is the overall high-level picture of .NET 4 TPL:

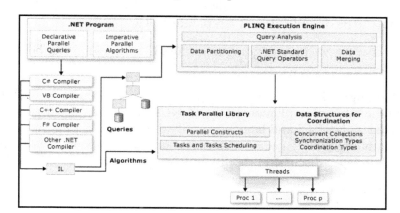

On the syntactic level, .NET TPL is conceptually divided into two:

- Declarative parallel queries (for example, PLINQ)
- Imperative parallel (for example, `Parallel.ForEach`, with an additional parameter to maintain state consistency)

This picture is valid for .NET 4.5 and it is still valid for .NET 4.6/4.6.1 as it illustrates the high-level of .NET TPL that includes data flow parallelism, which starts in .NET 4.5.

It is also worth noting that since .NET 4.5, there are the following new features in parallelism support:

- Debugging parallelism is easier with parallel debugging support.
- Dataflow libraries is essentially the same as F# `MailboxProcessor`.
- Coordinating data structures makes the existing concurrent data structures more concurrent-aware. This is essentially the same as the concurrent data structures that improve performance in .NET 4.5 and later.

For more information on what's new in .NET 4.5, 4.6 and 4.6.1, visit:

`https://msdn.microsoft.com/en-us/library/ms171868(v=vs.110).aspx`

For more information on what's new in .NET 4.5 specific to parallel programming, visit this Microsoft MSDN blog by .NET parallel team (formerly ParallelFX):

`https://blogs.msdn.microsoft.com/pfxteam/2011/09/17/whats-new-for-parallelism-in-net-4-5/`

There is a comparable message-passing agent library in .NET TPL; it is called *Dataflow*. The Dataflow library is not included in the original runtime distribution of .NET runtime and SDK. It is available to be downloaded as a separate NuGet package.

Throughout this chapter, we are not going to discuss Dataflow libraries because we are focusing on F# `MailboxProcessor`.

 Although .NET 4.0 is the starting release of .NET that has .NET TPL, some of the internal implementations of .NET TPL have bugs that have been fixed in .NET 4.5 and later, especially the parallel debugging support. Beginning with `Chapter 5`, *Advanced Concurrency Support in F#* all .NET TPL-related discussion should only be applied to .NET 4.5 and later.

In the next section, we will discuss more about the TPL, from task-based parallelism to data parallelism.

Overview of task-based parallelism

Let's visit task-based parallelism. The term *task* is actually the same concept of task as in the **Task based Asynchrony Pattern** (**TAP**) with one additional trait: it can run independently, as a concurrent unit. The consequence of a parallelized task as a concurrent unit is that it can run in parallel or may run as a chain of tasks some time in the future.

All the parallel task operations are available from the `System.Threading.Tasks.Parallel` class, under the `mscorlib.dll` assembly. This means that we can use it immediately without referencing any assembly other than `mscorlib.dll`.

This `Parallel` class has many `static` methods that provide support for task parallelism and data parallelism.

The task parallelism-related method in the `Parallel` class is the `Parallel.Invoke` method.

This method has the following overloaded signatures; the first signature is as follows:

```
static member Invoke :
        [<ParamArrayAttribute>] actions:Action[] -> unit
```

The second signature of `Parallel.Invoke` is as follows:

```
static member Invoke :
        parallelOptions:ParallelOptions *
```

```
[<ParamArrayAttribute>] actions:Action[] -> unit
```

The first signature defines `Invoke` to have one parameter–the parameter arrays of `Action` delegates. The `[<ParamArrayAttribute>]` is the same semantic as C#'s `param` keyword, but it has to be defined as an attribute parameter in F# to be used in a manner similar to `param` in C#.

The second signature defines two parameters: `ParallelOptions`, a class to further configure the behavior of the parallelism we want to run, and the parameter arrays of `Action` delegates.

The documentation on the `Parallel.Invoke` method is available at:

```
https://msdn.microsoft.com/en-us/library/system.threading.tasks.parallel.invoke
(v=vs.110).aspx
```

Using `Parallel.Invoke` in F# is quite simple. For example, we can parallelize two different processes, the first process being factorial, and the second process getting all of the running processes on your local machine.

The full sample code is as follows:

```
open System
open System.Diagnostics
open System.Threading.Tasks

let rec fact x =
    match x with
    | n when n < 2 -> 1
    | _ -> fact(x-1) * x
let factwrap x =
    let factresult = fact x
    ignore

let runningProcesses = fun () ->
    let processes = Process.GetProcesses()
    let processNames =
        processes
        |> Seq.map (fun p -> p.ProcessName)
    for name in processNames do
        Console.WriteLine(name)
```

The interesting fact about this code is how we interoperate with .NET `Action` delegate by simply instantiating a new `Action` delegate with the process we want to wrap as an `Action` delegate.

If we want to wrap a recursive function as an `Action` delegate, we need to wrap the function inside another function that always ignores the result, just as the `factwrap` function does. This is crucial, because `Action` delegate is a delegate that has no return value, or it returns a unit (`void` in C#).

We can then add the line to run `Parallel.Invoke` and our delegates of `factwrap` and `runningprocesses` in our existing `EntryPoint` of `main`:

```
[<EntryPoint>]
let main argv =
    let anyPerson1 = new Person(Name = "John Doe", Address="Baker Street",
IsMarried = false)
    let anyPerson2 = new Person(Name="Jane Doe", Address ="Arlington
Street", IsMarried = true)
    Console.WriteLine(anyPerson1.ToString())
    Console.WriteLine(anyPerson2.ToString())
    let anyperson3 = Person.Deserialize(anyPerson1.ToString())
    Console.WriteLine(anyperson3.ToString)
    Parallel.Invoke(new Action(ParallelInvokeSample01.factwrap 5), new
Action(ParallelInvokeSample01.runningProcesses))
    //printfn "%A" argv
    0 // return an integer exit code
```

The sample `Parallel.Invoke` contains two delegates to be parallelized. But we can add many delegates as well, more than one as implied by `ParamArrayAttribute` marking.

The parameter type of the array is the `Action[]` array. This means all of our functions must have a function body and return `void`, not just a result of a process. This is why the `fact` function must be wrapped into another function that runs `fact` and ignores the returning result, and the `runningProcesses` function body is explicitly contained within a lambda function that takes a unit as its parameter.

If we do not declare `runningProcesses` as explicitly declared within lambda, this function will be inferred to have a generic type as its parameter because F# needs an explicit declaration of the parameter type. And we will catch other compile errors because the `Action` delegate also requires a signature of a function that takes no parameter and returns nothing.

The following is the signature of the `Action` delegate:

```
type Action =
    delegate of unit -> unit
```

The `delegate` keyword in this sense is the .NET BCL delegate, not F# delegate. The delegate of F# represents an F# function, and this F# function will be compiled as an inheritance of F# `FastFunction`.

Let's dive into the IL of the `factwrap` function and the inside declaration of `Action`:

```
.class auto ansi serializable nested assembly beforefieldinit
factwrap@14<a>
        extends class
[FSharp.Core]Microsoft.FSharp.Core.FSharpFunc`2<!a,class
[FSharp.Core]Microsoft.FSharp.Core.Unit>
{
} // end of class factwrap@14
```

We now can see that it extends `Microsoft.Core.FSharpFunc<`T1,`T2>`, which takes two generic type parameters. `T1` is the parameter of the delegate and `T2` is the returning type. `T1` is typed as unit and `T2` is typed as unit as well.

Let's visit the second overload of `Parallel.Invoke` that has `ParallelOptions` as its parameter.

The documentation of the `Parallel.Options` class is available at:

https://msdn.microsoft.com/en-us/library/system.threading.tasks.paralleloptions (v=vs.110).aspx

The `ParallelOptions` class is basically a class to configure `Parallel.Invoke` further to meet custom concurrency requirements.

The following are the properties of `ParallelOptions`:

- `CancellationToken`, to pass `CancellationToken` to cancel the running of invoked actions.
- `MaxDegreeOfParallelism`, to get or set the maximum number of concurrent tasks enabled by this `ParallelOptions` instance.
- `TaskScheduler`, to get or set `TaskScheduler` associated with this `ParallelOptions` instance. Setting this property to null indicates that the current scheduler of the running thread from the current `threadpool` should be used.

We can also force the parallelism context to have a maximum degree of parallelism of 5 by passing this value to the property of `ParallelOptions.MaxDegreeOfParallelism`.

A quick sample of this (using our existing sample delegates) is as follows:

```
Parallel.Invoke(new ParallelOptions(MaxDegreeOfParallelism = 5),new
Action(ParallelInvokeSample01.factwrap 5), new
Action(ParallelInvokeSample01.runningProcesses))
```

We have now set the maximum degree of parallelism to 5, and this is not a pessimistic value because we are only passing two `Action` delegates. Setting this value to −1 will instruct `Parallel.Invoke` to run as parallelized to use available cores and available threads in the thread pool as often as possible.

Be careful when setting a value for the `MaxDegreeOfParallelism` property. MSDN Library has additional cautions:

- On many cores:

  When you know that a particular algorithm you're using won't scale beyond a certain number of cores. You can set the property to avoid wasting cycles on additional cores.

- On the implementation detail of the allocation of `thread` and `threadpool` resources:

  When you're running multiple algorithms concurrently and want to manually define how much of the system each algorithm can utilize. You can set a MaxDegreeOfParallelism value for each.

  When the thread pool's heuristics are unable to determine the right number of threads to use and could end up injecting too many threads. For example, in long-running loop body iterations, the thread pool might not be able to tell the difference between reasonable progress or livelock or deadlock, and might not be able to reclaim threads that were added to improve performance. In this case, you can set the property to ensure that you don't use more than a reasonable number of threads.

The lock in the parallel invocation (in the last bullet) implies that any global and shared state, if used inside a `Parallel.Invoke` delegate, is prone to an unpredictable state; therefore, a lock should be used. But locking objects in the middle of parallelism might bring deadlock itself because many threads are racing to modify and there is no guarantee which one will have an exclusive lock and will not block others.

To see further what goes on when we invoke delegates to be parallelized, we could leverage the existing parallel debugging tool in Visual Studio, available since Visual Studio 2012.

Quick start-using the parallel debugging tool in Visual Studio

Now let's use the parallel debugging capability of Visual Studio and .NET 4.5+. Put breakpoint in the line of `Parallel.Invoke` and inside `factwrap` and `runningProcesses`.

Press *F5* to run with debugging.

When it stops at `Parallel.Invoke`, open the **Parallel Stacks** visualizer by choosing **Debug | Windows | Parallel Stacks**. We also open **Tasks** by choosing **Debug | Windows | Tasks**:

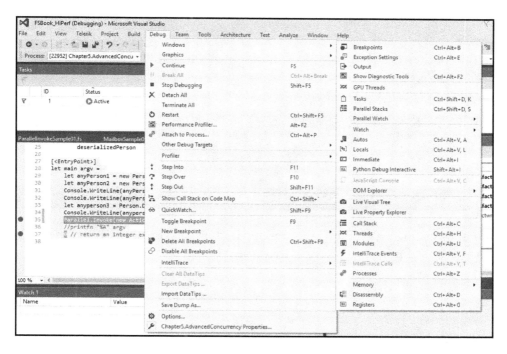

As visualized in the screenshot, the **Tasks** window already displays the current task of the active task.

Press `F11` to step into the next function. At the first round, it will go through `factwrap` and a new thread is created:

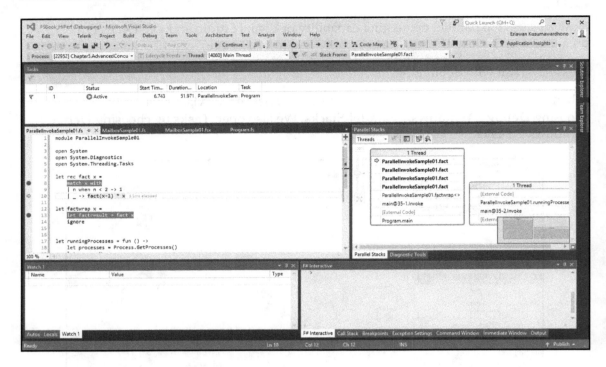

As `factwrap` is calling `fact`, the `fact` function body is also debugged for the number or parameter we passed into `factwrap`, in this case it is 5, as factorial of 5.

This is pictured nicely in **Parallel Stacks**:

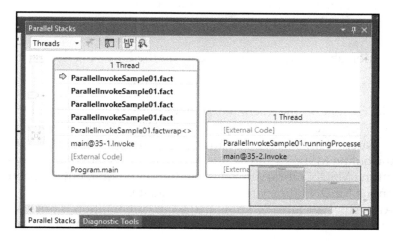

In the preceding screenshot, we can nicely see that it spawns a new thread to hold the `runningProcesses` delegate. In terms of the thread pool, all of these threads are in one thread pool, so it is efficiently executed within the same context of running the thread of the code that runs `Parallel.Invoke`.

As we go further into the `fact` function and leave the recursive, we can also see that **Parallel Stacks** displays the related call stack with the matched debug breakpoint:

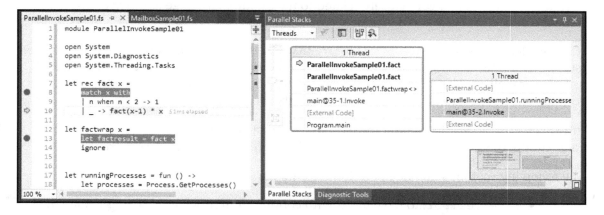

After it finishes executing the `Parallel.Invoke`, the current thread will go back to our entrypoint of `main`.

For more information on using parallel debugging (including multithread debugging) in Visual Studio, consult the following MSDN Library page:

```
https://msdn.microsoft.com/en-us/library/ms164746.aspx
```

For more information about **Parallel Stacks**, consult the following MSDN Library page:

```
https://msdn.microsoft.com/en-us/library/dd998398.aspx
```

 The current offline documentation of the MSDN Library in Visual Studio 2015 (opened with MS Help) section of Visual Studio debugging is not updated. It is not in sync with the latest documentation of Visual Studio in the online MSDN Library. It is highly recommended to always have the offline MSDN Library installed and updated first, but we should check the online MSDN Library for the latest update.

Also, since we already know that F# documentation is open source, we should also always check the online documentation for the latest update. Starting from this chapter, more resources will be emphasized on online MSDN Library.

Overview of data parallelism

Data parallelism in .NET TPL is actually a library of functions/methods that have parallel operations on certain data operations, such as enumerating data. It is can also be seen as declarative because it is very closely related to the existing language features of how F# iterates a collection (using F# `for` loop).

It is also clearly stated in the MSDN Library that this data parallelism is only for a collection (such as IEnumerable) and array, not for encapsulating operations to be parallelized, such as task parallelism. The main focus of data parallelism is parallelizing `for`, either `for` with counter or `foreach`, to directly iterate through the elements of the collection.

In F#, `foreach` is represented by the for .. in construct, and it's conceptually and contextually the same as `foreach` in C#/VB, although it is semantically different.

The following methods are the operations of data parallelism:

- `Parallel.For`, to have loops with counter (it may act as a starting value when incremented), and this `For` does not run sequentially as compared with the basic for
- `Parallel.ForEach`, to have `foreach` in parallel when iterating elements

The `Parallel.For` is related to the `for` loop of F# that has predefined from and stopping values to be counter for the loop.

For example, consider the following code snippet:

```
open System
open System.Threading.Tasks

let function1() =
  for i = 1 to 10 do
    Console.WriteLine("current datetime is" + DateTime.Now.ToString())
  printfn ""

Parallel.For(1,10, fun(iteration) ->
    Console.WriteLine("Iteration: " + iteration.ToString() + " current
datetime: " + DateTime.Now.ToString())
    printfn ""
    )
```

The `function1` will run sequentially from `1` to `10`, and it will always run synchronously, which means that the first iteration has to be finished first before running the next iterations. The rest of the iterations still have to wait; therefore, it is intentional and it is also trivial that the execution behavior of the first iteration blocks the next remaining iterations.

The `parallelFunction1` is a parallel version of `function1`. In the function body, we add the display of the current iterations by passing the counter into the output display.

We shall put the code as F# script, run the script inside Visual Studio **F# Interactive**, and immediately see the result:

Here, we can see the proof that there is no guarantee that the loop will execute sequentially. This is intentional because in parallelism, we do not care about the order of the executions, as we explored in the section, *Introducing concurrency support in F# 4* in `Chapter 4`, *Introduction to Concurrency in F#*.

Now, we visit the parallel pair of the F# `for .. in` loop, and the `Parallel.ForEach` method.

We now start from the simple sample of iterating a collection in F# using the `for .. in` loop and put it into parallel:

```
let seq1 = seq { for i in 1 .. 10 -> (i, i*i) }
for (a, asqr) in seq1 do
  printfn "%d squared is %d" a asqr

Parallel.ForEach(seq1, fun((a,asqr)) ->
  printfn "%d squared is %d" a asqr
    )
```

Again, run the code in **F# Interactive**, and we can compare the output:

```
F# Interactive
                                        LowestBreakIteration = null;}
>
1 squared is 1
2 squared is 4
3 squared is 9
4 squared is 16
5 squared is 25
6 squared is 36
7 squared is 49
8 squared is 64
9 squared is 81
10 squared is 100

val seq1 : seq<int * int>
val it : unit = ()


>
1 squared is 1
4 squared is 16
3 squared is 9
6 squared is 36
7 squared is 49
9 squared is 81
10 squared is 100
8 squared is 64
5 squared is 25
2 squared is 4
val it : ParallelLoopResult =
    System.Threading.Tasks.ParallelLoopResult {IsCompleted = true;
                                               LowestBreakIteration = null;}

>

Error List  Task List  Output  F# Interactive
```

Now, we have interoperability of .NET TPL's data parallelism in F#. As long as we carefully keep the process as simple as possible (without shared state), we can have a successful implementation of parallelism with a highly predictable result.

This is also a good example of minimizing unpredictability by keeping the side effects as minimal as possible. We can still use shared state, but then, we have to implement locking as well, and this will decrease the performance. The background reason for this decreasing performance is the same as having locks in an asynchronous workflow.

Common potential pitfalls in parallel programming

There are common pitfalls for parallel programming in .NET, and we should pay attention to these.

We know that we should avoid the following:

- Side effects in mutable states of an object. If a mutable state is used, a lock has to be implemented to ensure concurrency of the object state. This is also applied to shared states, because any shared state is also mutable as well.
- A side effect in the possibility of having an exception. If we do not catch any possible exception (especially exceptions related to blocking operations such as I/O), any exceptions thrown in the middle of any parallel processes will cancel the whole pipeline of the parallel process.
- COM objects, because we have to be careful when handling an object that has a different apartment model, such as COM objects.
- Side effects of mixing a UI thread with the current thread from a non-UI thread. In WPF, this can be mitigated by using WPF Dispatcher.

Now, let's try to handle mutable states in the next section.

Overview of handling mutable state

If we want to really have a mutable state, we can enclose it in a pair of `Monitor.Enter` and `Monitor.Exit` loops.

For example, we can code this using a simplified sample of how the lock in C#/VB is actually implemented:

```
open System.Threading

let lock (lockobj:obj) anyfunction =
  Monitor.Enter lockobj
  try
    anyfunction()
  finally
    // the code in the finally block will be executed after anyfunction is
completely finishing execution.
    // Therefore we can exit the monitor gracefully.
    Monitor.Exit lockobj
```

This watching state is the reason why .NET names the object to watch the state as `Monitor`.

We will not describe the `Monitor` object further because Monitor is part of an object locking mechanism that is not recommended in many cases of F# concurrency implementation. We shall focus only on the functional aspects of F# concurrency rather than dealing with mutable state, which is common for non-functional programming style code. For more information on .NET Monitor, visit the following link:

```
https://msdn.microsoft.com/en-us/library/system.threading.monitor(v=vs.110).asp
x
```

There is also a class in .NET BCL to allow mixing mutable state for simple operations, such as increment and decrement inside a parallel loop. The class is `System.Threading.Interlocked`, and it is also used internally in F# to implement asynchronous workflows in `Control.Async` and builders in the `FSharpAsyncBuilder` class.

The implementation of using `Interlocked` is not common, and we should be careful. This is why it has a limited kind of allowable operations. We can see a good sample implementation of leveraging `Interlocked` in the internal implementation of F# `Async.Parallel` code:

```
        static member Parallel (l: seq<Async<'T>>) =
            unprotectedPrimitive (fun args ->
                let tasks, result =
                    try
                        Seq.toArray l, None    // manually protect eval of
seq
                    with exn ->
                        let edi =
ExceptionDispatchInfo.RestoreOrCapture(exn)
```

```
                            null, Some(errorT args edi)

                  match result with
                  | Some r -> r
                  | None ->
                      if tasks.Length = 0 then args.cont [| |] else  // must not
be in a 'protect' if we call cont explicitly; if cont throws, it should
unwind the stack, preserving Dev10 behavior
                      protectedPrimitiveCore args (fun args ->
                          let ({ aux = aux } as args) = delimitSyncContext args
// manually resync
                          let count = ref tasks.Length
                          let firstExn = ref None
                          let results = Array.zeroCreate tasks.Length
                          // Attept to cancel the individual operations if an
exception happens on any of the other threads
                          let innerCTS = new LinkedSubSource(aux.token)
                          let trampolineHolder = aux.trampolineHolder
                          let finishTask(remaining) =
                              if (remaining = 0) then
                                  innerCTS.Dispose()
                                  match (!firstExn) with
                                  | None -> trampolineHolder.Protect(fun () ->
args.cont results)
                                  | Some (Choice1Of2 exn) ->
trampolineHolder.Protect(fun () -> aux.econt exn)
                                  | Some (Choice2Of2 cexn) ->
trampolineHolder.Protect(fun () -> aux.ccont cexn)
                              else
                                  FakeUnit

                          // recordSuccess and recordFailure between them
decrement count to 0 and
                          // as soon as 0 is reached dispose
innerCancellationSource
                          let recordSuccess i res =
                              results.[i] <- res;
                              finishTask(Interlocked.Decrement count)

                          let recordFailure exn =
                              // capture first exception and then decrement the
counter to avoid race when
                              // - thread 1 decremented counter and preempted by
the scheduler
                              // - thread 2 decremented counter and called
finishTask
                              // since exception is not yet captured - finishtask
will fall into success branch
```

[199]

```
                              match Interlocked.CompareExchange(firstExn, Some
exn, None) with
                | None ->
                              // signal cancellation before decrementing the
counter - this guarantees that no other thread can sneak to finishTask and
dispose innerCTS
                              // NOTE: Cancel may introduce reentrancy - i.e.
when handler registered for the cancellation token invokes cancel
continuation that will call 'recordFailure'
                              // to correctly handle this we need to return
decremented value, not the current value of 'count' otherwise we may invoke
finishTask with value '0' several times
                    innerCTS.Cancel()
                | _ -> ()
                finishTask(Interlocked.Decrement count)
```

In this code, `Interlocked.Decrement` is used to maintain or keep track of the state of the counter of the number of parallelized asynchronous workflows. The code flows nicely because F# has its own parallel asynchronous operation without depending on the .NET TPL `Parallel` class.

In the MSDN Library, there are additional aspects of common pitfalls of parallel programming available at the following page:

`https://msdn.microsoft.com/en-us/library/dd997392(v=vs.110).aspx`

Among those points, we should pay attention to the following examples in the MSDN Library article, in addition to the many samples of asynchrony and parallelism that we explored:

- Avoid over-parallelization. By using parallel loops, you incur the overhead costs of partitioning the source collection and synchronizing the worker threads. The benefits of parallelization are further limited by the number of processors and the cores on the computer. There is no speedup to be gained by running multiple compute-bound threads on just one processor. Therefore, you must be careful not to over-parallelize a loop. Also, too many parallelizations increase the overheads on the task scheduler and it may lead to a race condition on the thread affinities being obtained. Also, having overheads on a task scheduler will decrease the responsiveness of the running application.
- Avoid calls to non-thread-safe methods! This is extremely important, because writing to non-thread-safe instance methods from a parallel loop can lead to data corruption, which may or may not go undetected in your program. It can also lead to exceptions, for example, multiple parallel threads of calling `FileStream.WriteByte`. This point is closely related to avoiding mixing I/O

operations. It is also necessary to be aware that almost all of the operations in `Stream`, `File`, and `System.Web` classes are not thread-safe at all.

- Avoid changing thread affinity in the middle of any parallel operation. This might yield exceptions and not just unpredictable results/behaviors.

The most common scenario in which over-parallelization can occur is in nested loops. In most cases, it is best to parallelize only the outer loop unless one or more of the following conditions apply:

- The inner loop is known to be very long. You are performing an *expensive computation* on each order. The term expensive computation in this context means having complex calculations that will consume a lot of CPU cycles and also having a parallel computation inside a parallel computation or *complex nested parallelizations*.
- The target system is known to have enough processors to handle the number of threads that will be produced by parallelizing the operation. Having too many degrees of parallelism, especially if the number of parallelism is higher than the number of CPU core, will enforce other processes to wait indefinitely, and this waiting will also result in a deadlock condition.

We can also have a further reference to .NET parallelism from Microsoft by downloading the white paper titled *Patterns for Parallel Programming: Understanding and Applying Parallel Patterns with the .NET Framework 4* from the following official download link:

```
https://www.microsoft.com/en-us/download/details.aspx?id=19222
```

Summary

We have explored the advanced concurrency support in F# and .NET TPL. We also have enough knowledge about how we should handle side effects and also on using asynchronous for various cases and scenarios.

The main conclusion when implementing the best practices of leveraging concurrency in F# is that there is no silver bullet for all concurrency needs, and this includes avoiding the assumption that parallelized code always runs faster than non-parallel code after examining cases that may bring down the performance of parallel implementation in .NET TPL. These warning cases can be applied not just in F# but also in VB/C#.

We have understood asynchrony and parallelism. We will use this knowledge to optimize the type providers and avoid the pitfalls of implementing them in `Chapter 6`, *Optimizing Type Provider*.

6
Optimizing Type Provider

We now have a basic understanding of the basic and advanced concurrency features of F#. We also have enough tooling knowledge and hence, enough knowledge about tooling support in Visual Studio. Based on this knowledge, we can also enhance the performance optimizations when implementing and using other F# language features.

In this chapter, we will focus on bringing the previous knowledge into optimizing type provider. Type provider is a unique feature of F#; it was introduced in F# 3.0.

 Type provider was introduced in F# 3.0 release, at the same time as Visual Studio 2012 release. It is important to know that F# 3.0 is part of train releases of Visual Studio 2012, not Visual Studio 2013. Many external articles (including some blogs) outside the MSDN blogs and MSDN Library mistakenly assume that F# 3.0 has a type provider that comes with Visual Studio 2013. The release of F# that comes with Visual Studio 2013 is F# 3.1, not F# 3.0.

It is also important to first know what type provider is and the main goal or purposes of having or using it, before we optimize it. Knowing the concepts behind type provider will give us an insight of which part of optimizations are available for us when we use and implement type providers. This insight will also help us avoid pitfalls when dealing with type providers implementation in detail.

We now discuss these topics of optimizing type provider:

- Overview of F# type provider
- Best practices in implementing type provider
- Optimizing generative type provider
- Common pitfalls in type provider implementation

Overview of F# type provider

Before we go deeper into optimizing F# type providers, let's have a conceptual introduction to what a type provider is.

 From now on, F# type providers will be described as type providers, omitting the *F#* prefix. It is also common just to use type providers because type provider is a unique feature of F#.

Basically, type provider is a type of generators. It generates types (classes) to be used in code specific to special purposes. Some of the classes remain available in the runtime; some of them don't (get erased).

The type provider feature begins with F# 3.0 release, and it is the main theme of F# 3.0 release: solving the data manipulation problem. The specific *problem* in data manipulation problem is how we handle the data's metadata information while focusing on the correctness of syntaxes and type safety. The type safety, in this sense, does not have to be strict or even strong, it is also available as erased typed as object.

Using type provider implementations, we expect that when we use data, the information about the data itself (metadata) is available as we are using it. For example, having a type provider for SQL Server database will give us the table and the name of the column metadata to be available for us when we are using the type provider. This metadata information is available at development type immediately as the type provider is translating the schema information of SQL Server database metadata into types and properties available immediately.

This is the starting point of F# type provider documentation on MSDN Library:

```
https://docs.microsoft.com/en-us/dotnet/articles/fsharp/tutorials/type-provi
ders/index
```

In a simple definition, *type provider is a combination of language and library features that describe the information to represent data, including the types and its properties*. This is also one of the unique selling points of type providers: the ability to present type metadata of a data into the language immediately.

Type providers will provide the type resolution at compile time immediately, and this is different from the implementation of other code generators that perform type generations as well. This is also unique in F# compared to other managed programming languages on.NET such as C#/VB.

In the long definition, type provider is a design-time component that provides a computed space of types. Therefore, Intellisense is available immediately. All of the types are strongly typed at design time, and it can be carried on at runtime if the generative type provider strategy is used instead of the erased strategy that treats all of the generated types as objects (System.Object in .NET BCL).

Therefore, the following are the goals of type providers:

1. To provide more information on the data accessed from external source.
2. To provide more metadata information to be available immediately as part of the language, as type with its properties.
3. To make the type provided available as strongly typed in order to be used in the editor. This is possible because before the type provided is available in the editor, it is processed and compiled first; hence it is also available to be inferred.
4. To make the type provided to be explicitly available at compile time. This is crucial because a type provider must be available at compile time because the resulting type provided must be available immediately to be used when we type in the editor of Visual Studio, as related to point 3.

Point 3 is crucial because the type provider is doing its processing while in the editor as we type our code (as long as we compile our references and provide the type provider initialization first). This gives F# type provider strong and unique advantages.

The following are the unique advantages of type providers:

1. Type resolved is immediately available in the editor when writing code (in the IDE editing session).
2. Since type resolved is immediately available in the editor, type inference is also available immediately, and this gives us the availability of Visual Studio's Intellisense of the resulting generated type (either using erased or generative). This is closely related to the third goal of type providers: the type provided is available strongly typed.
3. The type provided includes not just properties but also additional necessary methods as well.
4. There is no code generation when providing type generation.
5. The implemented type provider is compatible with other managed programming languages as well, although the implementation of a type provider itself cannot be done outside an F# project.

Point 2 is crucial because if the type resolved does not provide the properties and the methods correctly, and if the metadata provided does not match the intention of the type providers, the type provider is not a good type provider and the resulting type might not work as expected.

Point 3 is important because of the fact that the resulting type provided is available immediately, not requiring us to rebuild the whole project (or related generated code's project).

We may conclude that the F# type provider can be used to tame the sea of information into more meaningful data with the agreed schema and metadata directly into our experience of writing the code, and this is also often mentioned in the documentation of Microsoft's Visual F#, and it was introduced particularly from F# creator Don Syme in his Build 2011 conference presentation session of F# 3.0.

For more information on Don Syme's Build 2011 F# 3.0 talk, this is the presentation's landing page on Channel 9:

```
https://channel9.msdn.com/Events/Build/BUILD2011/SAC-904T
```

The following diagram illustrates an abstract picture of F# type provider:

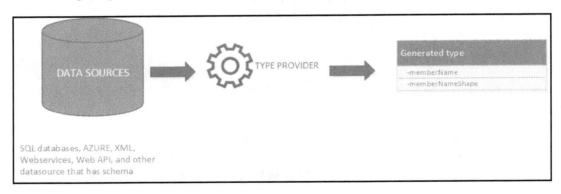

F# itself has type provider implementations built in since F# 3.0 under the `FSharp.Data.TypeProviders` namespace and the `FSharp.Data.TypeProviders.dll` assembly.

 We must use the `Microsoft.FSharp.Data.TypeProviders` namespace if it is going to be used in outside F# projects, because the compiled name is `Microsoft.FSharp.Data.TypeProviders`. This namespace name is not related to the name of the `FSharp.Data.TypeProviders` as assembly.

There are other type providers as well, and most outside F# type providers are managed under the governance of F# Foundations as community projects. All of these community projects are hosted on GitHub and we all are encouraged to contribute as well.

These are the ecosystems of F# type providers that we have in the first half of 2016:

- F# Data (for CSV, HTML, WorldBank)
- F# Data Toolbox (for Twitter and SAS)
- FSharp.Management (for WMI, Registry, Powershell, and Windows filesystem)
- Azure Storage type provider

To keep up with the latest development of these community projects under F# Foundations, please visit: `http://fsprojects.github.io/`.

We can conclude that there are some common scenarios where a type provider is the best fit:

- Accessing data from an external source in the form of a strong type JSON returned from web API. For example, World Bank data.
- Accessing data from predefined schema. For example, well-defined XML and its derivatives, such as XML DataSet (XSD) and XSL.
- Accessing data with predefined data format defined and documented. The way to access the data has a predefined protocol and its own query dialect. For example, returning data from Windows Management Instrumentation query (often called WMI query) using WMI protocol with its own query language, WQL.

Let's dive into the details of why the third advantage of type providers is important and comparison with other type generators as well.

Comparing the type provider with other type generators

F# type provider is not the only sample of advanced type generator. Type generators are commonly found in modern software platform ecosystems (including the tooling), such as .NET/Visual Studio, Java/Eclipse, and Mono/Xamarin Studio.

Type generators in F# type providers do not employ a code generator as compared to other type generator models. They rely on the compiler and tooling infrastructure at compile time. The type provided is not just immediately available but is also flexible to outside changes by simply rebuilding the project.

This is in contrast to many type generators that employ code generation strategy.

The following diagram illustrates the abstract working of these two type generators:

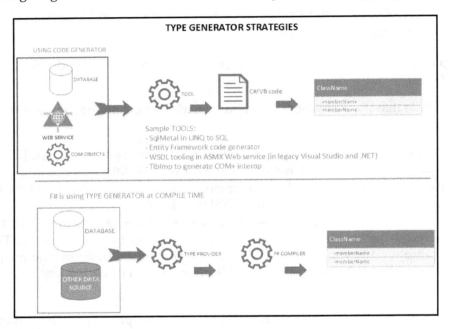

For example, Entity Framework 6 (using the database first and model first), SqlMetal in LINQ to SQL, TLBIMP to yield COM interop objects, and legacy web service reference (before Visual Studio 2010) are implemented using code generators.

Entity Framework 6's first database and model heavily rely on code generators to ensure the availability of the types mapped as classes from the underlying database, and this is normal and is intended as is because the mapping between database and the mapped object is manual, including the constructions of constraint mappings.

The design mode model uses a combination of EDMX and CSDL/SSDL files, which is completely generated as code, and we should not modify the CSDL file directly because it will always be overridden with the changes in EDMX file.

The same fact also applies with the WSDL/ASMX of the legacy web service in the previous version of Visual Studio before VS 2010. The ASMX file generated is also employing code generations, and they have their own translations that map the C#/VB code to the SOAP header envelopes. The resulting mapping code of WSDL/ASMX is closely linked as tightly integrated, and we should not modify the ASMX directly as we usually focus on the code behind the `asmx.cs` or the `asmx.vb` file. The modifications on the references of the ASMX will always override the generated references of the WSDL file, and this is quite cumbersome and might be error-prone because the code generations of the web services depend on the project that has the original ASMX.

Interoperability with other managed programming languages

The type provider is fully compatible with other managed programming languages that run on top of .NET CLR. Not just because it's implemented as managed language on top of CLR, but it is essentially the same CLR-compliant assembly.

But there is a caveat: when the F# type provider is used in other managed languages directly, it will not yield the Intellisense feature. Why? Because the type provided by F# type provider is available based on the specific attribute of `[<assembly:TypeProviderAssembly>]`, and this attribute is handled by F# compiler in Visual Studio IDE when the project is rebuilt.

This attribute in this assembly scope is important because this attribute is telling the F# compiler that *the type provided by F# type provider is added at compile time.*

It is important to know that only the F# compiler has the capability of adding additional type metadata as part of the resulting type provided using the attribute of `TypeProviderAssembly`. This means that we cannot use the F# type provider directly in other managed languages because their compilers must have the capability to identify the type provider-related assembly, and the whole compiler infrastructure has to match F# compiler infrastructure.

We can simply add references by adding our F# code that use the type library as a library/assembly references to our C#/VB projects.

Understanding the type provider building blocks

A predefined data source that has very good established documentations and strong conventions such as SQL Server database and **Windows Management Instrumentation (WMI)** is one of the best samples to have type provider implementations because all of the necessary descriptions of the data and the way to access it is documented extensively in detail.

For more information about WMI, consult the MSDN Library at

`https://msdn.microsoft.com/en-us/library/aa394572(v=vs.85).aspx`

Let's visit the minimum requirements of type provider implementation.

Minimum requirements of type providers

We have discussed the importance of certain restrictions on how a type provider should get the data. Now let's wrap the minimum requirements.

A successful type provider is expected to have the following traits:

1. The type provided must not be statically coded, it should be able to adapt immediately based on the defined parameters. For example, a connection string of a database server, which is then used to provide configuration for the type provided by SQL tables and its columns.
2. Related to point 1, the parameter to be used as base configuration must be specified. Therefore, there is no default parameterless constructor for any type provider because the configuration must be specified.
3. The schema mapping or the type and property mapping must be defined to be strongly typed even though the resulting type provided does not have to be strongly typed.
4. The mapping has to be carefully designed not to add irrelevant type information because it will add overheads on type instantiation. However, for erased type providers, the mapping properties and methods might be optional.
5. The provided type is always a type that has a setter and getter, and it is therefore not a standard F# type; it is actually a class. Related to the preceding point, the properties of the classes should be as simple as possible, and the class should only contain properties, not properties and methods.

Point 2 is crucial and very important. Fortunately, F# requires us by default to always use type providers with a constructor that has a parameter to be supplied. The parameter itself cannot be `null`; otherwise, the type provider cannot produce a type with metadata successfully and will always yield a breaking exception and undesirable results.

Point 3 of schema mapping defines how we implement the resulting type provided by a type provider. This is also defined as a general strategy for implementing type providers.

Strategies of type provider implementation

The type provider implementation strategies fall into the following two conceptual strategies:

- **Generative type providers**: The generated type provided is also available at runtime; therefore, the type metadata information of the type provided is always available at runtime. The assembly can be referenced by other assemblies because the type information metadata is kept. The reference is also fully compatible with other managed programming languages as well because the type metadata of the provided type is fully resolved and the assembly itself is fully available to use on top of the normal .NET CLR-compliant.

- **Erased type providers**: The generated type provided metadata is erased at runtime. This means the type provided metadata information is not available at runtime. The consequence of erased type provider is quite obvious: all generated types will always be typed as an object type at runtime. This is useful when generating type providers for semi-unstructured data and when the focus of resulting type provided metadata is less than the resulting data. This erased type strategy is also a recommended strategy to implement type providers for types that focus on the object's behaviors (the methods and the inherited methods) instead of the object's properties. Focusing on the object's behaviors means that we only care about what the object can do, instead of its properties and attributes.

These two strategies are also defined as how you implement a type provider because it must be chosen at first, as it will affect the returning type.

All of the returning provided types result as assemblies. Erased type and generative type provider requires more work in the sense of implementations because they require more careful planning on how the generated type is returned.

The next section will give us a deeper overview of choosing strategies.

Choosing strategies of type provider implementation

Before we dive deeper and start planning the implementation of type providers, we should choose one of the two strategies. There is no strategy that has a combination of both of them because this will again define the resulting provided type.

The high-level overview of the reason for choosing between erased and generative type provider is already provided by Microsoft in this MSDN Library:

```
https://docs.microsoft.com/en-us/dotnet/articles/fsharp/tutorials/type-provider
s/creating-a-type-provider
```

But unfortunately, the explanation on the reason for choosing the erased type provider is not quite clear. Check out the following definition:

> *When you are writing a provider for an information space that is so large and interconnected that it isn't technically feasible to generate real .NET types for the information space.*

This definition may look simple but it is not enough to quickly understand. The term *so large* should be more explained in detail, along with *interconnected*.

Why? The definition might have ambiguous meanings/semantics. These are the ambiguous semantics:

- In what sense is the data *so large*? The volume or the number of data?
- What is the meaning of interconnected? Is it connected by the data itself or does the data come from multiple sources?

The term large data and interconnected will be explained as part of the detailed reasons why we decide to use erased type provider.

Erased type provider is best for the following cases:

1. You don't care much about the format and the structure of the data returned. This also applies for unstructured data. Some common cases are if the metadata does not matter much and also if the data itself is unstructured. For example, having a type provider for Twitter feeds as it's mostly unstructured.

2. The volume of data is too large: you don't care about the type and the format of structure of the data because the volume of data to be mapped is so large, and it is not quite feasible or even efficient to try generating strong and strict type provided as the result. For example, the returning semi-structured data from World Bank or NASA Hubble images with metadata. This is a very huge dataset, and the volume for each data item for each row itself is already very large. From the perspective of NASA Hubble images, one image can have a size ranging from 100 MB to more than 500 MB, and one stream of data can be hundreds of images. In this case, it is also related to point 1 because most images are unstructured; therefore, it fits in point 1 and this point 2. This is also the same semantic in the term *so large*; it is so large in terms of the volume of data, *not in the number of data*.

3. You don't care about the format of the data because the format of the data itself often changes. This is common when getting data from querying social media. For example, querying data from Facebook using the Facebook API is quite challenging because Facebook keeps changing its API specifications almost once every year. Choosing a generative type provider is not fit for this because generative type provider implicitly requires us to have a tight coupling in the types and hence the assembly generated.

4. The data that you query contains heavy relations that links to themselves not just with normal JOIN clauses or SQL EQUI JOIN clauses but may also contain a recursive relation to itself. This scenario is common when we are defining a structure inside an unstructured data by examining the content of the data and extracting some part of it. For example, a tweet from a stream of Twitter may contain hashtags that might be linked, and the link might be loosely linked or it can be categorized into a higher category. This is the same as *interconnected* as defined in the MSDN documentation in the type provider tutorial.

When we define large datasets, we can argue about the size. But even in today's age of ubiquitous cheap large storage and high speed Internet (broadband), having to analyze data larger than 100 MB for each row is still very large and takes a lot of time to process even just to read it. This is crucial because the speed of storage can't keep up with the memory and CPU speed as the size of data to be read takes long time to process before it is put into memory. Also, type providers usually work best to handle data to be represented in the code and this will increase CPU time or I/O overheads because of the activities of querying large data and subsequently processing it into types with properties mapped from the data source.

For more definition on SQL EQUI JOIN clauses (including various SQL LEFT/RIGHT JOIN), visit MSDN Library at:

```
https://msdn.microsoft.com/en-us/library/ms177634.aspx
```

Grasping the basic concept of type provider is quite hard because you have to understand the internal works on how the type is provided and also how the type is constructed. It is easier to understand the concept by simultaneously looking at the documentation and also trying the samples of type providers.

It is also strongly recommended for all of us that in order to use the samples of type providers, we should use the built-in type provider in F#, `FSharp.Data.TypeProvider`. This is also very useful because this built-in type provider is supported by Microsoft.

The disadvantages of erased type provider are as follows:

- The returning type provider may be resolved as an object. This is intentional because of the erased nature of type provided.
- The assembly generated from an erased type provider is available in the F# project environment. This means that you cannot reference the erased type provider to other non-F# projects such as C#/VB projects, unless you combine the property of the erased type to have generative properties using normal CLR objects instead of F# record type.

A combination of erased and generative type providers is quite common in order to have an implementation of mixing the best advantages of both the strategies. We shall see that this is relevant in the next section of implementing our own custom type provider, later in this chapter.

A good sample of F# erased type provider implementation is the `FSharp.Extras` library provided by Forkmann.

The latest version of the library does not have the original type provider version included, but it is still there in the GitHub repo under the branch name of `VS2012`. This `VS2012` branch's library has type provider supports for the following:

- Regex (the regex model is using .NET BCL regex)
- XML
- Excel
- Registry
- JSON

We have grasped the reasoning behind erased type providers; let's visit the reasoning behind generative type providers.

Generative type providers are more powerful and this greater power comes with its own expenses: it requires more works to construct and it's also stricter than the erased type provider.

Now let's see the existing type provider (built-in) that F# has.

Sample usage of built-in type provider in F#

Let's try the existing F# type provider and put it in action.

The following is the list of existing F# type provider supports in F# 4.0 `FSharp.Data.TypeProviders` (with the type that serves) :

- SQL Server database (`SqlDataConnection`)
- Entity Framework (`SqlEntityConnection`)
- OData (`ODataService`)
- WSDL service (`WsdlService`)
- EDMX or the Entity Data Model design file (`EdmxFile`)

Of all the built-in type provider supports, the easiest one to use is the SQL Server database support, using `SqlDataConnection`.

Quick sample of using SqlDataConnection type provider

We are now going to use F# SQL Server database type provider using `SqlDataConnection` by referencing F# type provider's DLL assembly, `FSharp.Data.TypeProviders`.

The name of the SQL Server type provider is mentioned as SQL database provider, and this is misleading. This type provider can only be used for SQL Server database and not for other SQL-compliant databases such as Oracle, IBM DB2. Throughout the rest of this book, existing F# type providers for SQL will always be mentioned as SQL Server database type providers for the sake of clarity.

The following are the requirements before using
`FSharp.Data.TypeProviders.SqlDataConnection`:

1. Ensure that we have SQL Server 2008 R2 (or later) installed. We need this because we are going to access SQL Server database data. It is recommended to install the instance on your machine.

2. Ensure that .NET 4.6 is installed correctly. This is important because the `FSharp.Data.TypeProviders` assembly in F# 4.0 depends on .NET 4.5 and above.

3. Do not modify the F# target compiler without checking the .NET Framework target version. F# 4.0 in Visual Studio 2015 is recommended to work with .NET 4.6, not .NET 4.5.

Point 3 is quite subtle but it is extremely important: `FSharp.Data.TypeProviders`, F# tooling, F# compiler infrastructure, .NET Framework version in Visual Studio 2015 have a tight coupling. For example, `FSharp.Data.TypeProviders` has support for .NET 4.5 or later, but all of the F# projects in Visual Studio 2015 by default have a target for .NET 4.6 and so does the compiler of F# 4.0.

Although `FSharp.Data.TypeProviders` can be used in F# 3.0 projects in Visual Studio 2013, backporting `FSharp.Data.TypeProviders` in Visual Studio 2015 for use in Visual Studio 2013 might yield compatibility issues when compiling.

The F# 4.0 compiler itself might yield different warnings compared to F# 3.0 compiler. Using 4.0 version is highly recommended because it has bug fixes, especially bug fixes on very long time outstanding since version 2.0.

Consult the F# 4.0 release notes at GitHub at
`https://github.com/Microsoft/visualfsharp/blob/master/CHANGELOG.md`.

To quickly get started, we need a sample database to be deployed on SQL Server. We can use the popular Northwind sample database that was originally created for SQL Server 2000. Download the SQL Server 2000 sample database installer from this official Microsoft's download link:

`https://www.microsoft.com/en-us/download/details.aspx?id=23654`

Install the installer. Then, go to the installation path of the installer and open the file, `instnwnd.sql` in the SQL Server Management Studio and execute it by running the script.

If the execution of database creation succeeds, then the Northwind database will be available on the left of Management Studio's **Object Explorer**, as shown in the following screenshot:

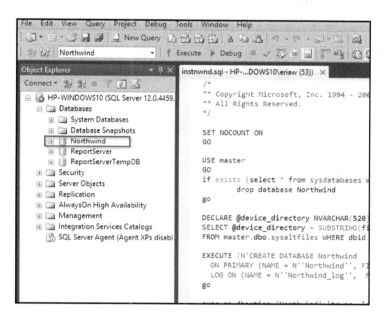

These are the steps required in Visual Studio:

1. Create a new F# class library project or console project. Do not create another type of F# project such as Silverlight or even Android, because it is not compatible with F# type provider target of .NET Framework 4.6.
2. Add references to `System.Data`, `System.Data.Linq`, and `System.Linq`. The physical DLL assembly filename for `System.Linq` is `System.Core.dll`, and the `System.Data` object's filename is `System.Data.dll`. `System.Data.Linq` is available in `System.Data.Linq.dll`.
3. Add references to `FSharp.Data.TypeProviders`. If you want to focus on F# interactive (scripting), then register the DLL manually using the `#r` directive.

4. Ensure that for built-in `System.Data`, `System`, and `Linq`, `System.Data.Linq` is properly referenced (as `System.Data.dll` and `System.Core.dll`).

   To ensure correct references, adding the references of `System.Core`, `System.Data`, `System.Data.Linq` is available in the **Framework** section under **Assemblies**:

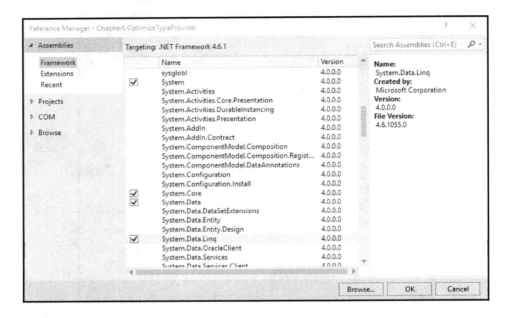

And adding reference to `FSharp.Data.TypeProviders` is available in the **Extensions** section under **Assemblies**:

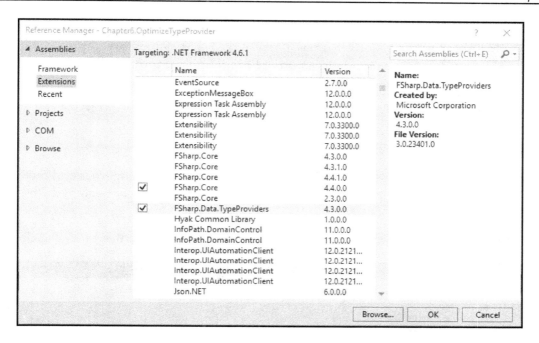

This is necessary because the F# built-in type provider assembly is not a part of .NET Framework 4.6 runtime distribution.

Create a new F# source code file and name it `SampleFSharpData`. By default, F# will treat this as a new file, which has a module declaration with the same name.

Type the following code after the module declaration:

```
open System
open System.Data
open System.Data.Linq
open Microsoft.FSharp.Data.TypeProviders
open Microsoft.FSharp.Linq

type NorthwindSchema = SqlDataConnection<"Integrated Security=SSPI;Persist
Security Info=False;Initial Catalog=Northwind;Data Source=localhost">
let nwdb = NorthwindShema.GetDataContext()
```

After the type declaration of `NorthwindSchema`, ensure that you have specified the connection string for the `SqlDataConnection`.

This `SqlDataConnection` is not related to `SqlConnection`, which is a part of ADO.NET's `System.Data.SqlClient` namespace. `SqlDataConnection` is a part of F# built-in type provider.

In order to quickly see the type provider in action, build or rebuild the project. Type this on the new line:

```
let customer = nwdb.Customers
```

At the time of typing *dot* after `nwdb`, Visual Studio will display the properties and methods of `nwdb`. The properties are actually the names of tables of the connected database, the Northwind.

This is the display of Visual Studio Intellisense, displaying the properties:

Now, let's continue to harness the SQL Server type provider by querying customer data. Change the code into this:

```
let customer = nwdb.Customers
let customerNameData =
    query { for c in customer do
            select c.ContactName }

let displayAllCustomerName () =
```

```
    for c in customerNameData do
        Console.WriteLine(c)
    ()
```

Let's call the `displayAllCustomerName` function. On the main `EntryPoint`, modify `EntryPoint` with the following code:

```
[<EntryPoint>]
let main argv =
    //printfn "%A" argv
    SampleFSharpData.displayAllCustomerName()
    0 // return an integer exit code
```

In the code of `customerNameData`, it contains an evaluation result of a LINQ query computation expression.

This LINQ query computation is essentially the same computation implementation of LINQ in F#. This query computation began with the release of F# 3.0 in Visual Studio 2012. For more information about F# LINQ query computation, consult the following link:

```
https://docs.microsoft.com/en-us/dotnet/articles/fsharp/language-reference/quer
y-expressions
```

Let's rebuild the project to ensure that re-references are correct and the dependencies are checked again. Run the code without debugging, and we will have a display of all the customer names:

We can also do additional queries such as adding the WHERE and ORDER BY clauses by translating them into LINQ in F#. For example:

```
let displayCustomerNameStartsWith prefix =
    let customerStartWith =
        query { for c in customer do
                where (c.ContactName.StartsWith(prefix))
                sortBy c.ContactName
                select c.ContactName}
    for c in customerStartWith do
        Console.WriteLine(c)
    ()
```

The WHERE clause is implemented as where and ORDER BY is implemented as sortBy.

Now let's use our little sample in another project with a different language, such as C#. This sample is also very simple but it is quite powerful because we will use our library that uses F# type providers with C#, although we cannot see the Intellisense provided by F# Type Provider compilation addition directly.

We need to perform the following steps before we use the F# sample type provider's code with C#:

1. Create a C# console project.
2. Add a reference of the previous F# class library project that we created with the SampleFSharpData module.
3. Add a reference of System.Data.Linq assembly.
4. Rebuild the project. This is important as you need to ensure that the added reference works well.

In the main method of Program.cs, add the calls to the displayCustomerNameStartsWith method. The main method should be coded as follows:

```
class Program
{
    static void Main(string[] args)
    {
        SampleFSharpData.displayCsutomerNameStartsWith("Maria");
    }
}
```

Run it, and we will have the same result as the previous F# project.

To check the inferred property of `NorthwindSchema` instances of `nwdb`, we can use the following code to test:

```
var customerData = from cust in SampleFSharpData.nwdb.Customers
                   orderby cust.ContactName
                   select cust;
foreach (var item in customerData)
{
    Console.WriteLine("Customer name = " + item.ContactName + ";
Company =" + item.CompanyName);
}
```

Now, we can see and prove that the F# type provider usages can be used in other managed programming languages as well, although it cannot be used directly. This interoperability sample is also a proof of point 5 of advantages of F# type provider.

It is also important to understand the implementation of `SqlDataConnection` because `SqlDataConnection` is a sample of a generative type provider because the generated type can be used with the full metadata information available (properties and methods).

For more information about using `FSharp.Data.TypeProviders.SqlDataConnection`, visit this MSDN Library:

`https://msdn.microsoft.com/en-us/visualfsharpdocs/conceptual/sqldataconnection-type-provider-%5bfsharp%5d`

`SqlDataConnection` itself is open source and is available with the other `FSharp.Data.TypeProviders` features. The GitHub repository of `FSharp.Data.TypeProviders` is available at `https://github.com/fsprojects/FSharp.Data.TypeProviders`.

Now let's go deeper into type providers by implementing our own type provider in various scenarios in the next section.

Implementing your own type provider

We already have enough knowledge on what a type provider is, the building blocks, and the nature of type providers, also understanding the nature of type provider implementations, including the implementation strategies, as we went deeper.

To ease the experience and our type provider building mindset, a real experience of quickly using it from existing samples has proven to be very useful. We have increased our intuition on how type provider works using samples from F# 4.0 built-in type provider features, `FSharp.Data.TypeProvider`.

Implementing your own type provider again is quite a bit tedious, especially when we are dealing with generative type providers as our choice of strategy.

The following are the common steps of implementing your own type provider:

1. Declare your type provider. The type provider must be `public`.
2. Mark your type provider's type with `TypeProviderAttribute`. You can simply use the abbreviated `TypeProvider`. This attribute is available in `Microsoft.FSharp.Core.CompilerServices`.
3. Implement the `ITypeProvider` interface. This interface is available in the `Microsoft.FSharp.Core.CompilerServices` namespace.
4. Implement the `IProvidedNamespace` interface. This interface is available in the `Microsoft.FSharp.Core.CompilerServices` namespace.
5. Implement your own code to handle a static parameter for the type provider.
6. Implement your own code to provide types, constructors, methods, properties, and fields, based on the static parameter used.

The `TypeProviderAttribute` provides hints for F# compiler to look for the necessary class that is intended as a type provider.

The `ITypeProvider` interface is essential and important because it provides the F# compiler the main entry point of the type provider implementation after having a hint of a type provider marked by `TypeProviderAttribute`.

Here are the `ITypeProvider` members and the added description (for clarification):

Abstract method	Quick remark
`ApplyStaticArguments`	Apply static parameters of this type provider to a provided type that accepts static arguments.
`Invalidate`	An event that is triggered when a type resolution semantic changes as part of initial type resolution of the provided type. It has the `IEvent` type.
`add_invalidate`	Add an event handler of `Invalidate`. It has the same semantic as the += syntax of C# event handler addition.

`remove_invalidate`	Remove an event handler of `Invalidate`. It has the same semantic as `-=`
`GetInvokerExpression`	Called by the compiler to ask for an expression tree to replace the given `System.Reflection.MethodBase` with. This is also important as `GetInvokerExpression` will be used as our entry point to provide reflection information of the methods that we are going to generate as part of the type that will be provided.
`GetGeneratedAssemblyContents`	Get the physical contents of the given logical assembly.
`GetNamespaces`	Return the namespace name that this type provider injects types into. This will be the namespace for all types provided. This is why it returns an array of `IProvidedNamespace`.
`GetStaticParameters`	Get all static parameters for this type provider.

To understand what the context of static parameters in type provider is, let's go back to the sample of using `SqlDataConnection`:

```
type NorthwindSchema = SqlDataConnection<"Integrated Security=SSPI;Persist
Security Info=False;Initial Catalog=Northwind;Data Source=localhost">
```

The string parameter in the `< >` brackets is the static parameter of the `SqlDataConnection` type provider. It is required in the case of `SqlDataConnection` because we need to apply the database connection string immediately when we are instantiating the `SqlDataConnection` type provider.

An invalidate event will be used by F# to trigger type resolution validation, and we can add many event handlers as needed.

Warning: It is highly recommended to add only F# event handlers within the F# syntax and semantics instead of C#/VB event handlers.

This is crucial because F# event handlers support implicit currying by default. Otherwise, undesirable results will occur, including unexpected memory leaks!

The implementation of code to provide types, constructors, methods, properties, and fields is tedious, not just implementing all members of `ITypeProvider` and `IProvidedNamespace`. We have to dive deeper into the inner workings of API in the .NET namespaces of `System.Reflection` and `System.Reflection.Emit`. This is crucial and important because types, constructors, methods, properties, and fields are all related to the reflection.

Fortunately, Microsoft and F# Foundation have provided a starter pack library to ease the creation of type providers from the start. The name of the NuGet package library is `FSharp.TypeProviders.StarterPack`, and we can simply use this library by adding it from NuGet.

To ensure the validity of the starter pack, use the `http://www.nuget.org` feed because this is the official NuGet repository that contains the commonly used .NET NuGet packages.

To use this NuGet, add this NuGet package on your project and accept the license agreement. If you have installed it successfully, Visual Studio will display the NuGet package under the **Installed** tab, as shown in the following screenshot:

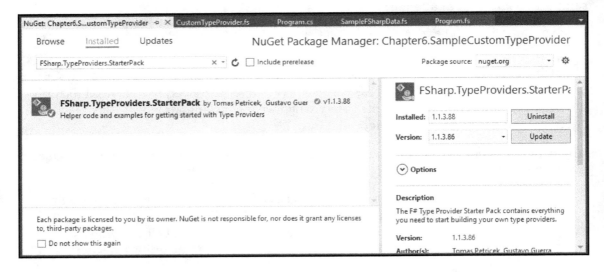

Now, let's dig deeper into building a type itself by looking at the internal working of this starter pack.

Building the type's building blocks

A type or a class in C#/VB is basically a blueprint of any object instance. It contains definitions of methods, properties, constructors, and other metadata of a class, such as the attributes applied on the type and its properties, methods, and constructors.

The .NET BCL provides us reflection API in the `System.Reflection` and `System.Reflection.Emit` namespaces. We can create the type's building blocks by lining up the calls to reflection APIs, but these calls to reflection API must have enough knowledge not just of ordinary methods/properties but also of the F# delegate, `FSharpFunc`.

Although the semantics are similar because of implementation in invoking the `Delegate` class of .NET BCL, the actual class used is different. Usually, to maintain high interoperability with other managed languages, we should use .NET's `Func` and `Action` instead of `FSharpFunc`.

As a common rule of thumb, *it is highly recommended to use Func and Action instead of F# FSharpFunc to provide a high degree of compatibility for the user of the type provider.* Having a high compatibility bar is important; otherwise, the type provider used will always need conversions from `FSharpFunc` to ordinary `Func` and `Action`, and this conversion will add overhead in using the resulting type provided.

By looking and examining the type provider starter pack, we see that it has organized the code into the following three files:

- `ProvidedTypes.fsi`: This file contains the type and function declarations
- `ProvidedTypes.fs`: This file contains code implementations
- `DebugProvidedTypes.fs`: This file contains helpers to simulate the running and debugging of type providers

We can further ease the development of our custom type provider by adding support for cross-targeting erased type provider or broader .NET **Portable Class Library** (**PCL**), while at the same time we focus on having a single entry of Factory method (based on Factory design pattern) of `ProvidedTypesContext.Create()`.

To add support for this cross-targeting erased type provider, we add these three files from the GitHub repo:

- `AssemblyReader.fs`: This file acts as a façade for reading .NET assemblies, including .NET PCL assemblies

- `AssemblyReaderReflection.fs`: This file act as a library of helper functions to deal with assembly reflection
- `ProvidedTypesContext.fs`: This file contains the entry of Factory method of the type provider, including the starting point of the `ProvidedTypesContext.Create()` method

After adding the preceding prerequisite files, ensure that `Program.fs` is ordered at the last file in the project.

This neat library provides the basic blocks: type provider base class, reflection metadata type helpers, and helpers to interact with type provider strategy. This library of classes of functions is also used as the infrastructure of how we generate type metadata because we need to prepare the necessary metadata generation infrastructure before we can implement a type generator. This infrastructure planning is crucial because a type is constructed with building blocks of assembly, parameters, methods, constructors, and properties.

At the time of writing this book, there were subtle but critical differences on the files of `FSharp.TypeProviders.StarterPack` distribution in the NuGet package and the current GitHub repo. If we only follow the NuGet package files, the current NuGet library requires us to manually wire the assembly reflection. The sample source code that complements this chapter is already correct to include the NuGet and the latest release on GitHub. It is strongly recommended to always use the prerequisite files from the source code, compared to using the files from the NuGet distribution.

Building type metadata infrastructure

Let's look at the type and function declarations first by focusing on the type provider base class. It is quite efficient because it has the implementations of `ITypeProvider` and `IProviderNamespace` for us to use.

The class name is `TypeProviderForNamespaces`. The type has checking for custom attributes as compiler directive. This is a must have because a type might have a custom attribute that may interfere with the F# compiler when it tries to process the type provider's type resolution.

Let's see the signature definition file (FSI) of `TypeProviderForNamespaces` (I have omitted the `FX_NO_LOCAL_FILESYSTEM` compiler constant check):

```
/// A base type providing default implementations of type provider
functionality when all provided
```

```
/// types are of type ProvidedTypeDefinition.
type TypeProviderForNamespaces =

    /// Initializes a type provider to provide the types in the given
namespace.
    new : namespaceName:string * types: ProvidedTypeDefinition list ->
TypeProviderForNamespaces

    /// Initializes a type provider
    new : unit -> TypeProviderForNamespaces

    /// Invoked by the type provider to add a namespace of provided types
in the specification of the type provider.
    member AddNamespace : namespaceName:string * types:
ProvidedTypeDefinition list -> unit

    /// Invoked by the type provider to get all provided namespaces with
their provided types.
    member Namespaces : seq<string * ProvidedTypeDefinition list>

    /// Invoked by the type provider to invalidate the information provided
by the provider
    member Invalidate : unit -> unit

    /// Invoked by the host of the type provider to get the static
parameters for a method.
    member GetStaticParametersForMethod : MethodBase -> ParameterInfo[]
    /// Invoked by the host of the type provider to apply the static
argumetns for a method.
    member ApplyStaticArgumentsForMethod : MethodBase * string * obj[] ->
MethodBase

    /// AssemblyResolve handler. Default implementation searches
<assemblyname>.dll file in registered folders
    abstract ResolveAssembly : ResolveEventArgs -> Assembly
    default ResolveAssembly : ResolveEventArgs -> Assembly

    /// Registers custom probing path that can be used for probing
assemblies
    member RegisterProbingFolder : folder: string -> unit

    /// Registers location of RuntimeAssembly (from TypeProviderConfig) as
probing folder
    member RegisterRuntimeAssemblyLocationAsProbingFolder : config:
TypeProviderConfig -> unit
```

Let's take a look inside the `TypeProviderForNamespaces.fs` file implementation (based on the signature defined in the preceding FSI signature).

We now visit the constructor implementation. The constructor signature is marked in the FSI by the notion of these `new` functions:

```
/// Initializes a type provider to provide the types in the given
namespace.
new : namespaceName:string * types: ProvidedTypeDefinition list ->
TypeProviderForNamespaces

/// Initializes a type provider
new : unit -> TypeProviderForNamespaces
```

These constructor definitions are implemented as follows:

```
new (namespaceName:string,types:list<ProvidedTypeDefinition>) = new
TypeProviderForNamespaces([(namespaceName,types)])
new () = new TypeProviderForNamespaces([])
```

The rest of the implementation code is strictly based on the signature convention. For example, the implementation of `Invalidate` is matched with the following signature:

```
member this.Invalidate() = invalidateE.Trigger(this,EventArgs())
```

The `Invalidate` is compliant with the signature of `unit -> unit`.

Now, let's discuss the details of the implementation of the `ITypeProvider` interface in `TypeProviderForNamespaces`. The F# language specification requires us to declare an interface implementation explicitly, and the implementation of interfaces used must be correctly indented.

The following code denotes an implementation of the `ITypeProvider` interface:

```
interface ITypeProvider with
```

The interesting part of the implementation of the `ITypeProvider` interface is the implementation of the `GetInvokerExpression` method. This method is implemented to traverse recursively (with a mutual recursive mechanism) to get the expression (as an expression tree of Abstract Syntax Tree) from the method that invoke it. Although the recursive is not required, using recursive in the implementation of this method is better.

The following code is an implementation of `GetInvokerExpression`:

```
    member __.GetInvokerExpression(methodBase, parameters) =
        let rec getInvokerExpression (methodBase : MethodBase)
parameters =
            match methodBase with
            | :? ProvidedMethod as m when (match
methodBase.DeclaringType with :? ProvidedTypeDefinition as pt ->
```

```
pt.IsErased | _ -> true) ->
                    m.GetInvokeCodeInternal false parameters
                    |> expand
            | :? ProvidedConstructor as m when (match
methodBase.DeclaringType with :? ProvidedTypeDefinition as pt ->
pt.IsErased | _ -> true) ->
                    m.GetInvokeCodeInternal false parameters
                    |> expand
            // Otherwise, assume this is a generative assembly and just
emit a call to the constructor or method
            | :? ConstructorInfo as cinfo ->
                Expr.NewObjectUnchecked(cinfo, Array.toList parameters)
            | :? System.Reflection.MethodInfo as minfo ->
                if minfo.IsStatic then
                    Expr.CallUnchecked(minfo, Array.toList parameters)
                else
                    Expr.CallUnchecked(parameters.[0], minfo,
Array.toList parameters.[1..])
            | _ -> failwith
("TypeProviderForNamespaces.GetInvokerExpression: not a
ProvidedMethod/ProvidedConstructor/ConstructorInfo/MethodInfo, name=" +
methodBase.Name + " class=" + methodBase.GetType().FullName)
        and expand expr =
            match expr with
            | NewObject(ctor, args) -> getInvokerExpression ctor [| for
arg in args -> expand arg|]
            | Call(inst, mi, args) ->
                let args =
                    [|
                        match inst with
                        | Some inst -> yield expand inst
                        | _ -> ()
                        yield! List.map expand args
                    |]
                getInvokerExpression mi args
            | ShapeCombinationUnchecked(shape, args) ->
RebuildShapeCombinationUnchecked(shape, List.map expand args)
            | ShapeVarUnchecked v -> Expr.Var v
            | ShapeLambdaUnchecked(v, body) -> Expr.Lambda(v, expand
body)
        getInvokerExpression methodBase parameters
```

The mutual recursive implementation of `GetInvokerExpression` is split into the following two parts:

- The first part is for the recognition of the wrapped objects, such as `ProvidedMethod` and `ProvidedConstructor`.

- The second part is for translating the expression from the first part into an actual invocation of the method or constructor.

For the first part, recursive is needed because the `methodBase` parameter at first is typed as `ProvidedMethod` or `ProvidedContructor`, then it will invoke the underlying method or constructor with the parameters passed by `parameters`.

This is important, and it is efficient because we do not have to loop through all the types of method implementation iteratively, and this recursive implementation means that it will give the desired method invoker information with the detailed granularity (either constructor, method, or lambda) as needed, without adding a break in the imperative `while` or `for` loop.

Then, let's look at the reflection metadata helper class's signature of the provided assembly, parameter, static parameter, constructor, and property in `ProvidedTypes.fsi`.

Implementing assembly to provide base assembly

First, we need to define the assembly. This is crucial as it is the first point we have to pay to attention because all of our types generated by type providers must have an assembly as the providers' host. The declaration signature to handle assembly generation is implemented in `ProvidedAssembly`. The following is the signature of `ProvidedAssembly`:

```
type ProvidedAssembly =
    /// Create a provided generated assembly
    new : assemblyFileName:string -> ProvidedAssembly

    /// Emit the given provided type definitions as part of the assembly
    /// and adjust the 'Assembly' property of all provided type definitions
to return that
    /// assembly.
    ///
    /// The assembly is only emitted when the Assembly property on the root
type is accessed for the first time.
    /// The host F# compiler does this when processing a generative type
declaration for the type.
    member AddTypes : types : ProvidedTypeDefinition list -> unit

    /// <summary>
    /// Emit the given nested provided type definitions as part of the
assembly.
    /// and adjust the 'Assembly' property of all provided type definitions
to return that
    /// assembly.
    /// </summary>
```

```
        /// <param name="enclosingTypeNames">A path of type names to wrap the
generated types. The generated types are then generated as nested
types.</param>
        member AddNestedTypes : types : ProvidedTypeDefinition list *
enclosingGeneratedTypeNames: string list -> unit

        static member RegisterGenerated : fileName:string -> Assembly
```

The implementation of `ProvidedAssembly` is as follows:

```
type ProvidedAssembly(assemblyFileName: string) =
    let theTypes = ResizeArray<_>()
    let assemblyGenerator = AssemblyGenerator(assemblyFileName)
    let assemblyLazy =
        lazy
            assemblyGenerator.Generate(theTypes |> Seq.toList)
            assemblyGenerator.Assembly
    let theAssemblyBytesLazy =
      lazy
        assemblyGenerator.GetFinalBytes()

    do
GlobalProvidedAssemblyElementsTable.theTable.Add(assemblyGenerator.Assembly
, theAssemblyBytesLazy)
```

For more information on what is a .NET assembly, visit:

```
https://docs.microsoft.com/en-us/dotnet/articles/standard/assembly-format
```

Implementing parameters for methods and constructors

The next step after handling the assembly is to examine the implementation of
`ProvidedParameter` (some comments removed):

```
type ProvidedParameter =
    inherit ParameterInfo
    new : parameterName: string * parameterType: Type * ?isOut:bool *
?optionalValue:obj -> ProvidedParameter
    member IsParamArray : bool with get,set

/// Represents a provided static parameter.
type ProvidedStaticParameter =
    inherit ParameterInfo
    new : parameterName: string * parameterType:Type *
?parameterDefaultValue:obj -> ProvidedStaticParameter

    /// Add XML documentation information to this provided constructor
    member AddXmlDoc           : xmlDoc: string -> unit
```

```
        /// Add XML documentation information to this provided constructor,
    where the computation of the documentation is delayed until necessary
        member AddXmlDocDelayed    : xmlDocFunction: (unit -> string) -> unit
```

We discussed the parameter first because the parameter resolution has to be defined carefully, since the parameter is a part of the method and constructor.

Implementing generated constructor

To have constructor support for our type provider, we must handle the construction of the reflection type of `ConstructorInfo`. This handling is done by `ProvidedConstructor`, which is a wrapper for `ConstructorInfo` and also extends `ConstructorInfo`.

The following code is the implementation of `ProvidedConstructor`:

```
type ProvidedConstructor =
    inherit ConstructorInfo

        /// Create a new provided constructor. It is not initially associated
    with any specific provided type definition.
        new : parameters: ProvidedParameter list -> ProvidedConstructor

        /// Add a 'System.Obsolete' attribute to this provided constructor
        member AddObsoleteAttribute : message: string * ?isError: bool -> unit
        member AddXmlDoc            : xmlDoc: string -> unit
        member AddXmlDocDelayed     : xmlDocFunction: (unit -> string) -> unit
        member AddXmlDocComputed    : xmlDocFunction: (unit -> string) -> unit
        member InvokeCode           : (Quotations.Expr list -> Quotations.Expr)
    with set

        /// FSharp.Data addition: this method is used by Debug.fs
        member internal GetInvokeCodeInternal : bool -> (Quotations.Expr [] ->
    Quotations.Expr)

        /// Set the target and arguments of the base constructor call. Only
    used for generated types.
        member BaseConstructorCall : (Quotations.Expr list -> ConstructorInfo *
    Quotations.Expr list) with set

        member IsImplicitCtor : bool with get,set

        member AddDefinitionLocation : line:int * column:int * filePath:string
    -> unit
        member IsTypeInitializer : bool with get,set
```

Implementing generated methods

Now, we can use the same constructor handling technique to implement the handling of a method implemented as `ProvidedMethod`. The following code is the signature of `ProvidedMethod` implementation:

```
type ProvidedMethod =
    inherit MethodInfo

    /// Create a new provided method. It is not initially associated with
any specific provided type definition.
    new : methodName:string * parameters: ProvidedParameter list *
returnType: Type -> ProvidedMethod

    member AddObsoleteAttribute : message: string * ?isError: bool -> unit

    member AddXmlDoc             : xmlDoc: string -> unit

    member AddXmlDocDelayed    : xmlDocFunction: (unit -> string) -> unit
    /// Add XML documentation information to this provided constructor
    member AddXmlDocComputed   : xmlDocFunction: (unit -> string) -> unit
    member AddMethodAttrs       : attributes:MethodAttributes -> unit

    member SetMethodAttrs       : attributes:MethodAttributes -> unit

    member IsStaticMethod       : bool with get, set

    member InvokeCode          : (Quotations.Expr list -> Quotations.Expr)
with set

    /// FSharp.Data addition: this method is used by Debug.fs
    member internal GetInvokeCodeInternal : bool -> (Quotations.Expr [] ->
Quotations.Expr)

    member AddDefinitionLocation : line:int * column:int * filePath:string
-> unit

    /// Add a custom attribute to the provided method definition.
    member AddCustomAttribute : CustomAttributeData -> unit

    member DefineStaticParameters    : parameters: ProvidedStaticParameter
list * instantiationFunction: (string -> obj[] -> ProvidedMethod) -> unit
```

Implementing generated properties

One of the natures of a type/class is the availability of properties (or attributes in the realm of OOP). Therefore, we need to handle the generation of properties as well, and the handling of properties is implemented in the `ProvidedProperty` class. This class extends `PropertyInfo`, and it also has additional functionalities that are quite similar to `ProvidedMethod`.

The following code is the implementation of `ProvidedProperty`:

```
type ProvidedProperty =
    inherit PropertyInfo

    /// Create a new provided type. It is not initially associated with any
    specific provided type definition.
    new   : propertyName: string * propertyType: Type *
?parameters:ProvidedParameter list -> ProvidedProperty

    member AddObsoleteAttribute : message: string * ?isError: bool -> unit

    /// Add XML documentation information to this provided constructor
    member AddXmlDoc          : xmlDoc: string -> unit

    member AddXmlDocDelayed   : xmlDocFunction: (unit -> string) -> unit
    member AddXmlDocComputed  : xmlDocFunction: (unit -> string) -> unit
    /// Get or set a flag indicating if the property is static.
    /// FSharp.Data addition: the getter is used by Debug.fs
    member IsStatic           : bool with get,set

    /// Set the quotation used to compute the implementation of gets of
    this property.
    member GetterCode         : (Quotations.Expr list -> Quotations.Expr)
with set

    /// Set the function used to compute the implementation of sets of this
    property.
    member SetterCode         : (Quotations.Expr list -> Quotations.Expr)
with set

    /// Add definition location information to the provided type
    definition.
    member AddDefinitionLocation : line:int * column:int * filePath:string
-> unit

    /// Add a custom attribute to the provided property definition.
    member AddCustomAttribute : CustomAttributeData -> unit
```

In the implementation of `ProvidedProperty`, we must handle all the characteristic traits and semantics of a property:

- Property setter.
- Property getter.
- Definition location of the property: This is very important, because the definition location of the property has the information of the type the property belongs to.

The visibility of a property and its setter and getter methods are handled further in the following override methods of `ProvidedProperty` in the `ProvidedTypes.fs` file:

```
override __.GetAccessors _nonPublic  = notRequired "nonPublic" propertyName
override __.GetGetMethod _nonPublic = if hasGetter() then getter.Force() :>
MethodInfo else null
override __.GetSetMethod _nonPublic = if hasSetter() then setter.Force() :>
MethodInfo else null
```

The methods, `hasGetter()` and `hasSetter()`, actually act as mini helper functions. These functions are implemented to check for the availability of the getter and setter in the property.

Again, the `ProvidedTypes.fsi` signature file is important, because it will give more meaningful information later when we are designing class libraries for others to use.

For more information about this FSI's signature file, visit:

```
https://docs.microsoft.com/en-us/dotnet/articles/fsharp/language-reference/sign
atures
```

We shall describe the significance of F# FSI more in Chapter 7, *Language Features and Constructs Optimization*.

Now, let's look at the implementation of the method provider, `ProvidedMethod`.

Basically, the `ProvidedMethod` class extends the `MethodInfo` class. Therefore, all of the operations and properties of `MethodInfo` are also available in `ProviderMethod`. The additional functionalities of `ProviderMethod` are implemented with the following design considerations:

- Handling of XML comment documentation of the method: This is implemented in the `AddXmlDoc`, `AddXmlDocDelayed`, and `AddXmlDocComputed` methods.

- Handling of special method attribute, the `ObsoleteAttribute`: This is not just a very useful feature, but it is also a necessary feature to warn the consumer of the method that the method should not be used anymore. This obsolete method handling is implemented in `AddObsoleteAttribute`.
- Handling the detection of `static` modifier on the method declaration: This is quite important, because the generation of a static method is different from a normal method and the handling should be explicit. The static detection is implemented in `IsStaticMethod`.

If we look back at the implementation of `ProvidedProperty` and `ProvidedConstructor`, the previous design considerations are also applied to `ProvidedProperty` and `ProvidedConstructor`, including the handling of the static modifier of a constructor, although F# does not support static constructors as part of F# language constructs specification directly.

`ObsoleteAttribute` can also be tuned further to enforce compile errors when the method is used. This attribute is useful and also strongly recommended to mark a feature that should not be used anymore, especially if the method has bugs.

For more information on the detailed usage of `ObsoleteAttribute`, visit MSDN Library at `https://msdn.microsoft.com/en-us/library/system.obsoleteattribute(v=vs.110).aspx`.

We are not going to dig deeper into the full implementation of this `ProviderMethod` type. We can add optimization to some methods. For example, we can optimize the `GetInvokeCodeInternal` method, a part of `ProviderMethod` methods operations.

The following is the original implementation of `GetInvokeCodeInternal`:

```
member __.GetInvokeCodeInternal isGenerated =
    match invokeCode with
    | Some f ->
        // FSharp.Data change: use the real variable names instead of
indices, to improve output of Debug.fs
        let paramNames =
            parameters
            |> List.map (fun p -> p.Name)
            |> List.append (if not isGenerated || isStatic() then [] else
["this"])
            |> Array.ofList
        QuotationSimplifier(isGenerated).TranslateQuotationToCode f
paramNames
    | None -> failwith (sprintf "ProvidedConstructor: no invoker for '%s'"
(nameText()))
```

We can further optimize the preceding code of `GetInvokeCodeInternal` to use PLINQ instead of non-parallel mapping of F#'s `List.map`.

To use PLINQ in our code, we must add a reference to `System.Linq` to tell the F# compiler to recognize classes within `System.Linq` namespace. We can insert the import of `System.Linq` namespace in the beginning of the open namespace declaration, so the namespace declarations in `ProvidedTypes.fs` file become like the following code:

```
open System
open System.Text
open System.IO
open System.Reflection
open System.Linq
open System.Linq.Expressions
open System.Collections.Generic
open Microsoft.FSharp.Quotations
open Microsoft.FSharp.Quotations.Patterns
open Microsoft.FSharp.Quotations.DerivedPatterns
open Microsoft.FSharp.Core.CompilerServices
```

We can now use parallel support in PLINQ at our disposal. To optimize the mapping using PLINQ, change the method body code of `GetInvokeCodeInternal` to the following:

```
member __.GetInvokeCodeInternal isGenerated =
    match invokeCode with
    | Some f ->
        // FSharp.Data change: use the real variable names instead of
indices, to improve output of Debug.fs
        let parallelizedSeq = System.Linq.Enumerable.Select(Seq.ofList
parameters, fun p -> p.Name).AsParallel()
        let paramlist = List.ofSeq parallelizedSeq
        let paramNames =
            paramlist
            |> List.append (if isStatic() then [] else ["this"])
            |> Array.ofList
        QuotationSimplifier(isGenerated).TranslateQuotationToCode f
paramNames
    | None -> failwith (sprintf "ProvidedConstructor: no invoker for
'%s'" (nameText()))
```

We have optimized the method provider to use PLINQ, to make the mapping of parameter to parameter name run faster because we do not care for the order of the parameter names. The call of `AsParallel` is actually an extension method. This extension method belongs to the `ParallelQuery` class.

The conversion of parameters (as F# list) into a sequence will add a small overhead but this overhead is highly compensated when we change the original map of `List.map` to use the PLINQ `Select` query because the `Select` method has the same semantic as the map in `List` and now the mapping is executed in parallel.

For more information about the `ParallelQuery` class, visit:
`https://msdn.microsoft.com/en-us/library/system.linq.parallelquery(v=vs.110).as px`.

For the generic parameterized version of `ParallelQuery`, visit:

`https://msdn.microsoft.com/en-us/library/dd383736(v=vs.110).aspx`

Although the generic type is not specified, the `ParallelQuery` class we used when calling the preceding `AsParallel` is inferred as calling a generic version of `ParallelQuery.AsParallel`. The type inference plays heavy lifting of the necessary flow of type information here.

It is highly recommended to always start from having the implementation of infrastructure of the type provider first, starting from preparing the assembly, parameters, methods, constructors, and properties, including other CLR type metadata information, such as adding supports for attributes and debug symbols.

The heavy lifting for reflection should be done carefully. In the next section, we can start implementing the basic custom type provider with minimum metadata supports.

Basic minimal implementation of type provider

Now, let's create a very simple type provider after we have done implementing all the necessary infrastructure of type metadata supports.

The easiest one is to create an erased type provider as a fundamental sample.

Let's create this sample named `BasicProvider`:

```
namespace ProviderImplementation

open System.Reflection
open Microsoft.FSharp.Quotations
open Microsoft.FSharp.Core.CompilerServices
open ProviderImplementation.ProvidedTypes

[<TypeProvider>]
type BasicProvider (config : TypeProviderConfig) as this =
```

```
    inherit TypeProviderForNamespaces ()

    let ns = "StaticProperty.Provided"
    let asm = Assembly.GetExecutingAssembly()
    let ctxt = ProvidedTypesContext.Create(config)

    let createTypes () =
        let myType = ctxt.ProvidedTypeDefinition(asm, ns, "MyType", Some
typeof<obj>)
        let myProp = ctxt.ProvidedProperty("MyProperty", typeof<string>,
IsStatic = true, getterCode = (fun args -> <@@ "Hello world" @@>))
        myType.AddMember(myProp)
        [myType]

    do
        this.AddNamespace(ns, createTypes())

[<assembly:TypeProviderAssembly>]
    do ()
```

Let's dive deeper into `BasicProvider`.

The following are the traits and reflection metadata of `BasicProvider`:

- `BasicProvider` type declaration has `TypeProviderAttribute` mark, as identified by using the abbreviated name of just `TypeProvider`.
- `BasicProvider` inherits from `TypeProviderNamespaces`. This class is available in the starter pack's helper of `ProvidedType.fs` file.
- The provided type has one property called `MyProperty` typed as `String`, and it has a static modifier. This means that this is a static property. We can also set this property to not static by setting `IsStatic` to `false`.
- The attribute's assembly scope declaration of `TypeProviderAssembly` means that this type's assembly is a part of `TypeProviderAssembly` and so is the project.

All these traits are matched with the requirements of the type provider implementation that we described in the previous section, *Minimum requirements of type providers*.

We have implemented a very simple custom type provider. It is quite simple in the sense that it has a basic support for namespace, assembly, public properties, and public methods.

Common pitfalls in implementing type provider

We now have enough knowledge of type provider, not just the concept of using a sample type provider and implementing a custom type provider but also that there might be pitfalls as well. In this section, the common pitfalls in type providers are wrapped as a simplified list with a simple explanation as well.

Common pitfalls in implementing type providers are quite subtle but these are important:

- Type provider strategy has to be planned first. The planning must also include the infrastructure to ease the metadata generation, whether it employs erased or generative strategy. *Do not* always assume that we can always provide generative type providers instantly. Failing to provide type resolution with the namespace will yield undesirable results, including erased type metadata.

- Reflection should use lazy implementation instead of an eager one. This lazy evaluation should not be combined with asynchronous reflection because cross-thread exception will occur and it can also lead to a deadlock as there is no guarantee that the reflection will return a CLR type that is fully CLS-compliant, from the type to the members (properties and methods).
- The use of any kind of TPL or PLINQ is encouraged when we are processing to give results as properties and members for each type provided, especially if we have to map a type to other types, such as the names of the properties.
- The implementation of type provider is not recommended for non CLI-compliant type, such as COM+ related types or types that are generated via `TLBIMP` of .NET SDK. An exception of cross-thread or even invalid object reference might occur, although the type generated may not be null.
- *Do not* use TPL/PLINQ when we are processing delegates. It might yield a memory leak because the delegate resolution is best handled as synchronous. This is quite subtle but important because there is no guarantee that the delegate is either unicast (normal delegate) or multicast.
- We should avoid F# units of measure implementation when a type with unit of measure is used as a type of the properties and parameters of the generated methods. Because in F#, any type that has *unit of measure is always erased at runtime*.

The last point about the use of unit of measurement is quite subtle because many F# developers tend to forget that the F# unit of measurement is an erased generic type.

Summary

We have the knowledge of type providers and insights of the internal working, while at the same time optimizing and avoiding the pitfalls of type provider implementations. We now have enough knowledge of the strategy behind choosing the erased and generative type providers at our disposal. It is quite important that we can optimize all of the internal language constructs, and not just know the functional programming style.

This is why we will now visit the optimization of the language syntaxes and semantics in `Chapter 7`, *Language Features and Constructs Optimization*.

7
Language Features and Constructs Optimization

When we code, it happens quite often that we are sunk into optimization details. We often have to focus on dealing with concurrency, performance/benchmark measurements, and profiling other elements such as memory consumptions. This focus on concurrency and performance/benchmark measurements is, of course, a big and important element of our code, especially concurrency. This topic has been described extensively in the previous two chapters: Chapter 4, *Introduction to Concurrency in F#* and Chapter 5, *Advanced Concurrency Support in F#*.

There are other elements in F# to be recognized as optimization opportunities, the language constructs that are commonly used in code and also advanced language constructs such as computation workflow. Language constructs, including the combination of semantics and syntax, are crucial too because we are directly dealing with them as we code. This chapter is dedicated to identifying performance optimizations in language features, focusing on language constructs.

Many F# language constructs are mostly trivial and they are already optimized, unless those constructs often require special care because of the subtlety of the implementation detail and also correctness, in the sense of having predictable results. Trivial constructs such as asynchronous workflow, list comprehension of `head::tail`, and list splicing are fully optimized, and often, to optimize further, we have to interop with other .NET libraries such as .NET TPL, in conjunction with F# asynchronous workflow, or dive further into the source code of F list.

When we are using F# collections, it's better to optimize on usage instead of optimizing the internal semantic implementations (the internal source code) as we already discussed in Chapter 3, *Optimizing Data Structures*.

This chapter focuses on subtle language constructs. We will now discuss these topics in optimizing language features and constructs:

- Overview of F# language features and constructs optimizations
- Optimizing common F# language constructs
- Optimizing inline functions
- Identifying tail call in recursive constructs

Overview of language features and constructs optimization

F# as a functional programming language has lots of language features. These language features also define the unique traits of F# itself, differentiating from other languages such as C#/VB.NET.

For example, the following are the F# language features related to functional programming:

- Pattern matching
- Active pattern
- Type inference (including type inference generalization)
- Inline function (also called function inlining)
- Discriminated union

Discriminated union is a language feature and it is also a type that is unique to F# implementation, although it is compatible with C#/VB.NET. The best practices of using discriminated union are already discussed in Chapter 3, *Optimizing Data Structures*.

By a simple definition, a language feature has the following elements:

- Syntax, the keyword and the usage
- Constructs, the overall unification of syntax and the contextual usage, especially when used within other language elements
- Semantics, the actual context and meaning of the code that has the constructs

We all know what syntax is. But constructs are quite subtle. The term *constructs* comes from the fact that syntaxes with identifiers and arguments forms a composite code that is heavily related to the syntaxes.

For example, let's examine the `if` syntax:

```
if boolean-expression then expression1 [ else expression2 ]
```

When we describe the syntax, it is by using an abstract concept such as `boolean-expression` or just an expression. We have highlighted the keywords for you: `if`, `then`, `else`.

Before we are going to use `if`, we have to understand the semantics of `if`.

The following information are the semantics of `if`:

- Within the `boolean-expression`, the expression has to be an expression that always evaluates to either true or false as this is also the nature of a Boolean type. It can be a direct value of Boolean itself, such as true or false, or it can be in the form of a symbol variable or as a function that evaluates to Boolean result.
- The expression after `then` means evaluate and execute the expression after the `then` keyword.
- The `else` keyword means to optionally evaluate and execute the expression if the `boolean-expression` is evaluated to be false.

The constructs of `if` as a sample is quite trivial, we just give a sample usage of `if` here:

```
if grade.Equals("A") then "Excellent"
```

The sample code means that the `if` construct uses the `if..then` construct, instead of the full `if..then..else` construct, as illustrated in this fugure:

```
if grade.Equals("A") then "Excellent"  ◄——————————  "if..then" constructs
if grade.Equals("A") then "Excellent" else "Not excellent"  ◄————  "if..then..else" constructs
```

Therefore, when we discuss constructs, it is often better to express it with a sample code, rather than using the abstract form of syntax usage and description.

If we look up and check F# documentation in MSDN Library, the syntax usage is defined using the common **Backus-Naur Form** (**BNF**) notation. This BNF notation is a notation to represent syntax definition and usage, originally taken from compiler theory in the realm of computer science discipline.

There are simplified and full notations of BNF, but for the sake of simplicity and to avoid confusion, we shall use simplified BNF. The simplified form is also commonly used in MSDN Library when describing programming language syntaxes, including those in F#, C#, VB, C++, JavaScript.

Some programming books use full BNF notation to describe syntax. It is also valid, but it is also quite confusing at the same time for people who are not from a computer science background. Throughout this book, we will describe syntax using the simplest form of BNF notation instead of the full BNF.

It is also quite common to use the angled brackets, [..], to denote optional syntax. In the context of our if syntax, the else keyword with the expression is also optional.

For more information on the overview of BNF notation, its variants, and the grammar of the syntax, check out this comprehensive article:

http://matt.might.net/articles/grammars-bnf-ebnf/

Optimizing common F# language constructs

When we are optimizing F# language constructs, the best way to start optimizing is to identify the most commonly used F# language constructs. This is quite subtle, but important, because commonly used F# language constructs are easier to understand and learn first rather than the rarely used or more advanced ones. However, we shall focus on the constructs that often have subtle performance impacts and recommended correctness to enforce predictable behaviors.

Predictable behaviors in the context of a running code means having predictable results on the entire flow of code, including when dealing with branches, switching execution contexts such as async and parallelisms, and having awareness on exceptions.

Let's visit the most commonly used F# constructs: active pattern, pattern matching, and delegate or function lambda in F#.

Best practices of interoperability of F# delegate with .NET delegate

Delegate in F#, as we have seen, is very useful and unique but at the same time it maintains the high compatibility bar with the .NET delegate.

As a matter of fact, the internal and actual implementation of F# delegates actually derives from the .NET Delegate class. This is important as F# has to be compatible with and maintain the underlying .NET CLR, and on the higher layer, compatible with .NET Base Class Library (BCL) that is defined in the mscorlib.dll and System.dll assemblies.

For normal functions implemented in F#, it should have planning in the future to define whether it will be compatible with C#/VB or is just available to be called from external F# compiled assemblies, or it is only used within its own compiled assembly.

The best practice rules with the related scenarios from the F# side are:

1. For functions that are planned to be called within their own assembly and do not have any direct use or reference to .NET delegate (for example, LINQ expression tree), always use F# delegates. This is faster than always mixing with the .NET delegate, although the function is always used within the assembly scope.

2. For a function that is planned to be available to be called from external assembly that is also implementing the whole F# compiled code and does not have any direct use or reference to a .NET delegate (for example, LINQ expression tree), always use F# delegates. It is still faster than .NET delegates.

3. For a function that is planned to be available to be called from any .NET delegate and does not have any direct use or reference to a .NET delegate (for example, LINQ expression tree), special care has to be taken into account, such as interoperability when the .NET delegate is calling the F# delegate.

4. For a function that is planned to be available to be called from any .NET delegate and also has calls to .NET delegate, use the .NET delegate model instead of F# delegate. This usage of .NET delegate is slightly slower than F# delegate, but the overall performance is compensated when the function is called many times from .NET delegate, while at the same time achieving the highest compatibility with .NET delegate and other managed languages, such as C#/VB.NET/managed C++.

Currently, there is no other known scenario for delegate interoperability other than the rules just mentioned. As long as we are aware about F# and other managed languages' feature parity, we are always guaranteed to have a high predictability. A best sample for this parity is the lambda function feature. This feature is available on both F# and most other managed languages such as C#/VB and IronPython.

Unfortunately, managed C++ has this full support for language lambda feature parity only since the release of Visual Studio 2013. It is good to know that Microsoft has provided extensive documentation on using this feature on managed C++.

For more information about lambda in C++, visit:

```
https://msdn.microsoft.com/en-us/library/dd293608.aspx
```

However, when doing interoperability with .NET delegate, avoid the following pitfalls:

1. Calling or mixing .NET delegates with normal asynchronous workflow. This will yield unpredictable behaviors because a .NET delegate is best suited within the Task Asynchrony Programming model of .NET Task asynchrony. F# has its own asynchrony without the need for using the same context switching model of .NET Task asynchrony.

2. Calling F# delegate/function that has implementation of asynchronous workflow from normal .NET method. This is fine, as long as the .NET method is not treated as asynchronous. But if the calling .NET method is implemented asynchronously, unpredictable behavior will always occur, and it might lead to race condition in the context switching.

3. *Do not* mix F# delegate within .NET unsafe methods. Unless we must have an unsafe implementation to a known Windows API, it is highly recommended to avoid this practice.

Let's do the real work of these delegates interoperability in the next section.

Passing a .NET delegate as an F# function

Let's start passing an F# function from C#, and this fits with scenario 4 for any function that is going to be called from C#.

For example, suppose we implement a function to get the row index of data from an `IEnumerable`:

```
open System.Collections.Generic

/// <summary>Get row index within a collection</summary>
let GetRowIndex (datasource: IEnumerable<'t>) (functionToFind: 't -> bool)
    : int =
    let paramcheck = datasource <> null
    match paramcheck with
    | true -> Seq.findIndex functionToFind datasource
    | _ -> -1
```

In our C# project, first add a reference to the assembly that has the implementation of `GetRowIndex`.

Then, we can import the namespace and use the F# function directly within C# using this sample:

```
using Microsoft.FSharp.Core;
```

```
using System.Diagnostics;

namespace Chapter7.DelegateInteropCSharp
{
    class Program
    {
        static void Main(string[] args)
        {
            var proclist = Process.GetProcesses();
            int index_devenv = FuncInterop.GetRowIndex(proclist,
FuncConvert.ToFSharpFunc((Process p) =>
p.ProcessName.Equals("explorer.exe")));
        }
    }
}
```

The preceding code will get all of the running process of our machine, then search for a process named `explorer.exe`.

When we pass a C#/VB delegate, it is actually a .NET delegate. But the lambda will evaluate as a different lambda that F# has; therefore, we have to convert our lambda expression parameter to `FSharpFunc` (F# lambda) before passing it.

`FuncConvert` is available in the `FSharp.Core` assembly under the namespace of `Microsoft.FSharp.Core.FuncConvert`. This helper class has enough converter methods that support all forms of .NET `Func`, as indicated by the signature symbol of `FuncConvert`:

```
[<AbstractClass>]
[<Sealed>]
type FuncConvert =
class
static member FuncFromTupled : ('T1 * 'T2 * 'T3 * 'T4 * 'T5 -> 'U) -> 'T1
-> 'T2 -> 'T3 -> 'T4 -> 'T5 -> 'U
static member FuncFromTupled : ('T1 * 'T2 * 'T3 * 'T4 -> 'U) -> 'T1 -> 'T2
-> 'T3 -> 'T4 -> 'U
static member FuncFromTupled : ('T1 * 'T2 * 'T3 -> 'U) -> 'T1 -> 'T2 -> 'T3
-> 'U
static member FuncFromTupled : ('T1 * 'T2 -> 'U) -> 'T1 -> 'T2 -> 'U
static member ToFSharpFunc : Converter<'T,'U> -> 'T -> 'U
static member ToFSharpFunc : Action<'T> -> 'T -> unit
end
```

For more information about F#`FuncConvert`, visit MSDN:

```
https://msdn.microsoft.com/en-us/visualfsharpdocs/conceptual/core.funcconver
t-class-%5Bfsharp%5D
```

Calling .NET delegate within F#

Now, what about calling a common .NET delegate, such as `Func<'T, 'U>`, in our F# code?

It is quite simple and straightforward, and it is also simpler than passing a .NET delegate as an F# delegate.

For example, we could call LINQ and pass the delegate parameter:

```
open System.Collections.Generic
open System.Linq
open System.Diagnostics
open System

let GetLargeProcesses() =
    Process.GetProcesses().Where(new Func<Process,bool>(fun proc ->
proc.WorkingSet64 > (8L * 1024L * 1024L))).ToList()
```

In the preceding code, the `Func` delegate is instantiated first, then the constructor is filled with the number of parameters and the correct type annotation, whether it is generic or not.

Best practices in pattern matching and active pattern

Pattern matching is one of the most commonly used language features/constructs. It is both a language feature and a language construct with syntax.

The starting syntax for pattern matching is as follows:

```
match expression with
| pattern [ when condition ] -> result-expression
```

The keyword `match` means to match the expression with the pattern below the `match` keyword. It is highly required for the patterns to be matched in order to have the same indentation as the `match` declaration.

Not all kinds of functional language patterns are supported, and this is already defined in F# 4.0 language specification. The full specification of F# 4.0 predefined/supported patterns of pattern matching is documented at:

https://docs.microsoft.com/en-us/dotnet/articles/fsharp/language-reference/pattern-matching

The easiest pattern to use is the constant pattern. The constant value means that the expression will be inferred as a type of the constant pattern as long as the pattern is consistently defining all the patterns and uses the same type of constant.

For example, let's write a code to convert *ABC* grade to the commentary report. Using pattern matching, this is the code:

```
let SimpleGradePattern grade =
    match grade with
    | "A" -> "Excellent"
    | "B" -> "Very good"
    | "C" -> "Good"
    | "D" -> "Bad"
    | "E" -> "Very Bad"
    | _ -> "undefined"
```

The grade parameter is inferred by the mostly used types of the constant patterns, typed as string. This pattern matching usage is common, and it is also easier to understand and easier to reason than using different types as constants. These common pattern matching uses of constants are also faster to compile because the type used as constants value.

To test on the type of grade parameter and the return type, we can use F# interactive. Simply highlight the code of SimpleGradePattern and press *Alt + Enter*. Then the type will be inferred as string -> string, as illustrated in the following screenshot:

```
 5    let SimpleGradePattern grade =
 6        match grade with
 7        | "A" -> "Excellent"
 8        | "B" -> "Very good"
 9        | "C" -> "Good"
10        | "D" -> "Bad"
11        | "E" -> "Very Bad"
12        | _ -> "undefined"
13
```
100 %

F# Interactive

```
Microsoft (R) F# Interactive version 14.0.23413.0
Copyright (c) Microsoft Corporation. All Rights Reserved.

For help type #help;;

>

val SimpleGradePattern : grade:string -> string

>
```

This inferred type is a proof that type inference flows nicely in a consistent way, as indicated by the use of string constants. The use of _ in the last pattern specifies that we should take care of the other patterns not mentioned, regardless of the content of the grade parameter. Omitting this will result in compile error because F# compiler always checks for all possible conditions in pattern matching and requires that all possible conditions in pattern matching must be handled.

Comparing constant pattern matching with if constructs

Some developers, especially when dealing with pattern matching, always compare pattern matching with a similar common language construct, the `if` construct.

The `if` condition construct is also supported in F#. It has an additional syntactic sugar, the `elif` keyword, to define that an else is immediately followed by the `if` construct. This `elif` keyword is the same as having the `else if` syntax.

The use of `if` is common in non-functional programming languages, especially in OOP languages such as C#/VB.NET/C++, because it implicitly enforces imperative as is usually found in OOP languages as well.

The `if` syntax in F# is defined as follows:

```
if boolean-expression then expression1 [ else expression2 ]
```

The following explains the syntax and semantics of the `if` constructs:

- The keywords `if` and `then` are required because they define the condition to evaluate and also what to do if the condition is evaluated as true.
- `boolean-expression` means that the expression is an expression that will result as Boolean, either true or false. This is required, and `boolean-expression` has to comply with the F# language specification for `boolean-expression`.
- The `else` construct is optional, and it does not have to be in the same line.

The official documentation of F# `if` specification is available at:

https://docs.microsoft.com/en-us/dotnet/articles/fsharp/language-reference/conditional-expressions-if-then-else.

Now, let's go back to our grade pattern. We are now going to convert our grade to use `if` instead of using pattern matching.

The code to convert our grade has to be written well to capture all of the semantics of `SimpleGradePattern`. There are many ways to write the code using `if`, but we are going to leverage `elif` in F#. This is the code:

```
let SimpleGradeNoPattern (grade:String) =
    if grade.Equals("A") then "Excellent"
    elif grade.Equals("B") then "Very Good"
    elif grade.Equals("C") then "Good"
    elif grade.Equals("D") then "Bad"
    elif grade.Equals("E") then "Very Bad"
    else "undefined"
```

To make the comparison more interesting, let's add more functions to test and to sample these constructs, comparing `if` with pattern matching.

First, we will use the `Stopwatch` object from .NET BCL of `System.Diagnostics`, by importing the namespace first, with the `System` namespace as well:

```
open System
open System.Diagnostics
```

Now, we will write a function to test the one pass running of `SimpleGradePattern` and `SimpleGradeNoPattern`:

```
let GradeBenchmarkTest() =
    let mutable swtimer = new Stopwatch()
    swtimer.Reset()
    swtimer.Start()
    for i = 1 to 5000000 do
        SimpleGradePattern "B" |> ignore
    swtimer.Stop()
    let timerSimpleGradePattern = swtimer.Elapsed
    swtimer.Reset()
    swtimer.Start()
    for i = 1 to 5000000 do
        SimpleGradeNoPattern "B" |> ignore
    swtimer.Stop()
    let timerSimpleGradeNoPattern = swtimer.Elapsed
    //Console.WriteLine("Elapsed SimpleGradePattern "B" =" +
timerSimpleGradePattern.Milliseconds.ToString()+" ms") |> ignore
    //Console.WriteLine("Elapsed SimpleGradeNoPattern "B" =" +
timerSimpleGradeNoPattern.Milliseconds.ToString()+" ms") |> ignore
    new
Tuple<Int32,Int32>(timerSimpleGradePattern.Milliseconds,timerSimpleGradeNoP
attern.Milliseconds)
```

The preceding code has the following notable elements of semantics and flows:

- The use of stopwatch `swtimer` as mutable. This is important because `swtimer` will be used and changed many times inside the scope of our `GradeBenchmarkTest` function.
- The stopwatch needs to be reset every time it is stopped and is going to be used again because we need to ensure that the timespan result at the initial start is reset to 0.
- The result of the stopwatch will be available after it is stopped, and it is stored in the `Elapsed` property, typed as `TimeSpan`.
- The use of `5000000` times iteration using `for..to` loop. The number of iterations is important because the nature of today's processor is so fast, and most sampling ends in milliseconds. Less than 1,000,000 sampling will yield less than 10 ms, and it will be hard to differentiate between pattern matching and `if` usage.
- We are using the same parameter of B to ensure that the code will evaluate as semantically the same (from the perspective of parameter and result).
- We are returning the milliseconds result as `Tuple`, which has two fields to contain `timerSimpleGradePattern` and `timerSimpleGradeNoPattern` results. The direct use of .NET Tuple instead of F# Tuple is chosen because this will ensure that the returning result will be used easily by the calling function.

The `Elapsed` property is using `TimeSpan` because it is used to store *the duration of time spanned*. This is important because `TimeSpan` can have a resolution from hours to milliseconds.

For more information on `TimeSpan`, consult the following page:

`https://msdn.microsoft.com/en-us/library/system.timespan(v=vs.110).aspx`

Now, we need further samples to get the average execution time of both constant pattern matching and `if` usage. To simplify calculating the average, we shall call `GradeBenchmarkTest` within a frequency value as defined by function parameter.

The following code tests the statistical sampling of the benchmark:

```
let GradeBenchmarkSamplingTest (freq:Int32) : unit =
    let mutable TotalPatternMatch : Int32 = 0
    let mutable TotalNoPatternMatch : Int32 = 0
    for i = 1 to freq do
        //Console.WriteLine("Sampling "+i.ToString()+" of
"+freq.ToString())
        let result = GradeBenchmarkTest()
        TotalPatternMatch <- TotalPatternMatch + result.Item1
```

```
        TotalNoPatternMatch <- TotalNoPatternMatch + result.Item2
    let AveragePatternMatch = TotalPatternMatch / freq
    let AverageNoPatternMatch = TotalNoPatternMatch / freq
    Console.WriteLine("Average Pattern match result for "+freq.ToString()+"
times = "+AveragePatternMatch.ToString()+"ms")
    Console.WriteLine("Average No Pattern match result for
"+freq.ToString()+" times = "+AverageNoPatternMatch.ToString()+"ms")
    ()
```

Let's run it by putting the benchmark to test by putting `GradeBenchmarkSamplingTest` with a high enough frequency sampling:

```
[<EntryPoint>]
let main argv =
    //printfn "%A" argv
    PatternMatching.SimpleGradePattern "B" |> ignore
    Console.WriteLine("Pattern Matching test")
    PatternMatching.GradeBenchmarkSamplingTest 30
    0 // return an integer exit code
```

To minimize friction with debugging, run without debugging by pressing *Ctrl + F5* and this is one of the sample displays:

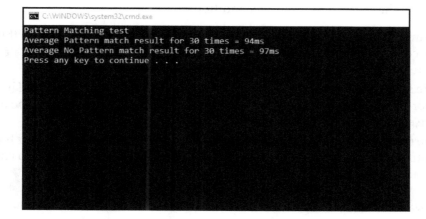

On my machine, under the configuration of core i7 4th generation with 16 GB of RAM, the `SimpleGradePattern` function (with constant pattern matching) is outperforming `SimpleGradeNoPattern` by a narrow margin results:

Sampling	SimpleGradePattern	SimpleGradeNoPattern
1	96 ms	97 ms
2	97 ms	97 ms
3	98 ms	99 ms
4	96 ms	98 ms
5	97 ms	100 ms
6	96 ms	99 ms
7	97 ms	100 ms

The results on your own machine may vary, but this result highly depends on the specifications of your machine, including CPU and RAM.

In order to successfully execute and sample timing sensitive benchmark, it is highly recommended to have the following preconditions:

1. Windows Update is turned off. On Windows 10, the best way to do this is to disconnect all your networks as Windows 10 will always try to update every time you are connected to any internet/network.
2. We should always run the benchmarked code without debugging. This will give more accurate results because the Visual Studio debugger will not be loaded, and the execution will be faster.
3. Turn off any Windows notifications. There are overheads when you have many notifications running in background, and this may affect one or two cores on your system.

On an average, `SimpleGradePattern` is 1 to 3 ms faster than `SimpleGradeNoPattern`. If you run this again, results may vary but in the overall condition, using pattern matching is better than using `if`. To understand why, we shall dive deeper into the resulting IL.

Let's dive into the IL of `SimpleGradePattern`:

```
.method public static string  SimpleGradePattern(string grade) cil managed
{
  // Code size       116 (0x74)
  .maxstack  4
  .locals init ([0] string V_0)
```

```
IL_0000:   nop
IL_0001:   ldarg.0
IL_0002:   stloc.0
IL_0003:   ldloc.0
IL_0004:   ldstr       "A"
IL_0009:   call        bool [mscorlib]System.String::Equals(string,
                                                             string)
IL_000e:   brfalse.s   IL_0012
IL_0010:   br.s        IL_0050
IL_0012:   ldloc.0
IL_0013:   ldstr       "B"
IL_0018:   call        bool [mscorlib]System.String::Equals(string,
                                                             string)
IL_001d:   brfalse.s   IL_0021
IL_001f:   br.s        IL_0056
IL_0021:   ldloc.0
IL_0022:   ldstr       "C"
IL_0027:   call        bool [mscorlib]System.String::Equals(string,
                                                             string)
IL_002c:   brfalse.s   IL_0030
IL_002e:   br.s        IL_005c
IL_0030:   ldloc.0
IL_0031:   ldstr       "D"
IL_0036:   call        bool [mscorlib]System.String::Equals(string,
                                                             string)
IL_003b:   brfalse.s   IL_003f
IL_003d:   br.s        IL_0062
IL_003f:   ldloc.0
IL_0040:   ldstr       "E"
IL_0045:   call        bool [mscorlib]System.String::Equals(string,
                                                             string)
IL_004a:   brfalse.s   IL_004e
IL_004c:   br.s        IL_0068
IL_004e:   br.s        IL_006e
IL_0050:   ldstr       "Excellent"
IL_0055:   ret
IL_0056:   ldstr       "Very good"
IL_005b:   ret
IL_005c:   ldstr       "Good"
IL_0061:   ret
IL_0062:   ldstr       "Bad"
IL_0067:   ret
IL_0068:   ldstr       "Very Bad"
IL_006d:   ret
IL_006e:   ldstr       "undefined"
IL_0073:   ret
} // end of method PatternMatching::SimpleGradePattern
```

The IL code in `SimpleGradePattern` is divided into two sections: the first section handles the conditions and the second section (after `br.s` in the line segment `IL_004e`) handles the return value as the destination of branches before `IL_004e`.

Let's dive into the IL of `SimpleGradeNoPattern`:

```
.method public static string  SimpleGradeNoPattern(string grade) cil
managed
{
  // Code size       122 (0x7a)
  .maxstack  4
  IL_0000:  nop
  IL_0001:  ldarg.0
  IL_0002:  ldstr      "A"
  IL_0007:  callvirt   instance bool
[mscorlib]System.String::Equals(string)
  IL_000c:  brfalse.s  IL_0010
  IL_000e:  br.s       IL_0012
  IL_0010:  br.s       IL_0018
  IL_0012:  ldstr      "Excellent"
  IL_0017:  ret
  IL_0018:  ldarg.0
  IL_0019:  ldstr      "B"
  IL_001e:  callvirt   instance bool
[mscorlib]System.String::Equals(string)
  IL_0023:  brfalse.s  IL_0027
  IL_0025:  br.s       IL_0029
  IL_0027:  br.s       IL_002f
  IL_0029:  ldstr      "Very Good"
  IL_002e:  ret
  IL_002f:  ldarg.0
  IL_0030:  ldstr      "C"
  IL_0035:  callvirt   instance bool
[mscorlib]System.String::Equals(string)
  IL_003a:  brfalse.s  IL_003e
  IL_003c:  br.s       IL_0040
  IL_003e:  br.s       IL_0046
  IL_0040:  ldstr      "Good"
  IL_0045:  ret
  IL_0046:  ldarg.0
  IL_0047:  ldstr      "D"
  IL_004c:  callvirt   instance bool
[mscorlib]System.String::Equals(string)
  IL_0051:  brfalse.s  IL_0055
  IL_0053:  br.s       IL_0057
  IL_0055:  br.s       IL_005d
  IL_0057:  ldstr      "Bad"
```

```
IL_005c:    ret
IL_005d:    ldarg.0
IL_005e:    ldstr       "E"
IL_0063:    callvirt    instance bool
[mscorlib]System.String::Equals(string)
IL_0068:    brfalse.s   IL_006c
IL_006a:    br.s        IL_006e
IL_006c:    br.s        IL_0074
IL_006e:    ldstr       "Very Bad"
IL_0073:    ret
IL_0074:    ldstr       "undefined"
IL_0079:    ret
} // end of method PatternMatching::SimpleGradeNoPattern
```

After reading the IL of `SimpleGradeNoPattern`, we come to the following conclusions:

1. All of the conditions of A to E (including `undefined`) are stored onto heap. This is normal and this is the nature of string, it being a reference type. Storing onto heap is indicated by the instruction of `ldstr`.

2. All of the patterns in the pattern matching results need a storage. The storage is prepared using `stloc`. This IL instruction will prepare stack storage, then all the condition results (the Boolean result) of A to E are stored onto the same stack. There is a stack allocation overhead at the first initialization, but this is compensated by using stack to load the value after the stack is allocated by calling `ldloc`.

3. In the code that uses `if`, the conditions result of A to E are loaded onto heap. This is needed for `if` because it needs a different location for each `if`, and it's faster to allocate the heap at the initial declaration in `if` because it will avoid stack allocation overhead. Then, the flow branches to the next instructions.

4. String in both the codes is evaluated using calls to the `System.String.Equals()` method. However, the interesting fact is the use of `call` in `SimpleGradePattern` instead of `callvirt`. This is subtle but different; `call` is used to call a static method of `String.Equals()`, while `callvirt` requires instantiation of string before calling `String.Equals()`. A static call is always faster to execute than method instance calls.

This narrow result of benchmark clearly shows and proves that using constant pattern matching is faster than the sequences of `if`, although it shows a small amount of difference in milliseconds.

We can safely conclude that it is common best practice to use pattern matching instead of `if` constructs for patterns that have the same data type and the patterns used are easily evaluated.

The results will be more apparent if the patterns used have many patterns, for example:

- 52 patterns of poker cards
- 7 days of a week
- 12 months of a year

And the semantic of pattern matching always enforces correctness by always enforcing us to evaluate all the possible outcomes. For example, in `SimpleGradePattern` there can be input outside `A` to `E`, and we can consider outside of these inputs as undefined or invalid. If we do not provide this information to satisfy the outside predefined conditions, we will have a compile error, and the code will not run even on F# interactive mode.

If we use too many patterns to be matched, then the code execution will be slower to compile and execute because F# compiler will try to parse the patterns used and search for unused/unidentified patterns; then, the IL code generated will add more overhead on branching, and branches with too many fall downs are not effective because later conditions will always be evaluated longer before the first conditions.

To relate to our example code of `SampleGradePattern`, the `E` condition is always treated to be evaluated after `A` to `D`. Therefore, too many patterns (especially above 10 patterns) will not be efficient, and later conditions, especially patterns nearing the end, will always be evaluated longer after previous conditions are evaluated.

To mitigate the slow execution problems of many patterns to be matched, it is better to refactor it and then we could use one of these:

1. A dictionary of key and value. The key will have to be treated like a unique primary key, and the value can be anything as long as it has relations to its key. This value can then be extended to be typed as delegates or F# functions to be executed when we search for a key that has values as actions to be executed.
2. A list of data typed as `KeyValue` pairs and this F# list is more efficient than the .NET dictionary because it will be stored as a linked list, with immutability coming by default and known recursive support by `head::tail`.

At the time of writing this book, .NET 4.6.1 does not have support for built-in read-only dictionary. Although we can use read-only collections that are parts of Microsoft's NuGet of `Immutable.Collections`, it is better to use F# list because of the nature of immutability, and it's faster to access than a .NET list as linked list. It is faster to access because the linked list implementation of F# list is faster than a normal .NET list in nature and it has support for recursive access within head and tails.

Best practices in using active patterns

Active pattern is one of the language constructs in F# that is very useful. It is often used in pattern matching and embedded within `if` constructs.

There are only two kinds of active patterns in F#: complete active pattern and partial active pattern. A complete active pattern is an active pattern that contains more than one identifier whereas a partial active pattern only has one identifier and the _ identifier to denote the rest of the conditions, much similar to the use of _ in pattern matching.

The syntax for active pattern is as follows:

```
// Complete active pattern definition.
let (|identifer1|identifier2|...|) [ arguments ] = expression
// Partial active pattern definition.
let (|identifier|_|) [ arguments ] = expression
```

For example, we can define an active pattern to contain even and odd number as pattern of *even* and *odd* like this:

```
let (|Even|Odd|) anumber = if anumber % 2 = 0 then Even else Odd
```

The operator `%` in F# means modulo, so the condition checks if modulo 2 equals 0 or not. If it equals 0 then it will be resolved as `Even`, otherwise (else) `Odd`.

We can then harness active patterns within pattern matching, for example:

```
let TestEvenNumber anumber =
    match anumber with
    | Odd -> "Odd number"
    | Even -> "Even number"
```

Now within our entry point of main, we can test with the following:

```
Console.WriteLine(ActivePatterns.TestEvenNumber 5)
Console.WriteLine(ActivePatterns.TestEvenNumber 6)
```

Run the code without debugging, and this is the result:

How does the pattern translate into raw IL? Let's dive into IL. Looking at the layout of the resulting output of IL Disassembler (ILDASM), we see this:

```
ActivePatterns
    .class public abstract auto ansi sealed
    .custom instance void [FSharp.Core]Microsoft.FSharp.Core.CompilationMappingAttribute::.ctor(valu
    TestEvenNumber : string(int32)
    |Even|Odd| : class [FSharp.Core]Microsoft.FSharp.Core.FSharpChoice`2<class [FSharp.Core]Micro
```

Based on the preceding picture, we can see the following interesting parts:

1. The module that holds our code, `ActivePatterns`, is defined as `public static class`.
2. The active pattern is defined as a method. The method references to a class of `Microsoft.FSharp.Core.FSharpChoice` with two generic type parameters (indicated by `'2`)
3. The function that performs the test–the `TestEvenNumber`.

Let's dump the IL of `Even|Odd`:

```
.method public specialname static class
[FSharp.Core]Microsoft.FSharp.Core.FSharpChoice`2<class
[FSharp.Core]Microsoft.FSharp.Core.Unit,class
[FSharp.Core]Microsoft.FSharp.Core.Unit>
        '|Even|Odd|'(int32 anumber) cil managed
{
  // Code size       24 (0x18)
  .maxstack  8
  IL_0000:  nop
  IL_0001:  ldarg.0
  IL_0002:  ldc.i4.2
```

```
  IL_0003:   rem
  IL_0004:   brtrue.s    IL_0008
  IL_0006:   br.s        IL_000a
  IL_0008:   br.s        IL_0011
  IL_000a:   ldnull
  IL_000b:   call        class
[FSharp.Core]Microsoft.FSharp.Core.FSharpChoice`2<!0,!1> class
[FSharp.Core]Microsoft.FSharp.Core.FSharpChoice`2<class
[FSharp.Core]Microsoft.FSharp.Core.Unit,class
[FSharp.Core]Microsoft.FSharp.Core.Unit>::NewChoice1Of2(!0)
  IL_0010:   ret
  IL_0011:   ldnull
  IL_0012:   call        class
[FSharp.Core]Microsoft.FSharp.Core.FSharpChoice`2<!0,!1> class
[FSharp.Core]Microsoft.FSharp.Core.FSharpChoice`2<class
[FSharp.Core]Microsoft.FSharp.Core.Unit,class
[FSharp.Core]Microsoft.FSharp.Core.Unit>::NewChoice2Of2(!1)
  IL_0017:   ret
} // end of method ActivePatterns::'|Even|Odd|'
```

Now, let's examine `TestEvenNumber`:

```
.method public static string  TestEvenNumber(int32 anumber) cil managed
{
  // Code size        32 (0x20)
  .maxstack   3
  .locals init ([0] int32 V_0,
           [1] class
[FSharp.Core]Microsoft.FSharp.Core.FSharpChoice`2<class
[FSharp.Core]Microsoft.FSharp.Core.Unit,class
[FSharp.Core]Microsoft.FSharp.Core.Unit> V_1)
  IL_0000:   nop
  IL_0001:   ldarg.0
  IL_0002:   stloc.0
  IL_0003:   ldloc.0
  IL_0004:   call        class
[FSharp.Core]Microsoft.FSharp.Core.FSharpChoice`2<class
[FSharp.Core]Microsoft.FSharp.Core.Unit,class
[FSharp.Core]Microsoft.FSharp.Core.Unit>
ActivePatterns::'|Even|Odd|'(int32)
  IL_0009:   stloc.1
  IL_000a:   ldloc.1
  IL_000b:   isinst      class
[FSharp.Core]Microsoft.FSharp.Core.FSharpChoice`2/Choice1Of2<class
[FSharp.Core]Microsoft.FSharp.Core.Unit,class
[FSharp.Core]Microsoft.FSharp.Core.Unit>
  IL_0010:   brfalse.s   IL_0014
  IL_0012:   br.s        IL_001a
```

```
    IL_0014:   ldstr      "Odd number"
    IL_0019:   ret
    IL_001a:   ldstr      "Even number"
    IL_001f:   ret
} // end of method ActivePatterns::TestEvenNumber
```

Yes, the Even|Odd class is defined based on registering the Even and Odd passed as parameters for FSharpChoice class. In F# code, this class is called Core.Choice<'T1, 'T2> because it has two generic parameterized types, and it is documented as a helper class to define active patterns.

We can deduce that there is a limit to the number of active patterns defined. The limit of the number of patterns is 7, as defined by active pattern documentation:

> *There can be up to seven partitions in an active pattern definition.*

The documentation for active pattern is available at:

```
https://docs.microsoft.com/en-us/dotnet/articles/fsharp/language-reference/active-patterns
```

F# Choice is powerful because it is used heavily in active patterns to effectively express our patterns as choices, which are then passed to Choice1of2 and Choice2of2 to be processed as the result of a choice. The kind of Choice class used depends on how many patterns we have as active patterns.

For example, three patterns used means that it will be translated into calls to the Choice<'T1, 'T2, 'T3> class, which then calls Choice1of3, Choice2of3, and Choice2of3 as needed.

Interestingly enough, all F# Choice classes are declared as discriminated unions. For example, F# Choice<'T1, 'T2> is declared as follows:

```
[<StructuralEquality>]
[<StructuralComparison>]
type Choice<'T1,'T2> =
| Choice1Of2 of 'T1
| Choice2Of2 of 'T2
with
interface IStructuralEquatable
interface IComparable
interface IComparable
interface IStructuralComparable
end
```

This means that `Choice` can also have the benefit of discriminated unions without having to redefine inner classes that go intermingled with generics embedded.

The most commonly used active patterns are patterns of two and three. This includes the implicit leverage of `Core.Choice<'T1,'T2>` and `Core.Choice<'T1,'T2,'T3>`.

For more information about `Core.Choice<'T1,'T2>` and `Core.Choice<'T1,'T2,'T3>`, visit the following links:

- `https://msdn.microsoft.com/en-us/visualfsharpdocs/conceptual/core.choi`
  `ce%5b'tl,'t2%5d-union-%5bfsharp%5d`
- `https://msdn.microsoft.com/en-us/visualfsharpdocs/conceptual/core.choi`
  `ce%5b'tl,'t2,'t3%5d-union-%5bfsharp%5d`

For the sake of correctness, the use of active patterns combined with pattern matching is recommended as long as the active pattern used is simple enough and the nature of the active pattern is a complete active pattern.

The use of partial active patterns is not recommended because:

- The rest of the unevaluated conditions will always be a fallback. This fallback of all unevaluated conditions might imply an uncaught error or exception, and this is not a good practice. All the conditions should be carefully thought and then handled as this will provide clear reasoning.
- Because of the nature of unevaluated conditions, any exceptions that may happen might be uncaught after the pattern is passed to the code that uses the active pattern. This uncaught exception is harder to resolve because our code is not in the correct context of where the exception should be caught.

Considerations in catching exceptions in active patterns

Uncaught exceptions in active pattern, no matter how subtle it is, are always expensive. The call stack preparations and the state will always lead to undesirable effects such as losing the previous states, including not evaluating the rest of the active patterns we have. Losing the previous states, especially losing the current execution state before the exception happened always leads us to execution termination, unless the exception is caught.

Catching an exception itself is expensive, but having an uncaught exception is more dangerous as it will always force our code to be halted/terminated. Propagating and then displaying the exception information (including stack traces) is common in many software applications that have GUI, in order to give user the information of what exception is caught.

In .NET BCL, the stack traces are represented in the `StackFrame` class. It will by default be always instantiated when we catch any exception. This is one of the many reasons *why catching exceptions is expensive*, because it will implicitly instantiate `StackFrame`, building information based on the current stack and call site and then hooking up the information. Hooking up the call site and the `StackFrame` itself takes some CPU overhead as it goes back and forth to the hooking up pointers and v-table of call stacks.

The `StackFrame` class is available under the `System.Diagnostics` namespace within the assembly of `mscorlib.dll`. For more information about .NET `StackFrame`, visit:

```
https://msdn.microsoft.com/en-us/library/system.diagnostics.stackframe(v=vs.110
).aspx
```

Now, let's turn our focus to optimizing one of the subtle language constructs of F#: inline functions.

Optimizing inline functions

F# has features of inline functions since F# 1.9, although the previous version already had it as experimental.

The definition of inline function is quite non-trivial: an inline function is a function that is *integrated* into the calling code. The word integrated must have a clear context; what kind of integration? It is integrated in the sense that the type is not generalized, but it is compiled accordingly when the inline function is used within other functions. The inline function body is embedded directly. This function embedding will be discussed in detail in the next section.

Before we discuss in-depth about inline functions, let's first examine the background of the importance and relevance of inline functions in the next section.

Background overview of inline functions and related type inferences

To understand this integration, we must know the background of how functions and arguments are evaluated first, especially if the arguments have no type annotation at all. When an F# function declaration has type annotations, the mechanism is simpler because the compiler will not perform any automatic generalization strategy at all. The evaluation of functions and its arguments are part of type inference mechanisms in F#, including automatic generalizations and inline functions.

Automatic generalization strategy is unique in F#, it is powerful but at the same time will put the burden of type inference on the compiler.

When there are type annotations applied in the function argument's declaration, heavy automatic generalization will not always occur. If the type annotation itself contains a normal generic type annotation such as `T, then the generalization is done partially because of the availability of existing type annotations in the declarations.

F# has further optimizations to use instead of having normal generic generalizations (including automatic generalizations) using inline functions. This inline function feature is a well-known and powerful feature of F#, although it is rarely used.

Overview of F# type inference mechanism of generic type inference

The most known aspect when writing a function declaration is writing the parameters without any type annotation at all. F# compiler infers the type using the following algorithm:

- If the function body contains expressions that employ common arithmetic operators such as additions and multiplications, the type will be inferred as Int32 by default. Any calculation that involves a rational number (for example, 2.5) will perform a type inference resulting as Double.
- If the function body contains more complex statements such as if and try...with, the type inference will perform an *automatic generalization*. The resulting signature will be similar to a C#/VB method that has generic types as parameters.

Overview of automatic generalization in F#

Automatic generalization means that type inference will resolve as generic when it cannot further infer as concrete types. In F#, automatic generalizations mostly happen when the type inference cannot be inferred further not just by the content of the function body. When a more complex construct such as `if` is used, the generalization will try to infer generic type, and it has more complex algorithms to prevent more generalization from using too many generic types.

Compiling a function that resolves as generalized parameters will generate IL for generic types, and the number of generic types is determined by the function body itself.

Let's examine automatic generalization samples from the simplest one.

The following code has `if` in the function body:

```
let greaterThan a b = if a > b then a else b
```

The type of `a` and `b` will be generalized and inferred to be typed as `'a`, because it assumes that `a` and `b` must have the same type due to the existence of > parameter in the function body.

This simple sample proves that automatic generalizations depend on the signature declaration and the function body.

For functions with type annotations that use normal generic type annotations, F# will try to check for the existence of a simple arithmetic expression and will infer it as long as the arithmetic expression does not contain another recursive call.

However, using generalization in a generic type will have its own disadvantages because generic type resolution is resolved at compile time but the user of the function might have a different use of concrete type, and this will add overheads in the compilation time and also small overheads when it is run. The runtime will always try to keep the original generalized type as is, and there is a chance that some type will be bound using late binding strategy instead of early binding.

For example, the `greaterThan` function might be called with different concrete types as long as the type inferred implements the > operator:

```
let intCompare = greaterThan 5 2
let strCompare = greaterThan "you" "me"
```

The late binding of type resolution will always add overhead to the overall performance, although it rarely occurs.

[270]

Do not mix late binding with dynamic typing. Late binding is different from dynamic typing; in dynamic binding, type resolution is done at runtime instead of compile time. Therefore, in dynamic typing languages, type resolution always happens at runtime, and it is mostly done using techniques such as combination of dynamic type resolution and call site caching.

To minimize the overheads of type binding at runtime (although the type resolution is done at compile time), F# has other features to replace the type of the parameter as a concrete type when the function is called by another function that has a concrete type resolved. This is called inline function, and it is described in the next section.

Best practices in implementing inline functions

F# supports *statically typed parameters*, not just normal parameters. The term, *static type parameters,* means that the type parameters are replaced with the concrete types at compile time instead of runtime.

This means an increased performance because the type is already filled in and there is no further generic type translation at runtime. It also increases correctness and predictability because the type is already inferred at compile time, minimizing the overhead of normal generic type materialization into a concrete type and at the same time providing a guarantee to be strongly typed at runtime.

There is a caveat: once we have declared the generic type parameter to be statically typed, we cannot mix with the normal generic type.

The syntax for this statically typed parameter uses a caret, the ^ symbol instead of the normal apostrophe ' symbol. Take for example the following function signature:

```
^T -> ^U
```

The statically typed parameter can be used only in conjunction with inline functions and methods.

In function/member declaration, a statically typed parameter is for all generic types used, so again there is no mixing with normal/common generics. For example:

```
val inline NonStructural< ^T > : IComparer< ^T > when ^T : (static member (
< ) : ^T * ^T    -> bool) and ^T : (static member ( > ) : ^T * ^T    ->
bool)
```

The `static` type flows into all usage, including at the declaration of the interface implementation used, the signature of the discriminated union, and the declaration of type constraints.

Let's start exploring inline functions. In this sample, we create a multiplication inline function:

```
let inline inlinemul a b = a * b
```

In the preceding code, we have an inline `inlinemul` function that takes a and b as parameters.

The inline functions can be implemented in defining custom operators:

```
let inline (^*) a b = a * b
```

In the preceding code, we have the ^* operator that takes a and b as parameters. The resulting semantic of sample `mul` and ^* operator is the same, and it is also the same from the perspective of IL implementation.

First, we need to verify the signature based on the documentation. To check the signature of the previous `inlinemul` function, we can use F# interactive.

After evaluating both `mul` and ^* operator, we have the following signatures in **F# Interactive**:

```
F# Interactive

  Microsoft (R) F# Interactive version 14.0.23413.0
  Copyright (c) Microsoft Corporation. All Rights Reserved.

  For help type #help;;

  >
  val inline inlinemul :
    a: ^a -> b: ^b ->  ^c
       when ( ^a or  ^b) : (static member ( * ) :  ^a *  ^b ->  ^c)
  val inline ( ^* ) :
    a: ^a -> b: ^b ->  ^c
       when ( ^a or  ^b) : (static member ( * ) :  ^a *  ^b ->  ^c)

  >
```

All generic type parameters are declared with a caret prefix instead of using the common normal apostrophe/single quote, '.

Let's extract and examine the declaration of `inlinemul` (with line number added for clarity):

```
01: val inline inlinemul :
02:   a: ^a -> b: ^b ->   ^c
03:     when ( ^a or  ^b) : (static member ( * ) :   ^a *   ^b ->   ^c)
```

Reading the inline function declaration might not be quite trivial, but it is quite straightforward to understand because it has predefined semantics within some syntaxes.

The following explains the semantics:

1. Line 1 defines an inline function declaration definition.
2. Line 2 defines function arguments signature that has a signature of `^a -> ^b ->` `^c`. It has type definitions to the effect that parameters a, b, and c are generic type parameters that are statically typed.
3. Line 3 defines constraints (using `when` keyword) for `^a` or `^b` to the effect that it must have a static member of the `*` operator implemented within the `^a` or `^b`. It means that `^a` or `^b` must have implementations of the `*` operator which has arguments of a and b.

Now that we have grabbed the contextual meaning of the inline function semantics, it is easier to see that type inference also plays an important role inferring the operation of the function, going deeper into explicitly adding constraints to define that the operator must be implemented in the generic type.

This constraint gives the meaning and reasoning why it is called statically typed parameter.

C# has comparable generic constraints keyword that are similar to F#'s `when` keyword, the generic constraint limiting of `where` keyword. This `where` keyword in the generic type constraint declaration/definition is different from the `where` keyword in LINQ because the `where` keyword in LINQ is actually translated into call to `Enumerable.Where` or `Queryable.Where`, depending on which LINQ provider is used.

Based on the definition of inline functions, the type will be made available at compile time: therefore, the type resolution is done at compile time. This will add some overhead, especially if the inline function contains complex operations.

Let's see these inline functions used by other functions, by creating quick symbolic properties to test them:

```
let MulDoubleTest = inlinemul 5.2 10.7
```

```
let MulIntTest = inlinemul 5 12

let InlineOpMultiplyTest = 6 ^* 10
```

Let's put these inline functions and the test functions inside a module, called `InlineFunctions`. Now, let's see the generated IL of the `InlineFunctions` module by using ILDASM:

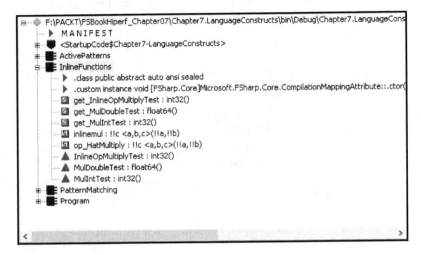

The compiled inline functions are compiled under the following names:

- The `inlinemul` function is compiled as `inlinemul: !!c <a,b,c>(!!a a, !!b b)`

- The inline `^*` operator is compiled as `op_HatMultiply: !!c <a,b,c>(!!a a, !!b b)`

Let's look at the IL of `inlinemul`:

```
.method public static !!c  inlinemul<a,b,c>(!!a a, !!b b) cil managed
{
  .custom instance void
[FSharp.Core]Microsoft.FSharp.Core.CompilationArgumentCountsAttribute::.cto
r(int32[]) = ( 01 00 02 00 00 00 01 00 00 00 01 00 00 00 00 00 )
  // Code size        13 (0xd)
  .maxstack  4
  .locals init ([0] !!a V_0,
           [1] !!b V_1)
  IL_0000:  nop
  IL_0001:  ldarg.0
  IL_0002:  stloc.0
```

```
IL_0003:    ldarg.1
IL_0004:    stloc.1
IL_0005:    ldloc.0
IL_0006:    ldloc.1
IL_0007:    call       !!2
[FSharp.Core]Microsoft.FSharp.Core.LanguagePrimitives::MultiplyDynamic<!!0,
!!1,!!2>(!!0,   !!1)
IL_000c:    ret
} // end of method InlineFunctions::inlinemul
```

The preceding IL is explained as follows:

1. The overall semantic of `inlinemul` and `op_HatMultiply` are basically the same because the body is using the same generated IL from the same expression of `a * b`.

2. Operator `^*` is compiled into IL as the `op_HatMultiply` function method.

3. The compiled prefix of `!!` in the parameter declaration means it is defined as compiled IL from statically typed parameter. It is unique in F# generated IL, and this might change in the future because it is considered as an implementation detail of how F# treats the statically typed parameters to be compiled into IL.

4. The parameters of `a` and `b` are allocated and stored onto the stack, which is then passed as a parameter to `LanguagePrimitives.MultiplyDynamic` because we are using multiplication in the function body.

5. The returning result is also marked as statically typed generics, compiled with the same `!!` prefix. Again, this is the implementation detail of emitted IL from F# compiler and this might change. But the same rule of thumb is applied in the IL: the compiler generates different IL for statically typed parameters and common generic type parameters.

Now, let's explore the IL of `inlinemul` usage, the `MulIntTest` property:

```
.property int32 MulIntTest()
{
  .custom instance void
[FSharp.Core]Microsoft.FSharp.Core.CompilationMappingAttribute::.ctor(value
type [FSharp.Core]Microsoft.FSharp.Core.SourceConstructFlags) = ( 01 00 09
00 00 00 00 00 )
  .get int32 InlineFunctions::get_MulIntTest()
} // end of property InlineFunctions::MulIntTest
```

We now see other proofs that F# type inference is powerful because this symbolic property is translated into a property with only a getter, as defined with .get getter declaration. This getter calls the get_MulIntTest method. The get_MulIntTest method is defined in the following IL:

```
.method public specialname static int32  get_MulIntTest() cil managed
{
  // Code size       6 (0x6)
  .maxstack  8
  IL_0000:  ldsfld     int32 '<StartupCode$Chapter7-
LanguageConstructs>'.$InlineFunctions::MulIntTest@9
  IL_0005:  ret
} // end of method InlineFunctions::get_MulIntTest
```

This ldsfld instruction means that the code pushes the value of MulIntTest@9 result onto the stack. Because of the fact that all operations are compiled into IL instructions that utilize the stack, the performance is quite fast.

However, if the implementation body of an inline function is more complex (more than one operator is involved), then all calls to the inline function will have large overheads of multiple calls to respective dynamic operators, which then has many indirections of having to specify the type information for the call site (the function that calls the inline function or inline operator). These overheads of stack allocations of type translations and call site stack frame allocations will decrease performance at the initial run.

We can also safely conclude that inline functions are best for functions that focus on simple generic types that incorporate simple arithmetic, although inline functions can speed up recursive operations, for example when dealing with operations that have a recursive nature of iterating head and tail of F# native list, a linked list.

Now that we understand the IL generated and the gory details of how the statically typed parameter works with inline functions, we now understand the integrated part of the inline function with the call site.

It is integrated in a sense that each usage of our inline functions will translate the type parameter from the call site, and each call site can have its own type, regardless of whether it is different or the same.

Identifying tail call in recursive constructs

One of the characteristics of a functional programming language is the common use of recursive constructs in many of the implementation of the functions; F# compiler itself is also a good sample of code that has many implementations of recursive constructs.

Functional programming languages always prefer to have recursive constructs instead of having loops or iterative constructs because recursive is better to use in the most complex calculations or in any operation that requires the ability to perform the same operation when the problem solving or calculation is broken into smaller problems.

Having recursive calls is quite common in F#, and it is recommended to optimize further to have tail call optimization, although the optimization may not be applied to all the cases.

Overview of recursion in functional programming

The use of recursion is more apparent in dealing with problems that require resolving problems into smaller problems with the same algorithm. This is why, in many cases, using iterations such as loop is not preferred because a loop will add more complexity in the form of exponential steps instead of relying on a return mechanism after resolving smaller problems.

For example, we can write a factorial function to be implemented using a loop, but then this loop becomes more complex to write because the number of loops might be large, and there will be overhead in the initial memory allocations instead of going deeper into performing the calculation recursively. Going deeper into performing the calculation or doing some processes requires a returning point to remember if the calculation is done and if the calculation is called by a previous calculation.

The consequences of this returning nature after finishing the final smallest problem require us to have a stack to store the locations and the state of the calculation. When the calculation takes long or deep levels of recursions, most codes will throw `StackOverflowException` because the stack allocation is exhausted.

F# has support for common recursive functions by marking it with the `rec` keyword as a requirement to indicate an explicit recursive function only if the function body contains a call to itself. This is the easiest concept of recursion: *a function that calls itself*. It is the most common because most of us get used to the idea of recursive in recursive functions, which is a function that calls itself.

However, in terms of a functional programming language, the traits of recursive constructs are broader:

1. A function that calls itself. This concept of a function that calls itself is the most common and also the easiest construct to understand. It is also by definition quite self-explanatory. This construct is also widely used not just in functional programming languages but also in non-functional programming languages, such as C#, VB, and C++.

2. A function that has a function as an argument, and then the function body contains a call to the function that is defined as an argument of the calling function. This trait might be confusing at first, but it is quite trivial when we see the examples later.

3. A function that contains flow branches that always end up with function calls to itself. This is quite similar to a function that takes a function as its parameter that contains a call to a function as its argument. In the end, both of the last expressions evaluated are functions, not constants or statements.

An example of point 1 is the most common, and it is also the most understood form of recursion.

For example, consider the following code for a factorial function:

```
let rec factorial n =
    match n with
    | 0 | 1 -> n
    | _ -> n * factorial (n-1)
```

In this factorial function, we implement the branching using pattern matching, and this is useful and more correct because all the conditions of possible values of n are checked.

Point 2 and point 3 require a deeper understanding of the nature of a curried function and how recursion does not stop at only one case of when a function calls itself, but also naturally has further optimizations that can be compiled as a loop or any other optimization such as a tail call optimization.

 The factorial function is one of the best examples to have the deciding factor of recursion. It is better to understand factorials as recursive instead of iterative.

If we call a factorial with a very large number, such as 50,000, the stack allocation will be quickly exhausted, and therefore there will be no more stack available for us. The function will throw StackOverflowException to inform that it is running out of stack and the stack that contains the returning state is full. In order to avoid or handle this exception, we can do one of these:

- We change the implementation to use a loop instead, but this is not feasible for all cases of recursion by nature.
- We can rely on compiler optimization because F# compiler will do its own optimization by translating common recursive functions into loop with IL optimization.

- We can use tail call optimization by implementing recursive with a specific pattern.

The last point, using tail call, is the most efficient optimization but it requires more understanding to implement it.

Tail call recursion in F# and .NET CLR

It is also common in many functional programming languages to have a tail call optimization in recursive constructs. Tail call recursion means that any recursion is optimized not to use stack instead of optimizing it to have a tail call.

F# supports both common recursion and tail call optimized recursion; tail call support is also available in .NET CLR.

What is tail call? A tail call means a function that has a call within a function whose result is immediately used as the output of the function. It is then a call that has a tail in its call to a function, usually as the last result of a calculation. The position is usually at the last position to mark the call; this is why it is called a tail call.

The definitive and full explanation of a tail call in F# is explained in this MSDN blog from the Visual F# team:

```
https://blogs.msdn.microsoft.com/fsharpteam/2011/07/08/tail-calls-in-f/
```

Identifying tail call optimized implementation

According to the MSDN blog, tail call is a call in tail position implemented recursively because the last expression is a function, not a composite expression, such as an addition between numbers.

A common sample of an expression that contains composite expression is the following function:

```
/// Computes the sum of a list of integers using recursion.
let rec sumList xs =
    match xs with
    | []     -> 0
    | y::ys -> y + sumList ys
```

The code tells us that the call to `sumList` is followed with a + operator; therefore, it is obvious that this calculation is not a simple call to only a function. Therefore, it is not implemented to have a tail call.

To prove that `sumList` does not have a tail call, let's look at the IL:

```
.method public static int32  sumList(class
[FSharp.Core]Microsoft.FSharp.Collections.FSharpList`1<int32> xs) cil
managed
{
  // Code size       40 (0x28)
  .maxstack  4
  .locals init ([0] class
[FSharp.Core]Microsoft.FSharp.Collections.FSharpList`1<int32> V_0,
          [1] class
[FSharp.Core]Microsoft.FSharp.Collections.FSharpList`1<int32> V_1,
          [2] class
[FSharp.Core]Microsoft.FSharp.Collections.FSharpList`1<int32> ys,
          [3] int32 y)
  IL_0000:  nop
  IL_0001:  ldarg.0
  IL_0002:  stloc.0
  IL_0003:  ldloc.0
  IL_0004:  call       instance class
[FSharp.Core]Microsoft.FSharp.Collections.FSharpList`1<!0> class
[FSharp.Core]Microsoft.FSharp.Collections.FSharpList`1<int32>::get_TailOrNu
ll()
  IL_0009:  brfalse.s  IL_000d
  IL_000b:  br.s       IL_000f
  IL_000d:  ldc.i4.0
  IL_000e:  ret
  IL_000f:  ldloc.0
  IL_0010:  stloc.1
  IL_0011:  ldloc.1
  IL_0012:  call       instance class
[FSharp.Core]Microsoft.FSharp.Collections.FSharpList`1<!0> class
[FSharp.Core]Microsoft.FSharp.Collections.FSharpList`1<int32>::get_TailOrNu
ll()
  IL_0017:  stloc.2
  IL_0018:  ldloc.1
  IL_0019:  call       instance !0 class
[FSharp.Core]Microsoft.FSharp.Collections.FSharpList`1<int32>::get_HeadOrDe
fault()
  IL_001e:  stloc.3
  IL_001f:  ldloc.3
  IL_0020:  ldloc.2
  IL_0021:  call       int32 TailcallSample::sumList(class
[FSharp.Core]Microsoft.FSharp.Collections.FSharpList`1<int32>)
  IL_0026:  add
  IL_0027:  ret
} // end of method TailcallSample::sumList
```

There is no tail call IL in the compiled `sumList` function. Although it is recursive in the code, `sumList` is compiled to use an iterative loop, as indicated by the `br.s` instruction at line `IL_000b` to call the `FSharpList,get_TailOrNull` function.

Let's try to implement the tail call function.

The tail call optimization is not available by default; we have to turn it on based on the project scope, not on the solution scope. To turn on tail call optimization, open the project's properties and select the **Build** tab. This tab contains all the properties of the F# project, including the runtime target of 32-bit and 64-bit. Set the checkbox of **Generate tail calls** as illustrated in the following screenshot:

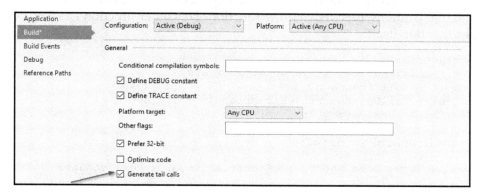

Let's examine the simplest function that has an argument that is typed as a function, then the main function body calls the function of the argument:

```
let apply f x = f x
```

This function is implemented to have tail call support because it minimizes stack allocation, while the recursion still applies. This is possible because it fits the pattern to have tail call as the last expression in a function.

Let's check the IL of `apply`:

```
method public static !!b  apply<a,b>(class
[FSharp.Core]Microsoft.FSharp.Core.FSharpFunc`2<!!a,!!b> f,
                           !!a x) cil managed
{
  .custom instance void
[FSharp.Core]Microsoft.FSharp.Core.CompilationArgumentCountsAttribute::.cto
r(int32[]) = ( 01 00 02 00 00 00 01 00 00 00 01 00 00 00 00 00 )
  // Code size       11 (0xb)
  .maxstack   8
```

```
    IL_0000:   nop
    IL_0001:   ldarg.0
    IL_0002:   ldarg.1
    IL_0003:   tail.
    IL_0005:   callvirt    instance !1 class
[FSharp.Core]Microsoft.FSharp.Core.FSharpFunc`2<!!a,!!b>::Invoke(!0)
    IL_000a:   ret
} // end of method TailcallSample::apply
```

Now, we have a tail call optimization, as indicated in line `IL_0003` that contains the `tail.` instruction.

Now let's apply tail call optimization to calculate the factorial. Let's create a new function of the factorial that contains a recursive inner function. This inner function has recursive calls to the inner function itself:

```
let accFactorial x =
    let rec TailCallRecursiveFactorial x acc =
        if x <= 1 then acc
        else TailCallRecursiveFactorial (x - 1) (acc * x)
    TailCallRecursiveFactorial x 1
```

And this is the IL of `accFactorial`:

```
.method public static int32  accFactorial(int32 x) cil managed
{
  // Code size       18 (0x12)
  .maxstack  5
  .locals init ([0] class
[FSharp.Core]Microsoft.FSharp.Core.FSharpFunc`2<int32,class
[FSharp.Core]Microsoft.FSharp.Core.FSharpFunc`2<int32,int32>>
TailCallRecursiveFactorial)
    IL_0000:  nop
    IL_0001:  newobj      instance void
TailcallSample/TailCallRecursiveFactorial@24::.ctor()
    IL_0006:  stloc.0
    IL_0007:  ldloc.0
    IL_0008:  ldarg.0
    IL_0009:  ldc.i4.1
    IL_000a:  tail.
    IL_000c:  call        !!0 class
[FSharp.Core]Microsoft.FSharp.Core.FSharpFunc`2<int32,int32>::InvokeFast<in
t32>(class [FSharp.Core]Microsoft.FSharp.Core.FSharpFunc`2<!0,class
[FSharp.Core]Microsoft.FSharp.Core.FSharpFunc`2<!1,!!0>>,
!0,
!1)
    IL_0011:  ret
} // end of method TailcallSample::accFactorial
```

[282]

We now have a tail call recursion in our function. In the next section, we will discuss the advantages of having tail call optimization.

Advantages of having tail call recursive implementation

Having tail call is a common technique in functional programming languages. Fortunately, F# is not just a single part of this tail call because tail call is also supported at the .NET runtime level, in a sense that the .NET CLR has IL support for tail call.

It is a very useful and powerful feature of F# because of the tight coupling of F# compiler and the generated IL on .NET; therefore, optimization is available in the compiled phase and in the runtime.

Let's compare the stack trace of our initial (unoptimized) factorial function with the optimized tail call factorial function:

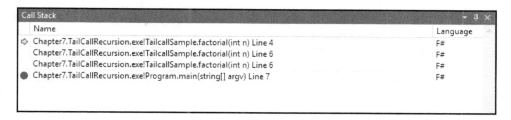

Let's look at `accFactorial`'s stack trace. Our tail call optimized function's stack trace shows that it has only one stack trace of `accFactorial`:

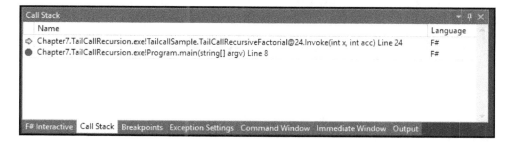

It proves that tail call optimization is very efficient because we only have one stack allocation. This is also faster than having no tail call optimization because there is minimal stack allocation overhead or is close to only having stack allocation once.

Although F#'s tail call optimization is a powerful optimization, its implementation is limited to specific cases, as described in the next section.

Limitations of tail call recursion in F#

There are limitations on how tail call is implemented, especially for F#-specific cases. Not all kinds of function can have tail call optimizations, mostly because of the nature of tail call itself.

The following are the limitations and restrictions of tail call optimization in F#:

1. Tail call optimizations will not be implemented on functions that return Unit (or void in C#/VB). This is important and natural because tail call relies on the returning the result from the last result of recursive function as a position to have tail call. The compiler will confuse the IL emission because F# has Unit, other languages such as C# that has void. Also all functions that return void are not compatible with F# functions that return Unit.
2. Tail call cannot be implemented within try...with constructs. It is also recommended that the exception handling should not be included in the body of the recursive function.
3. Tail call cannot be used to optimize calls to unsafe functions. Forcing to mix tail call with native unmanaged calls will yield unpredictable behavior and results.

The limitations just listed are simply not restrictions for all recursive cases specially exception handling.

Summary

We have enough knowledge to optimize common and subtle F# language constructs-from pattern matching combined with active pattern to the subtle F# features, such as inline functions, tail call recursion optimizations, and tail call identification. These constructs are features that make F# competitively unique in the .NET ecosystem.

Pattern matching and active patterns can be optimized without sacrificing correctness and functional style. We are now able to enforce type strictness by using statically typed generic parameters in conjunction with inline functions. Having tail calls in recursion optimization in F# is not only more efficient but also gives us a good exercise of optimizing at code level by identifying tail call semantics.

Now, it's time to optimize F# complex features and constructs that deserve a separate chapter: `Chapter 8`, *Optimizing Computation Expressions*.

8
Optimizing Computation Expressions

One of the most-used and unique features of F# is asynchronous workflow, and we have discussed this with the introduction to concurrency optimization in Chapter 4, *Introduction to Concurrency in F#*. The asynchronous workflow itself is actually an implementation of a computation expression, a feature that enables us to have a computation. This computation is, in fact, a sequence of workflows of functions that is composed sequentially and has bindings to bind or combine them.

The computation expression has many kinds of helper methods to implement, but using these helpers can be overkill, and it may have some overheads as well if it is not constructed properly. It is not as subtle and hard as the previous discussion on language constructs in Chapter 7, *Language Features and Constructs Optimization*.

In this chapter, we will focus our optimization on the implementation of computation workflows with the following topics:

- Quick introduction to F# computation workflow
- Walkthrough of an example implementation of simple computation workflow
- Design consideration in planning the computation workflow implementation
- Considerations of computation expression optimization

Quick introduction to F# computation expression

One of the quite subtle, but quite common, traits of a functional programming language is the availability of features to combine and compose functions into more sophisticated conceptual techniques that also encapsulate some side effects when combining functions. Some of these techniques are known as Monoids and Monads. These two come from the world of a subset of algebra, the category theory. This mathematical foundation gives the inspiration and also powerful concepts when composing and combining functions, including side effects.

For a more gentle introduction and information to Monads in functional programming, you could watch this MSDN Channel 9 interview with Microsoft's developer Brian Beckman:

```
https://channel9.msdn.com/Shows/Going+Deep/Brian-Beckman-Dont-fear-the-Monads
```

The best sample of F# computation expression is the asynchronous workflow. The term workflow in asynchronous workflow comes from the fact that it is implemented from the use of the computation expression feature to provide asynchronous computation. Asynchronous workflow is itself composed from functions with side effects such as switching the context execution of the current thread.

We already have discussed these F# concurrencies including asynchronous workflow cases in Chapter 4, *Introduction to Concurrency in F#* that asynchronous computations do not always equate to the needs of multithreading.

In F#, the composition of functions is done using builders. These builders are actually methods that help us construct a composition of functions. From the perspective of design patterns in OOP, these methods can be seen as helper methods or builder methods because they focus on building computation expressions.

Sometimes the composition of functions might contain conditional logic to handle side effects, such as threads, execution context (such as asynchronous workflow), I/O, and many more. The conditional logic is quite similar to workflow concepts whereas execution is always implemented as a sequence of steps. When conditional logic is needed, the execution always follows the branches of conditional logic based on the expression evaluated.

Earlier, F# language specification and MSDN Library mentioned computation expression as getting mixed with computation workflow. Since F# 3.0, the language specification is consistent and stricter to focus on computation expressions, not workflow.

Based on the official F# 4.0 language specification, the computation workflow syntax is often used by starting to have a construct using `builder-name` and the enclosing curly brackets as follows:

```
builder-name { expression }
```

The expression itself might be functions as defined (and also governed) by the builders of the computation expressions.

For an initial example of the computation expression syntax, let's revisit our own sample code for `async` workflow:

```
let fetchAsync(name, url:string) =
    async {
        try
            let uri = new System.Uri(url)
            let webClient = new WebClient()
            let! html = webClient.AsyncDownloadString(uri)
            printfn "Read %d characters for %s" html.Length name
        with
            | ex -> printfn "%s" (ex.Message);
    }
```

The preceding sample code uses `Control.AsyncBuilder`, a builder of `async`. The F# compiler will translate `AsyncBuilder` to a computation expression of `async`.

We will now go deeper into the fabric of computation expressions: builders of computation expressions. We will also create a simpler computation expression than asynchronous workflow as a starting sample in the next section.

Introduction to builders of computation expression

The notion, *builder*, also means that we construct a computation workflow by using the available builders when composing functions. These builders are actually methods that can be used when composing functions as a computation expression.

The following table briefly explains the commonly used builders in F# 4.0:

Method	Typical Signature	Remark
Bind	`M<'T> * ('T -> M<'U>) -> M<'U>`	Provide `let!` and `do!` in a computation expression. It is a basic method to compose functions.
Delay	`(unit -> M<'T>) -> M<'T>`	Wraps a computation expression as a function.
Return	`'T -> M<'T>`	Equivalent to `return` in computation expression.
ReturnFrom	`M<'T> -> M<'T>`	Equivalent to `return!` in computation expressions.
Run	`M<'T> -> M<'T>` or `M<'T> -> 'T`	Executes a computation expression.
TryWith	`M<'T> * (exn -> M<'T>) -> M<'T>`	Called for `try..with` to catch exception (`exn`) in a computation expression.
TryFinally	`M<'T> * (unit -> unit) -> M<'T>`	Called for `try..finally` in computation expression.
Using	`'T * ('T -> M<'U>) -> M<'U> when 'U :> IDisposable`	Called from `use` binding in computation expression. It is equivalent to `using!` in computation expression.
Yield	`'T -> M<'T>`	Called for `yield` in computation expression. It is conceptually the same as `yield` in C#/VB, but the semantic is different.
YieldFrom	`M<'T> -> M<'T>`	Called for `yield!` in computation expression. It is conceptually the same as `yield` in C#/VB, but the semantic is different.
Zero	`unit -> M<'T>`	Called when there is an empty `else` in the `if` condition (if there is an `if` statement in the computation expression). It is also called when the computation expression has an empty expression.

For more information about computation expression and the full list of builder methods, consult the official MSDN F# computation expression on the new Microsoft's docs:

```
https://docs.microsoft.com/en-us/dotnet/articles/fsharp/language-reference/comp
utation-expressions
```

We do not have to implement all of the builder methods because there are no definitive minimum requirements of a computation expression. However, we should have the basic requirements of understanding in order to use a computation expression implementation to be used easily. The following are the common requirements in terms of usage requirement with builder methods:

- A bind to compose functions. This `Bind` method will contain a composition of functions. An implementation of `Bind` is recommended because the expressions supported inside a computation expression are governed by the types defined in the `Bind` method. For example, composing functions that have the same generic type.
- A type to return. This requirement enforces us to implement `Return` or `ReturnFrom`. This is important because computation expressions must return a type, and it is recommended not to return `unit` (or `void` in .NET and C#).
- `Delay`, to wrap a computation expression as a function. It is also quite common to call the `Delay` method as a wrapper method.
- `Using`, to leverage the use of a type that implements `IDisposable`. This will be translated as `use` binding inside the computation workflow.
- `TryWith`, to handle exceptions inside a composition of functions of `Bind` or explicitly handle exceptions outside `Bind`.

The `Bind` method is crucial because it governs the type of generic type in the functions we are going to compose, but it is also enforcing all the types of the `let!` and `do!` functions inside a computation expression. Omitting `Bind` will make the computation expressions to be less complete because the main goal of a computation expression is the ability to compose expressions, not just returning the underlying type.

In the case of our previous sample code for asynchronous workflow, the following is the illustration of `Bind` as `let!` in an asynchronous workflow:

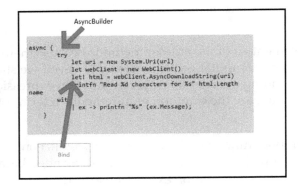

The default distribution of the F# core library already has samples of implementations of computation expressions with its own underlying type:

- LINQ query expressions support that returns `System.Linq.Enumerable<'T>`
- Asynchronous workflow returns `Async<'T>`

F# LINQ query expression is a little bit subtle, but actually it has implementation details similar to LINQ used in C#/VB. It is semantically the same; therefore, the performance characteristics are also similar to running LINQ in C#/VB. The difference between F# and C#/VB implementation is the type of delegates used: `FastFunc` in F#, `Func` in C#/VB.

This strong recommendation of F# function over `Func` is crucial and important because the method signature of all method builders use F# curried functions instead of the normal .NET method signature.

Using F# function/delegate over .NET Func

Usage of F# delegate instead of a normal .NET `Func` is also more efficient and more functional because of the immediate feature to have F# delegate as a function that supports currying; this allows for a higher order function after the availability of a partial function application.

When we are developing applications that use our own implementation of computation expressions, of course, it is faster and highly recommended to use F# function/delegate instead of using .NET Func. It is highly compatible with the rest of F# constructs/features, and it is faster to compile in F#. It is highly recommended due to the availability of function currying.

Proof that F# functions are optimized for supporting currying functions is available in the way F# supports higher order functions. Microsoft has documented this, and it is wrapped in a very nice walkthrough guide for functional programming traits/characteristics, focusing on function as first class values. The concept of function as first class values is then compared to classes and method as first class values of OOP.

The starting information about function as first class values and F# currying is available in this MSDN docs page of F# functional programming traits:

```
https://docs.microsoft.com/en-us/dotnet/articles/fsharp/introduction-to-functio
nal-programming/functions-as-first-class-values
```

On that page, we focus on the implied currying of F# in the section on curried function:

Currying is a process that transforms a function that has more than one parameter into a series of embedded functions, each of which has a single parameter. In F#, functions that have more than one parameter are inherently curried.

The implications of currying highly influence the language design of F#; hence, a special or unique F# function/delegate is needed. In the general .NET BCL, this F# unique implementation of a curried function is becoming very important and critical from the perspective of functional programming language architecture because Func does not support currying.

We are not going to dive deeper into the discussion of what is functional programming and the traits of functional programming language. Consult more of functional programming concepts in F# and the functional programming support in F# in the preceding MSDN docs page.

For example, let's examine the common (typical) signature of the Bind method:

```
M<'T> * ('T -> M<'U>) -> M<'U>
```

This signature means that the function returns M<'U> as its result, as indicated by the type signature after the last ->. The * between two types before the last -> means that the method takes two arguments—one is a normal type and the second parameter is a function that takes a generic T returns a type with a type of M<'U>.

The use of `*` in the signature of a method member of a class means that the types (before the resulting type) are seen as the arguments of a method.

The function of (`'T -> M<'U>`) means a function that takes one argument of `'T` and returns a result. This argument does not have to be one argument. We can also use more functions that have more than one argument, such as this:

```
'T -> 'U -> M<'V'>
```

Here, `M<'V'>` is the result.

The signature of `'T -> 'U` before the last -> means that the function has two arguments, typed generic T and U. We can then change and adapt the signature of `Bind` to be like this:

```
M<'T> -> ('T -> 'U -> M<'V>) -> M<'V>
```

We can then start to implement our `Bind` method. However, be careful as the `let!` and `do!` constructs are altered quite large, and it's better for us to implement computation expressions as simply as possible.

Relation of F# function computation expressions with arguments restriction

We can also use many arguments, but it is quite common to only use a function with one argument as long as the type is lined up well. If we use more than one argument, our `Bind` method implementation will be more complex, and it will always be harder to construct semantically correct computation expressions.

Not just the generic types have to be aligned carefully; it is also more complex to implement `Bind` with many parameters. The F# language specification also implies that the current F# 4.0 compiler (especially the lexer and parser) is preferred instead of using `Func`.

This complexity of having an implementation of `Bind` method with parameters will become clearer by having samples of computation expressions with `Bind`. The next section is the starting point of a sample of computation expression.

Walkthrough of planning and writing a computation expression

Let's start writing a very simple functional way of creating a **WPF (Windows Presentation Foundation)** window and composing WPF controls.

WPF is basically a UI framework implemented on top of DirectX 9.0c that starts from the release of .NET 3.0 as libraries of UI. It is still aggressively developed by Microsoft, and with the release of WPF comes the innovation of XAML as a declarative UI. It has been heavily supported since Visual Studio 2008, and now it is beginning to replace Windows Forms.

This slightly unfortunate fate of Windows Forms becomes more apparent with the introduction of Visual Studio 2012 and .NET 4.5; Windows Forms are no longer developed (although they are still supported in terms of bug fixes), but they have not yet been deprecated or become obsolete. It is considered as replacing Windows Forms because WPF is still developed heavily, at least not just in Visual Studio 2015/.NET 4.6.1, but it is also evident in the upcoming version of Visual Studio 2015, the Visual Studio 2017.

For more information about WPF, visit the official home page of WPF on MSDN at `https://msdn.microsoft.com/en-us/library/ms754130(v=vs.110).aspx`.

Before starting to implement WPF composition using computation expressions, we need to have some basic idea to understand the following (as design consideration plans) before having code implementations of WPF:

- All WPF control derives from `System.Windows.FrameworkElement`.

The WPF window is called `System.Windows.Window`.

- On the `Window`, all of the controls (typed as `UIElement`) to be put are usually laid on a container panel that is inherited from `System.Windows.Controls.Panel`.
- The adding of controls on `Panel` has to be carefully designed to exclude `Window` as it will not make sense if we add `Window` on to `Panel`, although `Window` inherits `System.Windows.Controls.Control` and `System.Windows.UIElement`.

There are special treatments of a `Panel` to be taken into account: the knowledge of what a `Panel` is and why it is not available to be used directly.

This is the proof that we cannot use `Panel` directly because `Panel` is implemented as an abstract class.

The following is the `System.Windows.Controls.Panel` declaration in F#:

```
[<AbstractClass>]
[<LocalizabilityAttribute(LocalizationCategory.Ignore)>]
[<ContentPropertyAttribute("Children")>]
type Panel =
    class
        inherit FrameworkElement
        interface IAddChild
    end
```

The `AbstractClass` attribute is the same semantic as marking the class as abstract class. Abstract class in F# is treated using the `AbstractClass` attribute, not as a keyword as in C#/VB:

```
[LocalizabilityAttribute(LocalizationCategory.Ignore)]
[ContentPropertyAttribute("Children")]
public abstract class Panel : FrameworkElement, IAddChild
```

To avoid confusion, we should know the OOP concept and keywords in F#, while at the same time relating and interoperating with OOP in C#/VB. This conceptual knowledge is increasingly relevant because it's quite common that in developing WPF application, we rely on inheritances and componentizations of OOP controls.

Before we start utilizing WPF, ensure that the following assemblies are referenced or registered (if you are in the scripting interactive mode):

- `WindowsBase`
- `PresentationCore`
- `PresentationFramework`
- `System.Xaml`

For scripting mode, these assemblies have to be registered first by directly registering the location of the DLL. In the following sample, we register the assemblies with 32-bit assemblies:

```
#r "C:\\Program Files (x86)\\Reference
Assemblies\\Microsoft\\Framework\\.NETFramework\\v4.6.1\\WindowsBase.dll"
#r "C:\\Program Files (x86)\\Reference
Assemblies\\Microsoft\\Framework\\.NETFramework\\v4.6.1\\PresentationCore.d
ll"
#r "C:\\Program Files (x86)\\Reference
Assemblies\\Microsoft\\Framework\\.NETFramework\\v4.6.1\\PresentationFramew
ork.dll"
#r "C:\\Program Files (x86)\\Reference
```

```
Assemblies\\Microsoft\\Framework\\.NETFramework\\v4.6.1\\System.Xaml.dll"
```

After registering all the required DLL assemblies, we should tell the F# compiler to scope the namespace of WPF to be available in our script:

```
open System
open System.Windows
open System.Windows.Controls
```

The open namespace is also useful because it will shorten our naming of WPF type not to use full type name with the namespace. It is semantically similar to the Using keyword in C# and Import in VB.

We can start from just creating Window with Panel, but we can also use an abstract class as a template for Window with Panel and Panel with controls because both Window and Panel extend FrameworkElement, as illustrated in this image:

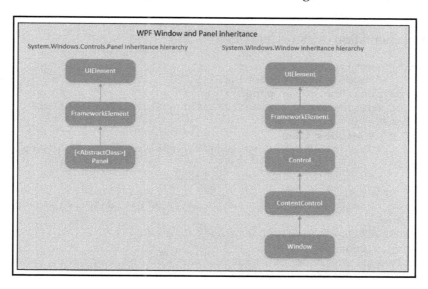

Next, we are going to implement our abstract class as a template for our builder:

```
[<AbstractClass>]
type IComposableControl<'a when 'a :> FrameworkElement> () =
    abstract Control : 'a
    abstract Bind : System.Windows.FrameworkElement *
(System.Windows.FrameworkElement -> 'a) -> 'a
    abstract Bind : IComposableControl<'b> *
(System.Windows.FrameworkElement -> 'a)  -> 'a
    member this.Return (e: unit)  = this.Control
```

```
member this.Zero () = this.Control
```

Based on the knowledge that `Window` and `Panel` inherit from the same `FrameworkElement`, we can continue to have the implementation of our own `Window` builder as a computation expression:

```
type WindowBuilder() =
    inherit IComposableControl<Window>()
    let win = Window(Topmost=true)
    override this.Control = win
    override this.Bind(c: FrameworkElement, body: FrameworkElement ->
Window) : Window =
        win.Content <- c
        body c
    override this.Bind(c: IComposableControl<'b>, body: FrameworkElement ->
Window) : Window =
        win.Content <- c.Control
        body c.Control
```

This is the implementation of `PanelBuilder`:

```
type PanelBuilder(panel: Panel) =
    inherit IComposableControl<Panel>()
    override this.Control = panel
    override this.Bind(c: FrameworkElement, body: FrameworkElement ->
Panel) : Panel=
        if c :? Window then
            raise (ArgumentException("Window cannot be added to panel"))
        else
            panel.Children.Add(c) |> ignore
            body c
    override this.Bind(c: IComposableControl<'b>, body: FrameworkElement ->
Panel) : Panel=
        panel.Children.Add(c.Control) |> ignore
        body c.Control
    // Implement the code for constructor with no argument.
    new() = PanelBuilder(StackPanel())
```

In the `PanelBuilder` implementation, we add type checking for `c` (as highlighted). If it is typed as `Window`, we should raise `System.ArgumentException` to inform us further that we cannot use `Window` to be added onto `Panel`. We can also return `null` as an option instead of `Exception`, but returning `null` is not recommended in F#, and it also adds more confusion on what is being added. Also, the code is not composed well. Any bad composition in `Bind` will always increase the unpredictability of the computation expression. Further information on this consideration is described in the next section.

Because of the fact that we derive `WindowBuilder` and `PanelBuilder` from the `IComposableControl` abstract class, we must also implement all of the abstract methods of `IComposableControl`. The implemented method must have an override modifier to denote that the method is an implementation of abstract methods from `IComposableControl`.

> We are not going to have a full discussion on OOP features of F# because it is outside the scope of this book.

For more information on abstract method and overrides, consult MSDN docs at `https://docs.microsoft.com/en-us/dotnet/articles/fsharp/language-reference/members/methods`.

Now that we have the builders implemented, we can set the builders in action:

```
let win =
    WindowBuilder()
        {   let! panel =
                PanelBuilder(StackPanel())
                    {   let! btn1 = Button(Content = "Hello")
                        let! btn2 = Button(Content = "World")
                        return () }
            return () }
do win.Show() // Pops up the window in FSI.
```

The preceding code will display the following window:

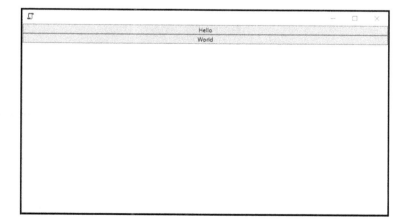

To test for `Zero`, we can simply test it by having an empty expression in the computation expression.

This is an example of `Zero` in our `WindowBuilder`:

```
let winzero = WindowBuilder()
                { Console.WriteLine("sample Zero") }
do winzero.Show()
```

There is a subtle feature, but we have used it and most of us are unaware: the builder object; when it is instantiated, the F# compiler will treat the instance as a keyword!

This translation of a computation expression instance becoming a keyword is already demonstrated by asynchronous workflow by instantiating `AsyncBuilder` as `async`. Therefore, the usage of `async` instance will be treated as a keyword.

In the case of `WindowBuilder`, the instance of `WindowBuilder` will be treated as a keyword too. For example, the following is a sample instance of `WindowBuilder`:

```
let windowexp = WindowBuilder()
let secondWindow = windowexp
                        {
                            let! panel =
                                PanelBuilder(StackPanel())
                                    {
                                        let! btn1 = Button(Content =
"Hello")
                                        let! btn2 = Button(Content =
"Second computation expression")
                                        return ()
                                    }
                            return ()
                        }
```

In Visual Studio, the preceding treatment of `windowexp` as a keyword is shown in the following screenshot:

```
58
59   let windowexp = WindowBuilder()
60   let secondWindow = windowexp
61                          {
62                              let! panel =
63                                  PanelBuilder(StackPanel())
64                                      {
65                                          let! btn1 = Button(Content = "Hello")
66                                          let! btn2 = Button(Content = "Second computation expression")
67                                          return ()
68                                      }
69                              return ()
70                          }
71
```

Now we have `windowexp` as an instance of `WindowBuilder()`, and we can use it as a `windowexp` computation expression keyword. This is shown by having a blue color just like the other F# keywords.

We have created a simple computation expression that has `Bind`, `Return`, and `Zero`. Let's peek into the implementation of a computation expression inside an asynchronous workflow.

The implementation of `AsyncBuilder` for an asynchronous computation also follows the same pattern as the implementation of `WindowBuilder` and `PanelBuilder`; it defines the method builder first, although the implementation does not use an abstract class.

It is quite easy to examine the implementation of F# asynchronous workflow because we can directly examine the source code. The following is the landing page of F# core libraries (`FSharp.Core`) source code, including the F# compiler implementation and F# tooling:

```
https://github.com/Microsoft/visualfsharp/tree/master/src
```

Let's look at the type declaration and the code of `AsyncBuilder` in the `control.fs` file:

```
type AsyncBuilder () =
    member b.Zero()                 = doneA
    member b.Delay(f)               = delayA(f)
    member b.Return(x)              = resultA(x)
    member b.ReturnFrom(x:Async<_>) = x
    member b.Bind(p1, p2)           = bindA p1 p2
    member b.Using(g, p)            = usingA g p
    member b.While(gd, prog)        = whileA gd prog
    member b.For(e, prog)           = forA e prog
    member b.Combine(p1, p2)        = sequentialA p1 p2
    member b.TryFinally(p, cf)      = tryFinallyA cf p
    member b.TryWith(p, cf)         = tryWithExnA cf p
```

All the members are implicitly `public static` methods, so it is again very succinct to quickly implement.

Let's visit the `Bind` method implementation, the `bindA`:

```
        // The primitive bind operation. Generate a process that runs the
first process, takes
        // its result, applies f and then runs the new process produced.
Hijack if necessary and
        // run 'f' with exception protection
        let bindA p1 f  =
            unprotectedPrimitive (fun args ->
                if args.aux.token.IsCancellationRequested then
```

```
                              cancelT args
                   else

                   let args =
                       let cont a = protectNoHijack args.aux.econt f a
        (fun p2 -> invokeA p2 args)
                            { cont=cont;
                              aux = args.aux
                            }
                       // Trampoline the continuation onto a new work item
        every so often
                       let trampoline = args.aux.trampolineHolder.Trampoline
                       if trampoline.IncrementBindCount() then
                           trampoline.Set(fun () -> invokeA p1 args)
                           FakeUnit
                       else
                           // NOTE: this must be a tailcall
                           invokeA p1 args)
```

If we want to check the signature of `AsyncBuilder.Bind`, the signature is in the `Controls.fsi` file. The following is the signature:

```
member Bind: computation: Async<'T> * binder: ('T -> Async<'U>) ->
Async<'U>
```

The `Bind` signature defines that the method takes two arguments: computation and binder. The computation argument is typed as `Async<'T>`, the binder is typed as `'T -> Async<'U>`, and the return type is `Async<'U>`, the generic parameter of `'U` is the underlying type. This `Bind` method is then called if we are using `let!` within the asynchronous workflow construct.

Understanding the use of type returned in computation expression

There is an apparent pattern of `let!`, `return`, and `return!` expressions in the computation expression. The use of the bang sign `!` as a suffix means that these expressions return the underlying type directly without any wrapper type. For example, `return!` will call the `ReturnFrom` method and `return` will call the `Return` method. In the case of F# asynchronous workflow, we can just see the signature comparison of `Return` and `ReturnFrom`:

```
member b.Return(x)            = resultA(x)
member b.ReturnFrom(x:Async<_>) = x
```

This is the explanation of the implication of the underlying type:

- The `ReturnFrom` will return the resulting type immediately without the wrapping type. In practice, it returns `'T` instead of `Async<'T>`.
- The `Return` method will return a type that wraps the underlying type. In the case of asynchronous workflow, `Return` will return `Async<'T>`, whereas the `Async` type wraps the type of `` `T ``.
- The concept of `ReturnFrom` is similar in .NET TPL to having `T` as the result of an operation of `Task<'T>`.

The F# way of composing a computation expression makes it easier to reason about returning the underlying type, but in .NET TPL, to get the `T` in `Task<T>`, we have to access the property as the result.

For example, this type wrap is shown when getting the result of `Task<T>` (in C#):

```
public static void Main()
{
    var t = Task<int>.Run( () => {
        for (int ctr = 0; ctr <= 1000000; ctr++) {
            if (ctr == max / 2 && DateTime.Now.Hour <= 12) {
                ctr++;
                break;
            }
        }
        return ctr;
    } );
    Console.WriteLine("Finished {0:N0} iterations.", t.Result);
}
```

As highlighted in the preceding code, the underlying result is contained in `t.Result` instead of `t` because `t` is typed as `Task<int>`. Therefore, the underlying type is typed as `int`; it is matched with the property declaration of `Task<T>.Result` documentation:

```
member Result : 'T with get
```

Other expressions such as `yield` and `yield!` have the same intention and behavior as `return`/`return!` and `let`/`let!` in terms of the type they return.

The asynchronous workflow and our own WPF computation expressions are samples of the common nature (also called *common behavior* in the realm of practical software engineering) of computation expressions. It is strongly recommended to follow this common nature of computation expression. Therefore, these traits of common nature of computation expression are not just best practices but also make more sense as predefined specifications for implementations. The predefined specifications for common code programming implementations are often called **design considerations**.

We will discuss the design considerations in the next section.

General computation expression design considerations

We have implemented a very simple computation expression using `Bind`, `Return`, and `Zero` as a starting sample.

We can conclude that the use of `Bind` will translate into `let!` as the result of `let!` expression will be composed nicely. The other translations are available on the official MSDN docs page of computation expression.

The translation of builder methods into syntaxes of language constructs such as `let!`, `return`, `return!`, and `do!` are samples of syntactic sugar. The **syntactic sugar** of a computation expression is the ability to translate the builder methods into very neat declarative expressions to combine expressions and functions nicely. It is quite easier to have computation expressions instead of directly calling the method builder after instantiating the builder object's constructor.

Based on the discussion in the previous sections, we have concluded that there are some aspects of best practices and some advice that must be taken into consideration.

The appropriate term for these aspects is *design considerations* because they serve as best practices and some initial actions to be avoided at the beginning of the implementation of a computation expression. The design considerations also include the related information on avoiding the pitfalls of computation expression because the design considerations include the related implementation patterns or background reasons behind each of the design considerations. Most of the reasons include pitfalls to avoid.

The following are the design considerations of computation expression implementations:

1. Always begin with the planned results and general outcomes of what you want to achieve. Not all builder methods have to be implemented because while any builder method implementation provides more powerful syntactic sugar and also more declarative constructs, it also adds compilation overheads, and therefore the generated IL could be more complex.

2. The signature of the used builder method must follow the same pattern recommendation as described in MSDN docs for F# computation expressions. This is crucial because any computation expression must have a high degree of predictability in the beginning by obeying or complying with the same signature recommendation of the builder method. For example, `Bind` must follow the signature of `M<'T> * ('T -> M<'U>) -> M<'U>` in order to have a predictable result.

3. *The focus of the computation expression is usually differentiated into three main focuses: on the requirement to return underlying type, on only combining operations in expressions/functions that usually return nothing or return F# Unit (void in C#), and on combining side effects.* This condition especially applies to the case of `Zero` method. The nature of computation workflow does not require to implement `Zero` for all cases. For example, a query computation expression (the `query { ... }` expression) does not require `Zero`, because it does not make sense to implement the `Zero` method because the main focus of a query expression is on not the underlying type, but rather on combining query expressions/functions of LINQ and trying to avoid side effects as much as possible. It makes sense in the case of asynchronous workflows and for `WindowBuilder/PanelBuilder` as combining asynchronous computations and adding UI controls have side effects.

4. Adding support for `Zero` means that we should be aware that the computation of `Zero` support might contain side effects. Therefore, the `Zero` method support should be added for computation expressions that have the predefined goal to include any side effect instead of composing pure functions or composing objects with a strict hierarchy. Asynchronous workflow is intended to combine functions and operations in a manner so as to have side effects; therefore we can safely include `Zero` support as well. `WindowBuilder/PanelBuilder` might not have side effects, but *all of the leverage in GUI layer, such as Windows Forms and WPF, always has side effects.* Sequence computation workflow, the `seq { ... }`, might have side effects, but the main goal is to focus on returning the underlying type. Therefore, `seq` computation expression does not have the requirement or necessity to implement `Zero`.

5. Adding support for `Combine` means that it is strongly recommended to add support for `Delay` because it is required based on the implementation body of the `Combine` method. But implementations of the `Delay` method builder will add more complexity because the result is not evaluated immediately. Such a behavior of not having evaluated immediately happens because the `Delay` method is always executed before the `Return/ReturnFrom` method. It can be optimized to be implemented with less complexity only if the method body of `Delay` contains simple expressions or if it simply contains a function because the nature of the `Delay` method is to wrap a function that contains our computation.

6. To shorten the instantiation of the computation expression builder, we can instantiate it under a module using the normal `let` syntax. F# will treat the instance of the builder as a keyword. *It is therefore strongly recommended to have only one instance that will be used as a keyword because it is bad practice to have many instances of a builder to have many keywords with the same semantic.* For example, we use `windowexp` as our instance of `WindowBuilder`, which can then be used by other F# library (DLL) or executable applications.

7. The instantiation of a computation expression must not be the same keyword in the existing pool of F# keywords. Otherwise, we will have unpredictable results and compile errors. This is crucial because we should not add more keywords in form of the name of type builders freely without checking the existing F# keywords.

8. Use an F# delegate/function (`FSharpFunc`) instead of .NET `Func` as much as possible, unless we are going to have an explicit use of .NET `Func` inside the implementation of the computation expression. For example: a query computation expression contains calls to LINQ's static methods, such as `Enumerable.Where` and `Orderable.OrderBy`, which requires .NET `System.Func` delegates.

9. The use of `Using` method builder is optional but we should use `Using` as much as possible if we are allowing the use of types (for the underlying type) that should be disposed immediately. The type that fits into this model is the type that implements `IDisposable`. But having this `Using` will add more complexity to our computation expression, and not all of the planning focuses (as described in point 3) require us to have implementations of `Using` method.

10. Do not use an implicit type as the underlying type of a computation expression for a type that has an implicit reference counting of events as part of event driven programming mode.. An example of this is the use of any `EventHandler` type (or a derived type) for the underlying type of a computation expression. Although there is no restriction on using event handler objects as the underlying type, there is no guarantee that we can always dereference the events from an event handler as the underlying type. Any event might have been added during the running of the computation expression, unless we also remember to dereference all of the referenced event objects, and this always adds more complexity to the implementation of the computation expression itself. Using the `IDisposable` pattern will not guarantee that any handled events are deregistered when the type is disposed.

11. If we use an implicit type as underlying type that is derived from reference-counting type such as `EventHandler`, the event registration (reference) and dereference have to be handled explicitly. This explicit reference/dereference implementation will guarantee that the reference to outside events that are referenced outside as delegates are registered and deregistered correctly.

12. Do not use inline functions on method builders. The context of inline functions does not fit into the context of a computation expression because inline functions will be inlined for every use of our method builder, and this is against the F# language specification. However, the nature of method builders prefers to have normal generic type parameters, which are then generalized instead of having an early optimization on the generic type inlined. Also, all of the method builders cannot be inlined easily because these methods only live within the type set by the computation expression builder type definition and can be used only within the scope of the computation expression when its instance is used. Fortunately, the F# compiler will catch this inline usage on builder methods early as a compile error.

It is good for us to have the preceding design guidelines when we are going to implement computation expressions, but they have their own implications and there are additional sub notes and more explanations on some points of the design consideration. The next section describes these implications with the additional explanations.

Implications of the design considerations of computation expression

The points in the design consideration are quite self-explanatory, but some points have to be explored further because they have some implications not just on the correctness and the clarity of the intention of the computation expression when used outside the scope of the assembly but also on the performance.

Let's discuss the points of the design considerations that have additional implications to be handled.

Point 2 defines that we must meet the specifications based on the signature of the commonly used method builder. This is important, especially on the crucial (required) methods that define the core intention and the requirement of the computation expression's focus as described in point 3 of computation expression focus. In the case of asynchronous workflow and `WindowBuilder/PanelBuilder`, all of them have to deal with the side effects, and therefore the implementation of `Bind`, `Return`, and `ReturnFrom` methods has to be implemented using the respective signature guidelines. Failing to comply with these signature guidelines will result as compile errors.

For example, if we try to have `yield` in our use of `PanelBuilder`, we will get a compile error.

Consider the following faulty code:

```
let testUnimplementedYieldWindow =
    windowexp
        {
            let! panel =
                PanelBuilder(StackPanel())
                    {
                        let! textblock01 = TextBox(Text = "test")
                        yield button = Button("World") // <- use to test
not implemented yield
                        return ()
                    }
            return ()
        }
```

The Visual Studio editor will display squiggle on the line with the `yield` declaration and also will complain that `yield` method has not been implemented yet, as shown in the following screenshot:

```
PanelBuilder(StackPanel())
    {
        let! textblock01 = TextBox(Text = "test")
        yield button = Button("World") // <- use to test not implemented yield
        return ()
                        This control construct may only be used if the computation expression builder defines a 'Yield' method
    }
rn ()
```

This error information from the F# compiler is crucial as currently, we have not yet implemented yield for `PanelBuilder`, although `yield` itself is a valid keyword in F# when used in a `for` loop outside a computation expression.

This simple quick test is also useful to prove that consistency in the implementation of a computation expression is very important so that we can be sure that our implementation of computation expression is correct in the sense that we have done the implementations based on the initial intention and design considerations. This is also why it is called *correctness*, not just consistency of the implementation and the usage.

Point 3 in the aspect of computation expression focuses implies that there is a certain deciding plan before implementing a computation expression. This focus plan will also provide guidelines on what method builder we should strongly implement and what method should not be implemented mainly based on how we are going to handle the side effects first.

Currently, there are no officially defined guidelines for computation expression method builder implementation in F# language specification. The main goal of the focus guideline is to have a starting focus plan on the implementation of computation expressions, which is then easily translated to what method builders we should implement.

Having the mindset to first focus on side effects is also critical and helpful. It also complies with the functional programming language common practices that we should treat side effects explicitly and identify them early in the beginning of the implementation.

We can then simplify the narrative description of point 3 with this illustration as the deciding flow (using UML 2 diagram notation):

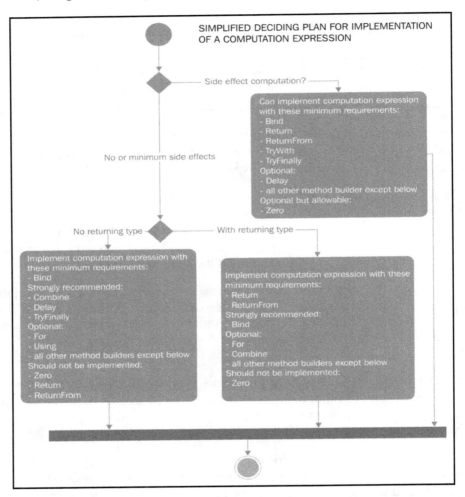

The preceding Unified Modeling Language (UML) activity diagram illustration is not meant to limit the creativity of the developer. In fact, there are no restrictions for the minimum method builders for many specific purposes beyond what we have in the illustration.

We leverage the UML activity diagram because we need to document or illustrate the flow of the deciding factor. UML itself is a software development standard diagram that focuses on documenting processes and system development (including application development), under the supervision of **Object Management Group** (**OMG**), a non-profit organization for standardizing documented processes and architecture.

For more information about UML 2 diagram, visit the official UML page at: `http://www.uml.org/`.

This is the landing page of UML 2 standards with various version histories at OMG: `http://www.omg.org/spec/UML/`.

The UML activity diagram is part of the UML 2.1 standard diagrams and notations.

The UML activity diagram is easier to understand than a flowchart because it can accommodate more conditional concerns (not just yes/no or true/false) and provides more support for event-driven and message passing agents. The most frequently used UML diagram is the activity diagram. Activity diagram is one of the many diagrams under the UML 2.1 umbrella standards. Currently, the UML standard has version 2.5, but still the widely used version in 2016 is UML 2.1. This book does not focus on how to create and use UML diagrams because it is beyond the scope of this book.

When we discuss the side effects in point 3, we should be aware that side effects are not just I/O or any other kind of outside API calls, such as interoperability with Win32 API; side effects such as exceptions, event-driven model, and any GUI library have to be taken into account as well to be carefully handled. When an event handler is instantiated within a computation expression, it is recommended to clear all event handlers of any events that we want to handle by setting them to `None` (`null` in C# semantic, `Nothing` in VB semantic). Otherwise, we will have occurrences of memory leaks even after we are done executing computation expressions.

Point 5 about the instantiation of computation expression is also a simple but meaningful proof of how we can easily add keywords to the existing F# keywords. It can lead to confusion because more keywords means more semantic and more contexts to be understood.

Point 8 about leveraging the `Using` method in a computation expression has to be implemented carefully. It is nice to have a use pattern for disposable objects, but many uses of disposable objects might lead to having additional overhead on garbage collector (GC) because of the overhead when disposing objects at the end of the computation expression lifetime. Also, having the `Using` method only can work for `IDisposable` objects, and this constraint will put a restriction on what kind of types to be used in the implementation of the `Using` method.

Point 9 is also important, although it is the last point in our design considerations because any use of types that have implicit reference counting as the underlying type (such as event handler) might be dangerous. Not that we cannot have the guarantee of always dereferencing references to other objects, such as events, but any action of dereferencing itself is always synchronous and it may slow down the running performance a bit.

Although dereferencing events of an event handler is as easy as setting it to `None`, but because of its sequential nature of synchronous executions, it cannot be used nicely in a parallel execution at all. This means that there is no option for parallelism when we have to do dereferencing.

Considerations of computation expression optimization

Computation expressions can be further optimized if we carefully implement the design planning. We have discussed the design considerations of a computation workflow in the previous section of this chapter, and we shall carry the considerations as a quick foundation to perform optimization.

The optimization of computation expression is quite hard because of the following factors as consequences of computation expression syntax translations:

1. Construction of computation expressions depends heavily on syntactic sugar that becomes language constructs. For example, `ReturnFrom` method is translated to a method that returns a result of the underlying type of a computation expression. Therefore, we must follow the strict guidelines of the asynchronous method builders to express translation; otherwise, we will get unpredictable results or even exceptions.

2. Composing the sequence of `let !` requires some wirings of a chained `Bind` method builder in the form of chaining `Bind` methods. This chaining of `Bind` method might be error-prone and it cannot be optimized further. Fortunately, we have a method builder in a computation expression called `Combine` to sequence multiple expressions (also called *sequencing expression* in the MSDN documentation of F#). However, the `Combine` method has to be carefully rewritten to match the signature requirement specification for `Combine`, then all of the necessary requirements of the related builder methods such as `Bind`, `Return`, and `ReturnFrom` must be aligned to match the type signature as well.

3. By default, the expression returned by expressions within a computation expression is not returned immediately because the order of execution might change based on what the implementation body of `Combine` and `Delay` is.

Points 2 and 3 are closely related to the design considerations, particularly to point 5 of the design considerations of computation expression that we discussed previously in this chapter.

To understand `Delay` and also to prove that it changes the execution order, we could compare two implementations of computation expressions: the first one without `Delay`, and the second one that has `Delay`.

This following code is implemented without the `Delay` method:

```
// without delay method
type ComputeExpression1Builder() =
  /// Combine two values
  member sm.Combine(a,b) = a + b
  /// Zero value
  /// sm.Zero()
  member sm.Zero() = 0
  /// Return a value
  /// sm.Yield expr
  member sm.Yield(a) = a
  /// For loop
  member sm.For(e, f) =
    Seq.fold(fun s x -> sm.Combine(s, f x)) (sm.Zero()) e
```

Let's test this `ComputeExpression1Builder` builder, using the following code:

```
let compute1 = ComputeExpression1Builder()
let computeEx1 x = compute1 { for x in [1 .. x] do yield x * x }
let computeEx1Result = computeEx1 50
```

Using **F# Interactive** mode, execute the preceding code. The **F# Interactive** window will display the following signature:

```
F# Interactive

>

type ComputeExpression1Builder =
  class
    new : unit -> ComputeExpression1Builder
    member Combine : a:int * b:int -> int
    member For : e:seq<'a> * f:('a -> int) -> int
    member Yield : a:'b -> 'b
    member Zero : unit -> int
  end

>

val compute1 : ComputeExpression1Builder
val computeEx1 : x:int -> int
val computeEx1Result : int = 42925

Error List  Task List  Output  F# Interactive
```

The following code is the same code as the previous one, but now it has the `Delay` method:

```fsharp
// Add delay method
type ComputeExpression2Builder() =
  /// Combine two values
  member sm.Combine(a,b) = a + b
  /// Zero value
  /// sm.Zero()
  member sm.Zero() = 0
  /// Return a value
  /// sm.Yield expr
  member sm.Yield(a) = a
  /// For loop
  member sm.For(e, f) =
     Seq.fold(fun s x -> sm.Combine(s, f x)) (sm.Zero()) e
  /// Delay a computation  member sm.Delay (f: unit -> int) =
System.Console.WriteLine("Test")     f()
```

The `Delay` method in the preceding code is implemented with type annotations. This is important because without type annotation, F# will set the signature to be generalized; this generalization is caused by automatic generalization. We need to minimize automatic generalization because we want to prevent type checking at the runtime when the generic parameter is bound because we already know that the method body of `Combine` will infer that the type of the underlying result type is `Int32`.

[314]

Use the following code to test `ComputeExpression2Builder`:

```
let compute2 = ComputeExpression2Builder()
let computeEx2 x = compute2 { for x in [1 .. x] do yield x * x }
let computeEx2Result = computeEx2 50
```

The following display of **F# Interactive** window proves that the `Delay` method wraps a function in a computation expression and affects the evaluation (as shown by the display of **Test** from `Console.WriteLine`):

```
F# Interactive
>

type ComputeExpression2Builder =
  class
    new : unit -> ComputeExpression2Builder
    member Combine : a:int * b:int -> int
    member Delay : f:(unit -> int) -> int
    member For : e:seq<'a> * f:('a -> int) -> int
    member Yield : a:'b -> 'b
    member Zero : unit -> int
  end

>
Test

val compute2 : ComputeExpression2Builder
val computeEx2 : x:int -> int
val computeEx2Result : int = 42925

>

◄

Error List   Task List   Output   F# Interactive
```

The preceding code has proved that the `Delay` method should be used carefully, and it may contain side effects that not just change the order of execution of `Yield` (or other returning result methods, such as `Return/ReturnFrom`), but it also might terminate the execution before returning the result of `Yield` because of the possibility of catching an exception.

This simple sample optimization case combined with the design considerations provides us careful and predictable behaviors. We now have increased awareness of what is going on inside a computation expression and how to minimize the overhead of having unnecessary or overkill usage of method builders.

Summary

The knowledge of the computation expression correctness is also useful as we are not sacrificing performance as well, while at the same time keeping the functional programming's best practices in place. Although the nature of builder methods in a computation expression implementation is mostly implemented using the object oriented principle, using instantiated computation expression gives us more expressiveness to make our code cleaner and better composed.

We have the knowledge of the optimization of F# code or applications, starting from identifying the performance aspects of the .NET runtime to the detail of F# performance characteristics, measurement with .NET tooling ecosystem, and optimization of all the aspects of the F# language ecosystem-from the compiler to the existing F# features.

We not only have an understanding of the general language features but also the knowledge of aligning compilers with concurrency, data structures, language constructs, and other sophisticated and powerful features, such as computation expression.

Index

.NET 4.5
  reference 185
.NET APM
  reference 141
.NET assembly
  reference 233
.NET BCL collection types
  reference 101
.NET BCL
  reference 63
.NET CLR
  reference 41
.NET CoreCLR
  reference 45
.NET delegate
  passing, as F# function 250
.NET Garbage Collector
  reference 63
.NET Monitor
  reference 198
.NET native
  reference 40
.NET TAP
  reference 151
.NET timers
  using 66, 67, 68, 69
.NET tools, in Visual Studio
  reference 45
.NET TPL
  reference 184

A

abstract method
  reference 299
active patterns

best practices 263, 264, 267
  reference 266
AOT
  reference 37
assembly language
  reference 90
Async.AwaitEvent
  reference 143
Async.FromBeginEnd
  reference 139
Async.Sleep
  reference 147
Async.StartChild
  reference 138
asynchronous callback 18
asynchronous concurrency 114
asynchronous flow
  implications 17
asynchronous operation
  ignoring, asynchronously 143
asynchronous primitives 116
Asynchronous Programming Model (APM) 133
asynchronous programming, in .NET TPL 151
asynchronous workflow
  about 122
  cancellation, handling in 147
  common conventions, for implementation 150
  delaying 144
  goals 123
  operations 133
  overview 124
  reference 132
  using, with Dispose pattern 127
auto properties, of F#
  reference 169
automatic generalization 269, 270

B

Backus-Naur Form (BNF) notation
  about 247
  reference 248
big O notation
  about 99
  reference 100
blocking thread
  trait 119, 121
blocking threads
  identifying 116
builders, of computation expression
  about 289
  Bind 290
  Delay 290
  Return 290
  ReturnFrom 290
  Run 290
  TryFinally 290
  TryWith 290
  Using 290
  Yield 290
  YieldFrom 290
  Zero 290

C

cancellation
  handling, in asynchronous workflow 147
child asynchronous workflow
  creating 136
CLR Profiler 4.5
  using 56, 57
CLR Profiler
  limitations 58, 59
  overview 57
  references 58
  working 58, 60, 62
Code generation phase 43
code indentation, F#
  reference 76
common bottlenecks, F# 14, 15
Common Language Infrastructure (CLI) 41
Common Language Runtime (CLR) 41
community projects, F# Foundations

reference 207
completor 136
computation expression design considerations
  about 304
  implications 308, 309, 312
computation expression optimization
  considerations 312, 313, 314
conceptual mappings
  of F# collection, to .NET BCL 100
concurrency, .NET
  about 20
  reference 20
concurrency, F# 4
  asynchronous 115
  building blocks 115
  parallel 115
concurrency, F#
  about 16, 17, 20, 114
  case samples 19
  features 21
  issues 18
constant pattern matching
  versus if constructs 254, 255, 256, 258, 260
constructs optimization
  overview 246, 247
Control.Async
  reference 133
coroutine
  about 159
  reference, for definition 159
currying
  about 293
  reference 293

D

data parallelism 194, 195
Debug mode
  versus Release mode 37
debugging, in F# 29, 30, 31, 32, 33, 34, 36
deserialization
  overview 167, 168, 170, 171
  requisites 172
developer command prompt, VS 2015
  reference 48
discriminated union

about 181, 246
reference 182
Dispose pattern
asynchronous workflow, using with 127
Dynamic Language Runtime (DLR)
about 82
reference 83
dynamic typing
versus static typing 82

E

early bound 84
erased type providers 211
disadvantages 214
implementation cases 212
evaluation strategy
involving, scenarios 109
exceptions, catching in active patterns
considerations 267, 268

F

F# 3.0 sample, CodePlex
reference 30
F# 4.0 release notes, GitHub
reference 216
F# 4.0
concurrency support 114
reference 11
F# asynchronous workflow support
for legacy .NET APM and EAP 138
F# code compilation 40
F# code
overview 8, 9, 10
relation, with F# assembly 12
F# collections
best practices 98
reference 99
F# compiler guide section
reference 43
F# compiler
processes 40, 41, 42
reference 21
F# computation expression
about 288, 289
planning 295, 296, 297

reference 291
writing 295, 297
F# Core Engineering group
reference 43
F# delegate
using, over .NET Func 292
F# documentation
reference 22
F# FSI
reference 29
F# function computation expressions
relation, with argument restriction 294
F# function
.NET delegate, passing as 250
F# interactive 22, 24, 25, 26, 27, 28
F# language constructs
optimizing 248
F# LINQ query computation
reference 221
F# List
versus .NET ListT 102
F# Map
versus DictionaryTKey,TValue 104
F# primitive types
reference 94
F# statically resolved type
reference 87
F# tooling, in Visual Studio
about 21
reference 21
F# tooling
reference 22
F#, in Visual Studio
capabilities 22
F#
characteristics 11
common bottlenecks 14, 15
common samples of misunderstood concurrent
problems 15
concurrency 16, 17
concurrency, features 21
immutability, versus mutability 13, 14
runtime characteristics 10, 11
unique characteristics 11, 12
fiber, in Windows API

reference 159
fire and forgot pattern
  about 156
  examples 157
first in first out (FIFO) 162
FSharp.Interop.Dynamic
  reference 82
FSI's signature file
  reference 237
FSSF
  reference 21
FsUnit GitHub repo
  reference 80
FsUnit
  reference 72
  used, for implementing unit tests 72, 75, 76
FuncConvert
  reference 251
function as first class values
  reference 293
functional programming
  reference 85
functions
  running, inside unit tests 70
future
  about 18
  reference 18

G

generated type providers 211
generic parameterized version, ParallelQuery
  reference 240
generic type, F# 86
global assembly cache (GAC) 75

H

heap 91

I

I/O
  background technical reason, of blocking nature
  117
IBM Websphere MQ
  reference 173
if constructs

versus constant pattern matching 254, 255, 256, 258, 260
if specification
  reference 254
IL and CLI standards, ECMA
  reference 41
IL Emit phase 43
IL tooling, in .NET 45
IL, in F#
  .NET Core IL 44
  about 43
  COM objects 44
  covariance/contravariance 44
  no PIA project and compile support 44
  Platform Invoke (P/Invoke) 44
  tailcall recursion 44
ILASM
  using 46, 47, 48, 49
ILDASM
  using 46, 47, 48, 49, 50, 56
inline functions
  implementation, best practices 271, 272, 273, 276
  optimizing 268
  overview 269
Intellisense 84
interactive support, F# 23, 24, 25, 26, 27, 28
interop, with .NET TPL 150
interoperability of F# delegate, with .NET delegate
  best practices 248, 250

J

JIT
  reference 37

L

lambda, in C++
  reference 249
language features
  active patterns 263, 264, 267
  elements 246
  overview 246, 247
  pattern matching 252, 253
last in first out (LIFO) 89
late bound 84

lazy computation, on types
    reference 108
legacy .NET EAP model
    reference 142
legacy models 135
Lexing 43

M

MailboxProcessor
    about 172, 175, 177
    features 178
    further implementations 180, 182
    lightweight aspects 173
    methods 178
    side effects, managing 183
    using 156
managed .NET bottlenecks 14
managed heap 62
memory allocations
    scenarios 110
memory storage allocation
    about 88
    heap 91
    register 88
    stack 89
message agent
    background case 156
    overview 163, 167
methods, MailboxProcessor
    Post 178
    PostAndAsyncReply 178
    PostAndReply 178
    PostAndTryAsyncReply 179
    Receive 179
    Scan 179
    Start 179
    TryPostAndReply 179
    TryReceive 179
    TryScan 179
monads
    about 122
    reference 288
MS Test 71
MSMQ
    reference 173

mutable state
    handling 197, 198

N

narrowing feature disparity
    reference 106
NuGet
    reference 74

O

Object Management Group (OMG) 311
ObsoleteAttribute
    reference 238
operations, in asynchronous workflow
    AsBeginEnd 133
    AwaitEvent 133
    AwaitIAsyncResult 133
    AwaitTask 133
    CancellationToken 133
    DefaultCancellationToken 134
    FromBeginEnd 134
    FromContinuations 134
    Ignore 134
    Parallel 134
    RunSynchronously 134
    Sleep 134
    Start 134
    StartAsTask 134
    StartChild 135
    StartChildAsTask 135
    StartImmediately 135
Orleans
    reference 115
overrides
    reference 299

P

parallel concurrency 114
parallel debugging tool
    using, in Visual Studio 191, 192, 193
parallel debugging
    reference 194
parallel programming, with .NET TPL
    about 184, 185
    data parallelism 194, 195

task-based parallelism 186, 188, 189
parallel programming
    common pitfalls 197
Parallel Stacks
    reference 194
Parallel.Invoke method
    reference 187
Parallel.Options class
    reference 189
ParallelQuery class
    reference 240
pattern matching
    best practices 252, 253
    reference 252
Portable Class Library (PCL) 227
Promises model 157
Promises
    samples 160

Q

quantitative measurements
    .NET timers 66, 67, 68, 69
    using 66

R

Read-Eval-Print-Loop (REPL) 22
recursion
    in functional programming 277
recursive constructs
    tail call, identifying in 276, 277
reference type
    about 85
    types 85
register 88
relational algebra
    reference 106
Release mode
    versus Debug mode 37
round-robin 159
runtime characteristics, F# 10, 11

S

serialization
    overview 167, 168, 169, 170
specifications, AMD

reference 121
specifications, Intel processors
    reference 121
SQL EQUI JOIN clauses
    reference 214
SQL Server 2000 sample database installer
    download link 216
SqlDataConnection type provider
    reference 223
    using 215, 216, 218, 223
stack
    about 89
    advantages 90
    disadvantages 90
StackFrame class
    reference 268
StackOverflowException
    reference 91
STAThread
    reference 153
static typing
    versus dynamic typing 82
System.Diagnostic.Stopwatch
    reference 69
System.Net.Socket
    reference 141
System.Threading.Tasks
    reference 151

T

tail call optimization 15
tail call optimized implementation
    identifying 279
tail call recursion, in .NET CLR 279
tail call recursion, in F#
    about 279
    limitations 284
tail call recursive implementation
    advantages 283
tail call recursive optimization 11
tail call
    identifying, in recursive constructs 276, 277
Task Parallel Library (TPL) 20
task-based parallelism
    overview 186

Test-Driven Development (TDD) 71
Thread apartment model
  reference 153
thread safe 13
thread synchronization, F#
  reference 20
timers
  reference 69
TimeSpan
  reference 256
Type checking 43
type inference mechanism
  of generic type inference 269
type inferences 269
type metadata infrastructure
  assembly, implementing to provide base
    assembly 232
  generated constructor, implementing 234
  generated methods, implementing 235
  generated properties, implementing 236, 238
  parameters, implementing for methods and
    constructors 233
type providers
  about 204, 206
  advantages 205
  basic minimal implementation 240
  building blocks 210
  building blocks, building 227
  common pitfalls, in implementations 242
  erased type providers 211
  generated type providers 211
  goals 205
  implementation strategies 211
  implementation strategies, selecting 212
  implementations 206
  implementing 224, 226
  interoperability, with other managed programming
    languages 209
  reference 204, 212
  requisites 210, 211
  sample usage 215
  SqlDataConnection 215, 216, 218, 223
  type metadata infrastructure, building 228
  versus type generators 207, 208, 209
type returned, in computation expression

uses 302
types, F#
  attributes 87
  best practices 82, 92
  classes 87
  delegates 87
  discriminated unions 87
  F# collections 87
  functions 87
  options 87
  overview 82
  primitive types 87
  records 87
  reference type 85
  static typing, versus dynamic typing 82
  structures 87
  unit type 87
  value type 85

U

UML 2 diagram
  reference 311
UML 2 standards
  reference 311
unit tests
  about 71
  functions, running inside 70
  implementing, FsUnit used 72, 75, 76
  in Visual Studio 71

V

value evaluation strategy
  selecting 106, 108, 109
value type 85
Visual Studio test runner
  reference 71
Visual Studio Testing Tool API
  reference 71
Visual Studio Unit Test Framework
  reference 75
Visual Studio
  parallel debugging tool, using in 191, 192, 193

W

WeakReference
  reference 97
Windows Management Instrumentation (WMI)
  about 210
  reference 210

Windows message loop, of Windows API
  reference 158
WPF (Windows Presentation Foundation)
  about 295
  reference 295
writer-reader model
  reference 174

www.ingramcontent.com/pod-product-compliance
Lightning Source LLC
Chambersburg PA
CBHW060923060326

40690CB00041B/3146